"Julie Goodspeed-Chadwick's latest contribution to our understanding of Assia Wevill's life is vital work. Built around crucial, newly accessible archival material, *Lives Revised* upends longstanding master narratives through a careful investigation of the early frameworks that have determined so much of our 'knowledge' about Wevill and Hughes. This is revelatory scholarship at its finest."

—JANET BADIA, author of *Sylvia Plath and the Mythology of Women Readers*

"Refusing to play the blame game, Goodspeed-Chadwick neither casts judgment on these tragically entangled writers nor pits them against one another. Instead, she seeks an empathetic understanding of Wevill, Hughes, and Plath. This book does not shy away from their disastrous decisions. But it insists on an ethical approach grounded in trauma studies—how would we respond to similar circumstances?"

—MARSHA BRYANT, author of *Women's Poetry and Popular Culture*

"Goodspeed-Chadwick's research is meticulous, yet this study wears that weight lightly. This study attends to Wevill and Hughes in all their complexities and lived experiences, seeking to pull back the layers of myth that have accrued to their stories. Grounding her analysis in painstaking archival work, Goodspeed-Chadwick makes a compelling argument for Wevill's significance."

—DEBORAH M. MIX, author of *A Vocabulary of Thinking: Gertrude Stein and Contemporary North American Women's Innovative Writing*

"In working so closely with new archival documents and in tandem with existing resources and scholarship, Goodspeed-Chadwick assimilates a vast amount of information for the modern reader of Assia Wevill and the other major literary figures with whom she intersects. *Lives Revised* further fills in pieces of the puzzle and brings us closer to a comprehensive portrait of Wevill."

—PETER K. STEINBERG, editor of *The Collected Prose of Sylvia Plath* and coeditor of *The Collected Writings of Assia Wevill* and *The Letters of Sylvia Plath*

"This deeply human study by the foremost expert on the life and writing of Assia Wevill does its subjects the great service of not only dismantling the lore surrounding them, but also explaining the processes of lore-making that have the potential to thwart our full participation in biographical narrative as a personally meaningful endeavor. Goodspeed-Chadwick's trauma-informed framework provides the ethical imperative and the tools to rethink the study of life writing and the default categories that shape—even warp—such work, particularly in writing about women and power. Her strategy of thoroughly analyzing a wide range of contrasting accounts from the archive is convincing. This book tells us what we don't know about Wevill, Hughes, and Plath, and in so doing illuminates the limits of biographical knowledge—and what happens when we fail to navigate those limits with humility and care for the pain of others."

—JANINE UTELL, author of *Literary Couples and Twentieth-Century Life Writing: Narrative and Intimacy*

"This book is a truly scholarly work, setting straight a bevy of misinformation disseminated through this past half-century of biography and criticism. Goodspeed-Chadwick draws on a great deal of archival and personally held material to *finally* create a full picture of not only Wevill and Hughes, but also of Plath. Any reader will benefit from her wealth of knowledge."

—LINDA WAGNER-MARTIN, author of *Sylvia Plath: A Biography* and *Sylvia Plath: A Literary Life* and editor of *Sylvia Plath: The Critical Heritage*

LIVES REVISED

WINNER OF THE
2025 LEWIS P. SIMPSON AWARD

JULIE GOODSPEED-CHADWICK

LIVES REVISED

ASSIA WEVILL
TED HUGHES
AND SYLVIA PLATH

LOUISIANA STATE UNIVERSITY PRESS
BATON ROUGE

Published with the assistance of Indiana University

Published by Louisiana State University Press
lsupress.org

Copyright © 2025 by Louisiana State University Press
All rights reserved. Except in the case of brief quotations used in articles or reviews, no part of this publication may be reproduced or transmitted in any format or by any means without written permission of Louisiana State University Press.

Designer: Barbara Neely Bourgoyne
Typeface: Whitman

Jacket illustration: Ted Hughes, Assia Wevill, and Shura Wevill, ca. 1966. Courtesy of the Stuart A. Rose Manuscript, Archives, and Rare Book Library, Emory University.

Library of Congress Cataloging-in-Publication Data
Names: Goodspeed-Chadwick, Julie, 1978– author
Title: Lives revised: Assia Wevill, Ted Hughes, and Sylvia Plath / Julie Goodspeed-Chadwick.
Description: Baton Rouge: Louisiana State University Press, 2025. |
  Includes bibliographical references and index.
Identifiers: LCCN 2025018345 (print) | LCCN 2025018346 (ebook) | ISBN 978-0-8071-8478-3 (cloth) | ISBN 978-0-8071-8524-7 (epub) | ISBN 978-0-8071-8525-4 (pdf)
Subjects: LCSH: Wevill, Assia, 1927–1969 | Hughes, Ted, 1930–1998 | Plath, Sylvia | Authors—Biography | Mistresses—Biography | Suicide victims—Biography | LCGFT: Biographies
Classification: LCC PR6073.E78 Z53 2025 (print) | LCC PR6073.E78 (ebook) | DDC 818/.5409 [B]—dc23/eng/20250416
LC record available at https://lccn.loc.gov/2025018345
LC ebook record available at https://lccn.loc.gov/2025018346

For Keith Chadwick,

Josephine Barbara Jean Chadwick,

Jude Valentine Chadwick, and

Ruby Mary Alice Chadwick

CONTENTS

Acknowledgments ix

I.
REAL-WORLD ENCOUNTERS

1. Setting the Scene 3
2. Assia and Hughes as Subjects in Interviews and the Lives of Other People 24

II.
THEIR LIVES AND THEIR WORDS

3. Assia 65
4. Ted Hughes 102

Conclusion 137

Notes 149

Works Cited 163

Index 175

ACKNOWLEDGMENTS

I am grateful to many people who supported this project. Without them, this would be a different book. From local to national to international support, I could not have written it without the following people, organizations, and entities.

In England, I extend my gratitude to the BBC, which made my dream of listening to the 1968 Radio 3 program come to life.

To Martin Baker, Assia's friend and now a friend to Peter and to me after *The Collected Writings of Assia Wevill*, I offer my great respect to him as a person and a literary, artistic professional. I hope that I was able to capture the spirit of his relationship with Assia and Shura successfully.

Without the support and friendship of Mr. Ira Chaikin and the generosity of the Estate of Assia Wevill, two of the three books I have had the privilege to work on would not exist. The Estate of Assia Wevill has played an instrumental role in supporting biographical work on Assia and solidifying her legacy. Thank you for allowing me to contribute to Assia's profile.

As always, thank you to Kathy Shoemaker, a crown jewel in the Emory crown, and deep gratitude to everyone associated with the superlative Stuart A. Rose Manuscript, Archives, and Rare Book Library at Emory University. The Rose Library is in a league of its own.

A jewel on the other side of the Atlantic is the British Library. The world-class expertise of Helen Melody and that of Kathleen Rowe is unparalleled. I am especially indebted to Helen and her expert approach to archival materials and knowledge about them. She is absolutely extraordinary.

A precious resource is time—time to research, read, and write—and I thank wholeheartedly Reinhold Hill and George Towers, two remarkable and brilliant men who support the important work of the humanities, and the IU Indianapolis Sabbatical Committee for providing me with a sabbatical that allowed the time necessary for the national and international archival work of this study.

To date, this book is, by far, the costliest of the ones I have written or been attached to, and I am relieved and proud that the project is completed, not least because it is the book that I wanted to read (prior to embarking on the project myself!). As a result, I am thankful for the following: the Indiana University Emergency Equity Fund for Research; Indiana University and the Office of the Vice President for International Affairs for the International Mobility Grant; Indiana University Columbus; Jason M. Kelly and Alicia L. Gahimer and the IU Indianapolis Arts and Humanities Institute (IAHI) and the IAHI Research/Creative Activity Large Grant; and Indiana University Research and the IU Grant-in-Aid for Research and Creative Activity.

Thank you to so many extraordinary people in the Indiana University system. Here are a few: Steven B. Chin (in memoriam), Naomi Cohenour, Cris Craig, Margie Ferguson, Brooke Hall, Vicki Kruse, Jay Lesandrini, Lori Montalbano, Michael Morrone, Dakota Myrick, Karissa Rector, Marsha VanNahmen, and Dan Youngblood. Special thanks to Lori for her excellent mentoring and leadership. Special thanks to Vicki for her outstanding support and talent. You all set the bar high, and you make the work I (and others) do as part of the IU system possible. Thank you to Emily Dill, the University Library of Columbus, and everyone associated with it for research assistance with this book.

I continue to be inspired by scholars and writers who maintain an unwavering belief in the beauty, power, and significance of literature and literary scholarship. Thank you to these trailblazers who in various ways inspired this project: Melissa Bradshaw, Marsha Bryant, Heather Clark, Deborah Cohn, Kathleen Connors, Gail Crowther, Luke Ferretter, Jessica Ferri, Amanda Golden, Anita Helle, Christoph Irmscher, Yehuda Koren, Karen V. Kukil, Gary Leising, Deborah M. Mix, Rai Peterson, Eilat Negev,

Carl Rollyson, Elaine Showalter, Peter K. Steinberg, Janine Utell, Linda Wagner-Martin, and David Wevill. Special thanks to Heather for her generosity, advice, encouragement, humor, inspiration, and the gift of a real friendship. Special thanks to Peter K. Steinberg: a true colleague and friend, the first reader of the first draft of this book, and someone I can count on outside of books.

To Janet Badia and Emily Van Duyne, you are colleagues and friends that make my world brighter. Working on the Plath book with you is a career highlight and something I prize. The work you produce is critically important, but to me, your sisterly friendship is even more so.

My writing group consists of writers who are stronger at writing than I am, and they are also my treasured colleagues and friends. I hold John Paul M. Kanwit, George Micajah Phillips, and Jennifer J. Smith in the highest esteem. Likewise, Diane Prenatt, once my professor and mentor and now my colleague and friend, earns my admiration and my friendship, too. The end of this book must be credited to Diane's influence, and, truth be told, her impact on my academic life is difficult to assess because it extends to almost thirty years.

Louisiana State University Press is my favorite press. James W. Long is a brilliant editor with an expert eye and is a joy to partner with in the pursuit and publication of literary scholarship. Everyone at LSU Press is unrivaled and deserves all the accolades the press receives and more: Catherine Kadair, Sunny Rosen, Jordyn Lofton, Sam Anselmo, Min Marcus (in order of when I encountered them), and everyone else at LSU Press whom I did not interact with directly but whose influence on the landscape of university press publishing is great. I admire everyone at LSU Press, and I am proud to publish under its banner. It remains my first choice with respect to publication. Thank you to the outside specialist readers the press secured for this book; your reports made it the best it could be. Thank you to Susan Murray for your incredible talent in critical reading and writing; I am grateful to you for your care in handling the manuscript.

Most of all, my gratitude and heart belong to my family. To my husband, Keith Chadwick, and to our children (who asked that I use their lovely full names)—Josephine Barbara Jean Chadwick, Jude Valentine

Chadwick, and Ruby Mary Alice Chadwick—the four of you are my sunshine and happiness, and I owe everything, including all the good in this book, to you. With the last three book projects, I brought a different nursing baby to the archive, and all three children had passports at very young ages as a result of my academic work. Without the love and support of my husband, none of this—researching abroad in a pandemic with young children, including a baby—could have been logistically possible. Although they were work trips and I was researching and otherwise working (presenting and writing), my family gamely traveled with me to Atlanta, Georgia; western Ireland; and London, England—so that I would not feel like I had to choose between them and my profession. While I am passionate about writing books and teaching and often feel that being a literature professor is a calling, it is, in large part, for my family that I work so hard. For their part, they have never complained about sacrifices attendant to my career, and while this book cannot make up for those, it is dedicated to them.

REAL-WORLD
ENCOUNTERS

I

1

SETTING THE SCENE

There is more to say about the lives of Ted Hughes and Assia Wevill. And there probably always will be, despite the fact that Hughes managed to distance himself from Assia,[1] his partner and the mother of one of his daughters, in all but his poetry and personal writing, the very types of writing that he may have held most dear. At the very least, he viewed poetry to be the most transformative genre with respect to trauma and healing, as well as the most revealing of the truths of his own life, as we see in his interviews with Drue Heinz of the *Paris Review* and with Yehuda Koren and Eilat Negev, Assia's biographers. As for Assia, what more could be said about her? Because her life exists in fragments—a number of letters, journal entries, notes, and other documents exist but amid gaps in documents and within the fragments of what we know of her life record—Assia's life and work have yet to be positioned and contextualized in a manner that allows us to grasp how remarkable a life she lived, in its early-second-wave feminist tendencies and in what it left us as legacies. Meanwhile, work on Assia inevitably leads to work on Hughes, and the impact made on his life and work by Assia cannot be underestimated, as both *Lover of Unreason* and *Reclaiming Assia Wevill*, books about Assia primarily and Hughes secondarily, show. All the same, Hughes's life and his contributions to literature and letters remain extraordinary achievements and, I would argue, become even more impressive when we consider the trauma he suffered and addressed, as well as the dedication to his art that he sustained throughout his life. It is the art and personal writing he produced about Assia that is at the heart of this book because that work signals the highlights and lowlights of a life lived truthfully in writing. Assia's own bold and audacious life writing and achievements gain in their poignancy and significance when we consider how they emerged and why they resonate: what we can glean from their narratives and stories and why, I suggest, they should matter to us in the twenty-first century.

Over the course of researching three books pertaining to Assia and through participating in countless wide-ranging discussions about her with scholars and general readers, I have come to the conclusion that there is still a lot we—myself included—do not know about Assia. As new biographical facts and stories emerge, we will need to revise and, I hope, complicate the basic plot summary of her life, one that has become mythic shorthand for a glamorous, dangerous, and bad woman: a woman who attracts and repels. When Plath's friend Clarissa Roche asks who Assia is, Harriet Rosenstein, who wanted to write a biography about Plath in the 1970s, readily responds that Assia partnered Hughes, died by suicide, and killed her daughter (Clarissa Roche, interview recording, November 20, 1973, part 3). The first two parts of this three-pronged definition fit Plath, too. But just as Plath's life and work are multifaceted, Assia's importance in literature and culture is greater than her role as a romantic partner, and the unconscionable, horrific decisions she made are illuminating in what they can show us about gender, mental illness, and trauma. On a different note, as Diane Middlebrook observes, the public becomes more interested in Plath and Hughes as details emerge about Assia (xvii). Her biographical story informs theirs, and that observation might lend even more importance to the project of fleshing out Assia's life and its contributions.

A purpose of this study is to show what has been buried in archives or held in private hands for a half century, namely, content that is relevant and significant in revising and amplifying our critical and literary understanding of the lives of Assia, Hughes, and Plath. Another purpose is to revise and refine the default plot in Plath studies and Hughes studies. That storyline presents Assia as an envious and destructive woman, alluring and seductive—just as this default storyline is both alluring and seductive— who triggers a chain of events that result in Plath's suicide. Ultimately, the master narrative goes, she is the perpetrator and the villain in the story.

To better serve biographical stories, this book makes available for the first time what is in the archives at the British Library and Emory University: the material that has not yet made it into publications. Perhaps readers will be able to use this material and cite it in their own critical and creative contributions, as well as in the classroom. The never-before-seen or never-before-cited material is packaged with scholarly context and analyses; the framework is informed by trauma studies and women's, gender, and sexuality studies. When we take on trauma-informed perspectives in connection with vulnerable women in precarious situations, we might better understand the cruelty of victim blaming and the ways in which power dynamics shape outcomes. Everyone suffers to varying degrees in the Assia Wevill–Sylvia Plath–Ted Hughes story.[2]

Biographies and biographical studies fascinate us because they reveal facts, details, and interpretations of lives lived in the real world. They can provide new takes on old subjects or reveal what was kept secret. "Biography," posits Janet Malcolm, "is the medium through which the remaining secrets of the famous dead are taken from them and dumped out in full view of the world" (9). Biography, as Hermione Lee pinpoints, crosses into and becomes synonymous with life writing (1). In one framing of what biography is, biographers strip their subject in a metaphorical examination of a dead body (1). In another, biographers construct a portrait that brings the subject to life "in all the totality, there-ness, and authenticity of their being" (3). Yet another approach highlights sympathy as a necessary component to an "ideal biography" (3). According to Lee, biography should be true; cover the whole story; include and reveal everything one can find out; identify all sources; understand that biography is a form of history and an investigation of identity; and create a story that has some value for the reader (6–18). "Any biographical narrative is an artificial construct, since it inevitably involves selection and shaping," writes Lee, who explains that she decided to focus on certain aspects of Virginia Woolf's life when writing a biography about her (122). Another biographical treatment may state up front why the subject matters, how the author feels about the subject, and what the approach is likely to be (125). This book is not a biography but a biographical study. All the same, it takes some of its cues from Hermione Lee specifically. Perhaps this biographical study of Assia and Hughes, with Assia as its primary focal point, will be accepted as a "resuscitation" or "a revisionist return": regardless, my approach strives to ground what we can know in "the social and cultural politics of its time and place" and to interrogate and bolster, modify, or dismantle received narratives, values, and the like (126). Inevitably, we will confront the "danger," to use Malcolm's word, associated with biographical work: the cracks in the facade of a biography, the "sound" or intimation of "doubts about the legitimacy of the biographical enterprise" (9–10). Avers Malcolm, "The biography-loving public does not want to hear that biography is a flawed genre" (10). In other words, biographers can never get the biographical story entirely right because there exists the potential for multiple retellings and revisions. Malcolm's approach is to lay out her experiences, values, and biases in tackling the Plath-Hughes biographical enterprise, and this study will follow suit to some degree to provide context and as much transparency as possible.

Ultimately, this book is a book about biography rather than a biography itself. The lives of Assia, Hughes, and, to a lesser extent, Plath are the case studies within which we can examine the very possibilities and challenges encountered and/or engendered in biographical study. Within this first chapter, I will give an overview of the who, what, when, where, why, and how of this book: the particulars concerning Assia and Hughes and what we can learn from them. The theoretical framework and the core ideas that underpin this book will be shared, and the anecdotes that brought this book into being will be recounted. Entitled "Real-World Encounters," part 1 considers who Assia and Hughes are, how we have approached and might come to approach them. Interviews, memoirs, and other text-based documents—the memories, stories, and reflections—from Assia and Hughes's contemporaries will be showcased and mined in order to present portraits of these larger-than-life figures. It has become clear to me that, much like a binary construction or opposition, we cannot truly make inroads on scholarship on either Assia or Hughes without the study of both. One informs the other and makes an impact in demonstrable fashion. Too, understanding our subjects from multiple vantage points enables us to grasp their complexity as well as recognize that there will be some aspects we will never be able to definitively ascertain. In this first section, I focus on text-based materials to bring to life Assia and Hughes as others portray them; these texts anchor my interpretations and conclusions. I do not wish to enter into conjectures or speculations on my own accord; rather, I wish to center and parse what we might call data that has not been thoroughly worked over. With newly opened archives and antifeminist barriers being breached, now is the time to embark on such work.

In part 2, "Their Lives and Their Words," I will draw upon Assia's and Hughes's own words in both published and unpublished texts. In this second section, we will become keenly aware of the gaps, of the missing facts, texts, and deceased and absent subjects who are continually animated and resonant in literary studies and cultural studies. It is in this section that I will delve into trauma studies and map the traumatic moments and ruptures that manifest in our text-based documents related to Assia and Hughes. We will see, finally, how trauma is a social justice issue that affects people across identity categories and that, perhaps, affects all of us, given our community affiliations, in some measure. As I understand it, trauma is a psychological and emotional injury, that which cannot be repressed indefinitely, and I will emphasize the gendered dimensions of traumatic experiences when applicable.

This book is indebted to the prodigious literary-critical biographies that paved the way for it. Two of these, *Ted Hughes: The Life of a Poet* by Elaine Feinstein and *Ted Hughes: The Unauthorised Life* by Sir Jonathan Bate, even discuss Assia, providing important information and provocative details, the very material that lends itself to and prompted the start of this book. Other biographies set examples for scope and approach. Gail Crowther's dual biography *Three-Martini Afternoons at the Ritz: The Rebellion of Sylvia Plath and Anne Sexton* powerfully braids together the biographies and contributions of two critically important writers, contextualizing their lives and writing in feminist fashion. Heather Clark's *Red Comet: The Short Life and Blazing Art of Sylvia Plath* displays the fruits of massive efforts involved in the researching of Plath and the interviewing of people related to her, revealing new details, facts, and events that carve out and fill in the panoramic picture we have of her from past scholarship. Her book, too, addresses Assia.[3] Additionally, feminist understanding and insight infuse Clark's biography, a finalist for the Pulitzer Prize for Biography, distinguishing it as one especially relevant for our time. Another influential book is Bate's dual biography of John Keats and F. Scott Fitzgerald, which eschews a "cradle to grave" narrative in favor of establishing parallels and convergences through "highly selective series of anecdotes, moments and scenes . . . [that reveal] their essence and . . . the wellsprings of their art" (5). In line with Bate's biographical approaches more generally, I, too, have elected to write about both published and unpublished source material, to more fully round out stories about lives that endure, and this current book builds upon my selection of anecdotes, moments, and scenes that display character qualities and patterns in the figures of Assia Wevill, Ted Hughes, and, to a lesser extent, Sylvia Plath. Their writing and the critical consideration of it take up significant space herein because all three were writers whose output presents us with biographical and literary legacies to mine, and the stories about them provide additional contexts to understand lives and texts.

Peter K. Steinberg captures his tremendous expertise and experience in working with the more than 1,400 letters by Plath he edited with Karen V. Kukil in "'They Will Come Asking for Our Letters': Editing *The Letters of Sylvia Plath*." This type of scholarship is critically important and pathbreaking feminist recovery work, and such scholarship inspires and fuels the mission of this book. With Plath, Steinberg and Kukil strive to "restore the narrative of [Plath's] life as she saw fit to relate it as well as reveal the range of her epistolary voices." Her letters, carefully transcribed, researched, and contextualized, "introduce readers to a fuller portrait of her life at the time" (308). This careful and exhaustive labor of researching, editing, and writing (Steinberg details the art of writing the copious footnotes in the hefty tomes of Plath's letters) infuses the books with a distinctive freshness and originality. Steinberg and Kukil make new stories about Plath possible in making new texts and scholarship public. Kukil articulates the philosophy underpinning her field-changing Plath books, the *Journals* and the two volumes of *Letters*: "I have always been careful to present Plath in the round—relying on her words and not editing her into my version of Sylvia Plath" (300). *The Unabridged Journals of Sylvia Plath* and *The Letters of Sylvia Plath*, volumes 1 and 2, have forever changed, shaped, and revitalized Plath studies. These books serve as testaments to the importance of recovering biographical and critical literary narratives, and the books that follow them are indebted to their trailblazing contributions.

The importance of reclaiming and reframing literary lives cannot be overemphasized because the biographical enterprise functions to consolidate and solidify literary reputations and future scholarly work, as Melanie Micir's book *The Passion Projects: Modernist Women, Intimate Archives, Unfinished Lives* shows. In tracking women's lives through writing across genres and archives from early modernism to midcentury writing, Micir arrives at this judgment: "the biographical impulse signals a shared ethical drive to develop a counternarrative of literary history grounded in women's lives," which becomes feminist recovery work (4). Perhaps because biography requires interpretation, Micir deduces that "biographical stories *are* analyses, not simply the historical building blocks with which to construct other, more literary-critical arguments" (6). While the present book strives to tackle both, this twinned mission dovetails with the feminist standpoint Micir also takes up: biography was and is "the generic terrain on which women battle for their inclusion in history" (7). My own passion for feminist recovery work, stemming from the book I authored about Assia Wevill (and Hughes and Plath) and the book I coedited, with Steinberg, of her writing across genres, prepared me for this ambitious project of tracking down and mapping biographical facts, stories, literary pieces, and, finally, a new narrative encompassing more than one life. Much of the material I cite has never before been written about or published, some of it has recently surfaced, and other sources are in private hands and otherwise not public.

Assia's characterization, whether as a historical figure, literary character, or biographical subject, continues to be polarizing. Perhaps because of this polarization in treatment and reception, establishing a definitive depiction of her or a storyline about her seems elusive and difficult. We should bear in mind that context matters. For example, the positionality of the authors or interviewees who speak about Assia, Plath, and Hughes, as well as events concerning them, should be taken into account when possible as we evaluate what was said.[4] As Annette Gordon-Reed, the prominent biographer, argues, "We are who we are in relation to other people"; biographical subjects are part of a network, she explains. To this end, we can review a letter by Brenda Hedden to Elizabeth Sigmund as a case in point. Hedden details what Hughes is like in crisis mode; he prefers to avoid a crisis, but when he cannot, he is, by turns, passive, secretive, devious, callous, and ruthless. Not a violent person himself, she posits, Hughes, instead, "had a tendency to arouse violence in response, which in women of course often turns to aggression turned in on themselves, as with both Sylvia and Assia" (correspondence).[5] This description of Plath and Assia suggests the harmful nature that is indicative of—but not exclusive to—trauma. Traumatized persons have two options when acting out in response to trauma: they can turn it outward and be violent, be the bully, or they can direct the violence consuming them further inward and destroy themselves. While Hedden may be a controversial person in both Hughes's life story and Assia's, she nevertheless occupies the position of an insider, given her romantic relationship with Hughes and her knowledge of and interactions with Assia. From Assia's perspective, no love was lost between Hedden and herself.[6]

We can see how interpersonal dynamics play out and are subsequently recorded in the biographical enterprise in the following instance. Assia worked with Julia Matcham, who served as art director at Colman, Prentice, and Varley, and Matcham most certainly harbored no affection for Assia. Indeed, in more than one letter, Matcham engages in faultfinding, criticizing Assia for everything from Plath's suicide to her rocky relationship with Hughes to her death. While she adumbrates what she understands of Assia's romantic life from her late twenties until her early forties to Elizabeth Sigmund and Linda Wagner-Martin, Matcham cannot reconcile the incomplete and flattened life (that of the femme fatale) she relates with the profound gaps that gape in the narrative—but it is an enticing story that she cannot refrain from taking up: "from my point of view," writes Matcham, "what happened unfolded like a fascinating novel, many pages of which are frustratingly missing" (correspondence). Seemingly desiring answers to what she has sketched as a sordid story, Matcham writes to Sigmund, "Obviously, I have continued to wonder about the gaps in my knowledge. Why did Ted leave Assia so quickly—Assia blamed Teds [sic] family. Why did Assia commit suicide, and why kill the child? . . . And what would Teds [sic] version be . . . ?" (correspondence). This book is dedicated to reflecting on these perennial questions, but it is also committed to enlarging the scope of how we think and talk about Assia and Hughes and considering why their biographical stories mean so much to us now. Part of the fascination may be with the abominations—no one discounts the tragedies of three lives needlessly lost, ostensibly for love—but the secrecy, the reticence, the taboo quality of the conversations swirling around Assia, especially in connection with Hughes, may add to that fascination. As Matcham shares, "To describe in a few lines some-ones [sic] character is almost certainly to do them an injustice and as [another co-worker says], one could write a book about Assia" (Matcham, Wagner-Martin MSS).

What may not have been conveyed in earlier work on Assia: she was remembered by a friend as cheerful and fun, not exactly what we associate with her stereotype. Acknowledging Assia's beauty, her friend remarks that everyone noticed Assia in a room; she attracted attention. Despite the attention, which may have opened up opportunities to discuss Plath, she did not talk about Plath to everyone; this unnamed friend never heard Assia speak about her. Summing up her friend, the interviewee asserts, "Assia was an intelligent person, not emotional." The friend goes on to state that everyone assumed Shura was Hughes's daughter with Assia and that emotional harmony, rather than sexual chemistry, would be the reason that Assia would have been attracted to Hughes (Orr [and Beben?]). Even in this interview, one in which Assia's personality is delineated, the interviewer presses the interviewee about Assia's sex life.[7] Archetypes and stereotypes are difficult to dismiss or thwart.

After Assia's death, Elizabeth Compton Sigmund, whose allegiance was to Plath, expressed in succinct fashion the archetype that has occluded study of Assia as a person and figure in literary and cultural studies. Declaring Assia "a witch with a terrible capacity for destruction," Sigmund elaborates on her take: Plath was frightened of Assia, of her alleged barrenness, abortions, hysterical emotions, and "feline smell" (interview recording, part 5). This association with the animalistic—the not human, specifically—leaves Assia in a space in which she can be attacked and scapegoated as that which is not deserving of the full breadth of her humanity. Sigmund's positionality with respect to Assia informs her opinions; just before intimating that Assia is less human than Plath, Sigmund sketches a scenario that features her vulnerable friend: forced into the competitive literary market, Plath felt very threatened and discussed "literary wars" with Sigmund, metaphorical battles in which everyone shot at her and, in Sigmund's words "every arrow went through" (interview recording, part 5). The memory of this scenario would be one that would cause Sigmund to rally to her friend's defense, if only in memory of her, and Assia, already positioned as a scapegoat, receives the brunt of the anger and dislike surely meant for Plath's attackers. A world hostile to women, in which other women are socialized to dislike and compete against each other, features in Elinor Klein's conversation with Rosenstein about who Assia was. Was she a competitive woman, wondered Klein, after Rosenstein expresses her incredulity that Assia would move into Plath's flat with Hughes after Plath died. If nothing else, she betrayed Plath as a "pretend friend," concludes Klein, a notion to which Rosenstein verbally assents (interview recording, undated, part 1), notwithstanding that Hughes tendered the invitation to live with him and that Assia assumed the role of caretaker of his children with Plath when no other suitable caretaker could be secured.

In many respects, the discussions that occur in the following pages are long overdue. It may seem impossible to fathom that Sigmund could say to Hughes at one point: "Everyone knows about Assia. Everyone knows everything because you're so public about it" (Sigmund, interview recording, part 1). In 2001, Feinstein drew a comparison between the famous Plath and the infamous Assia (if the latter happened to be recognized at all, it was for being bad). Feinstein observes, Assia presented "in some ways as fragmented and vulnerable a human being as Sylvia [Plath]. Very little has been written about Assia, partly because Ted discouraged it" (2). Matcham remarks in 1987, almost two decades after Assia died, "And how amazing it is that none of this has been publicly aired." She continues, "Ted and his friends seem to have chosen to save the public from the undoubted risk of making too harsh a judgement [sic] of him—even if in so-doing his dead wife's reputation is cruelly distorted" (correspondence). I would add that Assia's reputation was distorted and fabricated, too: she became a sort of caricature of an archetype. As she researched her biography on Plath, Linda Wagner-Martin wrote to Elizabeth Sigmund, also in 1987, wondering if "the whole story will ever be known." Ted Hughes and the family and friends who cared for him attempted to erase or minimize Assia's presence and impact on his life to spare him pain: "no one knows what those years in the 60s were like" for Hughes, Wagner-Martin notes, before "he lived happily ever after." No mention of Assia could be made in writing, concludes Wagner-Martin, because Ted and Olwyn Hughes forbade it. As Peter Porter comments, "In the name of a greater legend she had to be kept in the background."[8] Wagner-Martin advocates for a more complete, layered, complex narrative, informed and shaped by literary, feminist women writers, whom she invokes in an earlier paragraph: "There is room for us all, there is a need for us all" (correspondence).

 The inducement to secrecy must be attributed in part to the traumatic events Hughes endured. Trauma marred Hughes's life, and his ability to find his equilibrium and restore safety and community while telling his trauma story through his poetry sequences *Capriccio* (1990) and *Birthday Letters* (1998) constitute great feats of working toward healing, even if healing is an elusive and a recursive process. The aftermath of the suicides of Plath and Assia, combined with the death of his daughter Shura, was almost more than Hughes could bear. For that reason and to salvage his reputation in the aftermath of Plath's suicide, Hughes managed to keep quiet about Assia, except in personal writing and in poems or notes that were never published or that were so oblique as to keep secrets buried or obscured. Plath's suicide alone proved devastating. Richard Murphy confessed to being appalled by the consequences: how her family and friends suffered cruelly and remorselessly. In an oft-quoted passage from notes that Murphy wrote for a future biographer, he relates what Hughes confided in him about the breakup of the Plath-Hughes marriage: "What he [Ted] admitted was that after six or seven years that had been marvellously creative for him, the marriage had somehow become destructive: and he thought the best thing to do was to give it a rest by going to Spain for six months. Assia's name was not mentioned, but her role was implied" (copy of correspondence). What stands out to me is the last sentence: typically, when this sentence is cited, it is used as support for the femme fatale argument. However, the organization of the paragraph and the syntax are far more ambiguous than that. We know that Assia accompanied Hughes on a vacation to Spain after Hughes left Plath in Ireland. Might that be what is meant? After finding himself in a marriage that was no longer creative, that he views as destructive, Hughes wished to separate from Plath and explore Spain and a new life for a half year. Assia factored into that vision of a new life; to be sure, Hughes attempted to persuade Assia to leave David Wevill for a number of months and try out living with him, as we know from his letters to Assia in the early 1960s. From Olwyn Hughes's point of view, both interpretations ring true: "Ted was enamoured with Assia (who was actually very nice . . . if a bit femme fatale and desperate).[9] I think Ted was pretty desperate about the marriage long before Assia came along, although there was a strong bond" (Olwyn Hughes, correspondence).

    Assia first came to my attention when I was researching Plath. For me and many other Plath scholars, Assia resembled an enigma more than anything: who was she other than a caricature of a person, a flattened character, a woman reduced to a villain role who had little to offer outside of a beautiful and imperfect body? What can her story offer? In an interview with Rosenstein, who, at the time, was gathering materials for a Plath biography, an unnamed woman acquainted with Assia declared, "to understand Sylvia, one must understand Assia" (Orr [and Beben?]). Suzette Macedo, a friend to both Plath and Assia, maintains that Plath recognized Assia as her alter ego as well as the other woman (Helder Macedo, interview recording, December 1, 1973, side A). Rosenstein's understanding of this adage amounted to Plath and Assia serving as complementary and dichotomous figures (Orr [and Beben?]). In examining these constructions, we can learn a lot about what we value: what we like and do not like about women, what we uphold and what we denigrate or destroy in juxtaposing them. Perhaps we can think of them as binary oppositions, wherein seemingly opposite terms or concepts actually and mutually inform and define one another. In setting up Assia and Plath as foils, Rosenstein enacts this very dynamic in her interview with Winifred Davies, Plath's midwife and friend in Devon (interview recording, 1970, part 2). Referring to Plath, Rosenstein exclaims, "I get double stories on everything" (Fainlight, interview recording, undated, side A)—and these double stories about Plath and Assia will expand and test what we know (or think we know). Moreover, the opportunity to round out biographical stories, to establish fuller narratives about who, what, when, where, why, and how will be motivation enough to study these lives: in them, we learn more about contexts of literary texts, lives lived, and lessons we can process and apply.

Assia and Plath's contemporaries engaged in comparisons habitually. Typically, the two women were played off of each other, turning them into literary foils. For example, Leonard Baskin asserts that Assia was "the complete opposite of Sylvia" and speculates that Assia was the embodiment of Plath's Jewish self (interview recording). Making them into a literary convention had the effect of simplifying their complexity and humanity, however. To my earlier point, they shared similarities, both superficial and more profound. While beauty may reside in the eye of the beholder in a specific time and place, people who knew Assia and/or Plath point to Assia's physical beauty in interviews and elsewhere as a defining feature of her characterization in the mid-twentieth century. Plath, too, was cited as beautiful by people who knew her. In one of his interviews, David Compton uses that very word to describe Plath, stating that she was beautiful especially when she was enthusiastic (interview recording, undated).[10] Both experienced a sense of "rootlessness," to use Klein's word; she attended Smith College with Plath but did not know Assia (interview recording, undated, part 1). Assia thought of herself as displaced and rootless, culminating in the epitaph she crafted for herself in a draft of her last will and testament: "Here lies a lover of unreason and an exile" (*Collected Writings* 267).

Like Plath, Assia figured even more prominently in posthumous stories her contemporaries told among themselves: the story Clarissa Roche reveals about Plath reading Assia's name on a burning slip of paper (while burning Hughes's papers in a bonfire in her garden) originally did not feature Assia at all. Rather, Dido Merwin was the name Plath spotted, according to Roche (interview recording, November 20, 1973, part 3); Roche never heard Plath mention Assia (interview recording, November 20, 1973, part 2): whereas Suzette and Helder Macedo insist that Assia's name was inscribed on the paper (interview recording, parts 3 and 4). Assia, however, was aware of Plath's actions; taking Hughes's side, Assia engaged in histrionics, according to Suzette: Assia "distorted things very much" when, for example, she claimed that Plath had burned all of Hughes's poems. And, yet, overall, Plath "sensed something in Assia she liked very much," insists Helder Macedo (interview recording, December 1, 1973, side A). This comment asks us to consider how binary oppositions both oppose and inform: how they mutually define through similarities and differences. Too, such accounts ask us to continually revisit and revise stories we think we know.

At the same time that we begin to develop more complex stories about women, we will find that we must grapple with our ingrained, implicit biases about women and gender. It is still the case that a woman's sexuality defines her in a way a man's does not, and we default to binary thinking, even when speaking about women who both adhere to default standards of femininity and heterosexuality. Conventional logic, as informed by binaries, stipulates that we must have a bad actor to prove the goodness of the other actor in an equation. Thus, for decades now, we pit Plath against Assia: our admiration or love for Plath dictates, per a binary formula, that we must distance Assia from her, making the latter the repository of everything Plath was not. Because Assia occupies the negative position of the binary opposition involving her and Plath, we tend to hypersexualize her, as Rosenstein and Clarissa Roche do in their conversation about Plath and Assia, likely occurring in the early 1970s. Rosenstein insists, "Everyone is talking about Assia's . . . formidable sexuality," to which Roche replies, "All of this is upsetting" because Assia leads to Plath's "blotting out." "When Assia arrived," surmises Roche, "Sylvia must have felt like a nobody." In order to show her allegiance to Plath, Rosenstein speaks up: Plath was a "genius," she announces, and Assia was "merely a translator of poetry." Perhaps feeling like she is a bit unfair to Assia's memory and legacy, Rosenstein offers up remarks about Assia's physical appearance: she was a "magnificent beauty" and "totally unique." Now feeling like it is her turn to defend Plath, Roche adds that Plath is a beauty in her own right and she was "more beautiful at Smith" than at Devon, where "somehow or other she was different" (interview recording, undated).

In one of her poignant interviews with Rosenstein, Suzette Macedo invokes a complicated portrait of Assia. She depicts her friend engaged in a metaphorical "mad dance": to some extent, Macedo concedes, Assia created the situations in which she found herself; she enjoyed making a mess and could be "impossible." Despite the compliments she heaps on Assia in other interviews, Macedo, in an undated one, readily enumerates her friend's shortcomings: Assia "had a very malicious, mocking way" about her, and, eventually, her fabled beauty and glamour disappear. According to Macedo, "All of the glamour of Assia was gone, and I noticed how square she was." Her beautiful face aside, Assia resembled a German hausfrau, in Macedo's words. "She was marvelous," asserts Macedo, "but very empty in a way." Other adjectives used to characterize Assia by her friend include "heavy," "lost," and "defeated." States Macedo, "She was really a victim. She didn't know what was going to happen." In her interpretation of Assia's life, Macedo summarizes it thus: "She got herself into a situation she couldn't cope with. . . . Not what she planned for at all. . . . [She] was caught between forces she couldn't control" (interview recording, undated). This book will explore Assia's portraiture to, paradoxically, complicate it and make sense of it within the context of the very forces she did not understand and could not control. Assia's story is one that reveals the power, limitations, and enticements of gender, in addition to the punishments we dole out to women who are too beautiful, too successful, and too bold for our liking. In the pages that follow, we will encounter

Assia and the most influential person in her life, Ted Hughes, through the amassment of never-before cited stories, facts, and details in the hope that more robust and layered narratives emerge.

In the course of researching and writing this book, I realized that to write about Assia's life, I would also need to write about Hughes and Plath, recognizing that my own experiences, in preparing this study, would shape the presentation of the materials, as must be the case for all writers, who make decisions about how to cast the narrative page by page. Laura Marcus asserts, "Recounting one's life almost inevitably entails writing the life of an other or others; writing the life of another must surely entail the biographer's identifications with his or her subject, whether these are made explicit or not" (*Auto/Biographical Discourses* 273–74). Assia and Hughes wrote about each other, but each separately tells only part of their shared and individual stories. Moreover, any biographical writing about them entails distancing, partial information, and lenses we impose to make sense of lives that are not our own.

In an interview by Drue Heinz, published in the *Paris Review*, Hughes acknowledges that "throughout your life you have certain literary shocks" ("The Art of Poetry" 59); for him, the first literary shock is associated with his discovery and reading of folktales. (Later, he associates Assia with folktales.) For me, it was reading Louisa May Alcott's *Little Women* on my own when I was about ten years old: this was an entire novel, both serious and engaging, that centers women, girls, and their lives in a sweeping and moving manner, honoring—not one—but multiple female characters. I had always enjoyed reading, but I loved literature, I realized, after reading that book. In a rather similar fashion, I found myself astonished by Thomas Hardy's *Tess of the d'Urbervilles* when it was assigned during a "Rise of the Novels" course I took during my sophomore year of college. With *Tess*, the captivating writing, the gorgeous characterizations, and the sensitive treatments of trauma and Tess as a protagonist, portrayed as a tragic heroine, captured my heart and mind. However, I remember feeling confused as to why we concentrated on analyzing landscapes in the novel and not the sexual assault(s) of Tess and her ensuing traumatic downfall and demise. Even at nineteen years old, when I was not steeped in feminist theory or scholarship in women's, gender, and sexuality studies, that seemed a gross oversight and an injustice. Our silence in the class likely stemmed from our inability to know how to broach or talk about the subject, and because it was not addressed, it became taboo. Later on, years and years after my beloved mother suffered an untimely death, I came to understand that my commitment to feminist recovery efforts in literature originated with her. And maybe my love for biography and passion for feminist scholarship come from a place of wanting to make sense of lives: my own, my mother's, other women I know, and the women I research.

Mary Catherine Bateson claims, "Women today read and write biographies to gain perspective on their own lives" (5). That claim, I would venture to say, rests on the understanding that women's lives have something to teach us, something to tell us, first and foremost. Bateson also avers, "We need to look at multiple lives to test and shape our own" (16). My mother's life resonates with me in many ways. Unlike mine, her life was curtailed for various reasons, not least of which was the expectation that she would assume the roles of stay-at-home wife and mother after earning her college degree. When I was twenty-seven and about to sit for my doctoral comprehensive exams, she was dying from cancer at age fifty-two, having battled valiantly through experimental chemotherapy trials for three years, since she had been diagnosed as stage 4 at age forty-nine. I served as a primary caregiver during that time and had the privilege of caring for her. On her deathbed, she asked that I wait to have children, that I finish my Ph.D. (she never finished her graduate study as she learned she was pregnant with me), because she was concerned that my life would become circumscribed in the ways that hers had. Hers was a life of missed and forever deferred opportunities because of her gender, race, and marital-family status. I do not want to dig too much into my family history other than to express that I had another literary shock when I discovered Assia Wevill, whose own life had been circumscribed by gendered constraints and lack of support, whose own horizons must have felt smaller than those of her male counterparts, and who does not get a pass because we love to hate unacceptable women, to use Audre Lorde's words in "The Master's Tools Will Never Dismantle the Master's House"

(112). Conversely, my mother lived an exceptionally acceptable and conventional life, a to-be-expected and even model life for the women of her generation: she was a proverbial lady first and foremost, and her vistas were not any larger or better because of it.

In *Hooked: Art and Attachment*, Rita Felski provides the language and concepts with which to make sense of the mechanics of our attachment to literature and other media, why art pulls us in and why we find it so compelling. When we discover ourselves partial to a literary text, when we realize we have feelings about it, Felski declares that these feelings authenticate the text: it really matters, she writes, and it conveys heft (28). While we do not frequently address affective labor in critical writing in literary studies, it is addressed in the classroom (28), where literature undergoes critical examinations in conversations. Whether in writing or teaching, attachment to literature and what it means and offers to us—its "mattering," to use Felski's word—may stem from an eclectic mix of sources. According to Felski, "This mattering can be aesthetic, political, emotional, ethical, intellectual, or any combination of these" (35). In asserting that we need to develop our justifications for the study of literature and art so that we can better articulate why it is important rather than assuming it is a given, we should start by figuring out what attachments people do have and working from there (35). That information will provide us with enough data to investigate the layers of meaning, importance, significance, and relevance of the particular literary text. The last word I will add to this conversation is allegiance, in the way that Felski uses it. Allegiance can be "partial, qualified, or ambivalent," and when we are able to identify what leads us to hold this allegiance, we can understand how it aids us in shaping our responses to and assessments of the piece of literature (96). Here, I would suggest that our allegiance might also be activated not only with a literary work that invites attachment but also to an author whose identity and life story might be brought to bear as a layer attached to the writing. Surely, my witnessing and understanding of the circumscription of women's lives would factor into how I approach Assia's life and artistic contributions, combined with my research and my scholarship in literary studies and trauma studies. Because, as Felski rightly remarks, gender or biological sex alone do not guarantee identification, attachment, or allegiance (98).

This book concentrates on written texts and audio recordings related to Assia Wevill, Ted Hughes, and Sylvia Plath in this order, from the primary focus to those of lesser concentration. Fortunately, Sylvia Plath does not need recovery, even if we will always be engaged in reframing the meanings and relevance of her life and work in our own time. To some extent, this book deals with ghostly presences as audio recordings, interviews, memoirs, and photographs create the illusion of vibrant, alive people, contributing in significant ways to the world and leading their lives as best they could in numerous challenging circumstances, and, not least, leaving us with stories we can learn from and build on in our classrooms, in our interpretations of lives, and in our discussions of writing and values. I think about Emma Tennant's story depicting Hughes looking out a window in England in fall 1978—nine years after Assia and their daughter Shura died—and he is thinking about Shura: "A girl—it's how she would have looked now. She was a child, Shura. Walking past. That's all" (199). While memories might be all Hughes has left of Shura, we have much more: memories and various media that depict what various people thought mattered and what did not, what was worth fighting for and what finally was not, what was most valued and devalued. Out of these riches, we can identify and parse narratives and values that continue to resonate all these years later. The year in which Hughes muses on what Shura would look like as a thirteen-year-old girl is the year I was born, and it gives me pause to recognize that these lives were lives lived not all that long ago. Timeliness may be one aspect of relevance, but there are countless reasons why we care, and perhaps others can take up why we do. One of the aims of this book in studying the art of "composing a life" is "to find a way to take what is simply ugly and, instead of trying to deny it, to use it in the broader design" (Bateson 211). By no means are Assia or Ted Hughes (or Sylvia Plath) perfect people, but we have much to gain from revisiting what we think we know and learning from new materials and perspectives.

Though we are making inroads when it comes to how we value women's lives and contributions—their legacies in arts and culture—much remains to be done. What we have accomplished with respect to Assia is staggering; we have written her back into history, arts and letters, and culture in more multifaceted ways, working to correct a misogynistic turn in Plath studies and Hughes studies. What is not understandable, at this point in Plath and Hughes studies, is the unkind way we still need to castigate and diminish Assia in order to, finally, establish her as "less than" Plath, "less than" good, and, therefore, not worthy of our attention. Ultimately, with this mindset, we refrain from plumbing the depths of sexist, misogynistic, patriarchal politics that straightjacket women, that stratify women into good and bad as they benefit a larger system of exploitation of women's vulnerability and contributions, inside and outside the home.

There remains much we have not uncovered, do not know, and cannot imagine at the present time. Filling in the record as best we can enables us to better approach lives and literature that are grounded in and indebted to biographies, lives really lived. And that, finally, is the goal: to support, produce, and encourage a world in which we promote diversity, equity, justice, inclusion, and belonging. Focusing on Assia as a case study allows us to surface the issues, values, and debates that frame our literary study and that inform and govern the world in which we live. In studying Assia and Hughes, we make and extract meaning; what we find is that we have clues, then, that show us where we are and that orient us in women's, gender, and sexuality studies as well as critical race and ethnic studies. We, then, can decide how we will move forward because we cannot stay where we are, ethically or otherwise. What Maggie Nelson argues about Freud applies to constructing and weaving biographical narratives about Assia and Hughes: "the problems come when [Freud] succumbs—or we succumb—to the temptation to mastery rather than reminding ourselves that we are a deep play in the makeshift" (68). My approach to these lives is just that: to approach rather than to master.

If it is true, as Annette Kolodny holds, that we assign literary value because of a canon, then it is ever more critical that we interrogate what we include and sanction in reading, teaching, and writing about canonical literature and what is absent. The canon helps us to make sense of a version of literary history and culture. As Kolodny contends, our interest in literary history or a canon stems from "our need to call up and utilize the past on behalf of a better understanding of the present" (303). Surmises Lillian S. Robinson, recognizing the embeddedness of phallogocentrism in the canon, "it is probably quite accurate to think of the canon as an entirely gentlemanly artifact" (154). Therefore, we might be mindful in acknowledging the following when using labels such as "major" and "minor" with authors and their works: the act of distinguishing between major and minor reflects subjective assessments of readers and the "successful critical promotion" of an author (Robinson 153). Without positive subjective assessment and effective critical promotion, an author remains minor. Whether or not the canon can still be equated to a gentlemanly artifact, it is productive to problematize canonical authors and problematic texts to open up conversations about what we uphold and what we unwittingly communicate when making the texts come alive in scholarly books or classrooms. For it follows that what we read and study will play a part in helping us make sense of and navigate our own lives. "Plath," observes Middlebrook, "had always drawn her notions of how to live from literature" (189).[11] If this approach holds true for many, then it behooves us to investigate what is at stake in literary discourses and what we want to champion.[12] This book provides the results of research for others to make up their own minds about significant lives and fascinating texts—and how we should move forward.

2

ASSIA AND HUGHES AS SUBJECTS IN INTERVIEWS AND THE LIVES OF OTHER PEOPLE

The wealth of materials—public, private, and archived—that have emerged since *Reclaiming Assia Wevill* and *The Collected Writings of Assia Wevill* were published, as well as the revisiting of archived materials, made this book possible. With this new constellation of materials, we can piece together storylines from the archives, from interviews recorded shortly after events took place in the middle of the twentieth century to diary accounts to letters. These records document and lend themselves to the work of substantiating the narrative arcs exhibited within these pages. In this book, I do not pretend to establish the true reasons Hughes had affairs or why Plath's marriage ended and Assia's never began with Hughes. Instead, I will provide careful research coverage through archival materials and scholarship that makes accessible what is available for us to know, so that others can fashion new stories, scholarship, creative projects, and conversations from this scholarship. Old stories die hard, and we need new ones.

For the first time in many instances, details, facts, and new pieces of information and stories emerge from the archive and elsewhere to be fixed in print. We learn about motivations and subjective accounts, helping us to recognize the biases that undergird perceptions. For instance, it is well known that Al Alvarez detested Assia and did not allow an opportunity to pass in which he might denigrate her. For example, in his memoir, he writes, "Assia was a rapacious woman with a delicate, sultry face that seemed out of proportion with her heavy figure, and she made a pass at every man she met so automatically that it was hard to feel flattered" (235).[1] We need to unpack this quotation before we move on. First of all, Alvarez states that Assia was greedy, wanting everything for herself: ironically, Assia settled for far less than what she wanted. Second, in fat-shaming her, Alvarez demonstrates his hostility and sexism simultaneously: Assia's virtues are embodied only, and, according to Alvarez's reasoning, her beautiful face cannot compensate for her fat body, thereby implying that Assia should be thought of as less than beautiful or worthy for what Alvarez denigrates as a fat body. Ironically, he also faults her for her flirting or for making sexual overtures, and, yet, Alvarez's anger and mean-spiritedness toward Assia and her memory stem from the fact that she rejected his romantic advances and spurned him. She did not make a pass at him apparently. Alvarez never forgave Assia for ultimately rejecting him; he proposed marriage to her on July 27, 1962, but she had already declared she was sick of him to her friend Nathaniel Tarn on July 16 and subsequently turned down his marriage proposal (Nathaniel Tarn Papers).[2] However, Alvarez "had not grown sick of her. He was in love with Assia to the point of obsession," writes Jonathan Bate (*Ted Hughes* 316). For the rebuff, Alvarez skewered Assia for decades in print and in conversation. As an influential man in literature and culture, Alvarez wielded much power in creating and maintaining master narratives and plots. One such plot: Assia, as a jealous and vengeful femme fatale, precipitated a chain reaction of tragedies, starting with Plath's death. This master narrative makes her the scapegoat, thereby relieving anyone else, including Plath, Hughes, and Alvarez himself, of culpability. Such a narrative, showcasing such a plot, led Wagner-Martin to write to Elizabeth Sigmund on February 11, 1987, twenty-four years to the day that Plath died, "What a beast Assia must have been, or that was Alvarez's take. But, yes, trapped in her own web finally. And that is only sorrow again" (correspondence, item 37). Carl Rollyson recounts a conversation he had with Alvarez: "Ted and Assia often turned up in black, Al Alvarez told me, a couple bound together and riven apart by Sylvia who always stood between them, exerting a power that Sylvia herself could not imagine except in her commanding poetry" (120). Alvarez clearly did not censor his thoughts and feelings about Assia to biographers, and he carried a particular agenda, influenced by his positionality, with respect to Assia, Plath, and Hughes.

The perspective sketched above aligns with the manner in which literary London treated Assia. As Heather Clark documents, the public thought of Assia as a pariah, and, in 1969, the year Assia died, David Wevill observed to a contemporary that Assia was "blamed and never forgiven" for any transgressions concerning Plath and Hughes (Wevill qtd. in Clark, *Red Comet* 912). So hostile but also so very unrelenting was literary London in its scapegoating of Assia that even the scapegoat came around to believing that she must be at fault, as Assia's friend Mira Hamermesh avers, "She never, never thought otherwise" (Hamermesh qtd. in Clark, *Red Comet* 914).

People who knew Assia offer 360-degree perspectives that enrich our understanding of her as an actual person rather than as a stock character. And these friends understand better than anyone the extremity of Assia's situation, then and now. Tarn befriended Assia and worked with her professionally.[3] In those capacities, he became well acquainted with her and even assumed the role of her confidant.[4] On February 22, 2020, I attended a session dedicated to Tarn's life and work at the Louisville Conference on Literature and Culture since 1900 and managed to talk with Tarn for about twenty minutes afterward. During the panel session itself, in which he participated, Tarn argued that myths and symbols are all we have left in the end, as we see in T. S. Eliot's work: "There is no world outside poetry," Tarn maintains. For the purposes of this book, these arguments are prescient and anticipate the difficulty of piecing together coherent narratives about Assia and her life with Ted Hughes. Much of what I tracked down revolves around myths and symbols, and the lives we explore herein are rooted in the world of poetry, as Tarn might phrase it. Referring to Assia during his formal presentation, Tarn says, "David Wevill's wife[5] got involved in the appalling nightmare of Ted Hughes–Sylvia Plath," and he declares vehemently, "That trio [Plath–Hughes–Assia Wevill] has been the curse of British poetry for the last 20 years, and no one can talk about anything else."[6] He offers the papers in his Stanford archive as an example: the only reason people read them is to read about Plath, he asserts. The fate of American poetry, he says, is in the hands of London, a sentiment he first heard in San Francisco years ago. The panel discussion and informal interview show me that, a half century after she died, Assia's life story continues to resonate in academia in transatlantic fashion; in this instance, it is used to gesture to the influence of British literary circles (or triangles) on American literature and letters.

It is the case that Tarn's diary brings to light private details that Assia ostensibly related to him about her life, as well as the lives of David Wevill, Hughes, and Plath. In July 1962, months after the fateful May 18–20, 1962, visit the Wevills made to Hughes and Plath at Court Green, when and where the attraction between Hughes and Assia appears to have started, Assia confides to Tarn that Plath indicated that she did not care for Assia, that Plath "hated" her, actually, to use Tarn's word for what Assia told him, and that Plath wanted her to depart early that weekend. By October 1962, when the full-blown romance between Hughes and Assia served as the catalyst that broke up the Hughes-Plath marriage, Assia informed Tarn about Plath hiring detectives to investigate her because Plath was naming Assia as a correspondent in the divorce suit Plath intended to file. In an unguarded moment, Assia tells Tarn she cares about Hughes and names the qualities he has that attract her: "charity, energy, love, genius" (Nathaniel Tarn Papers). On February 12, 1963, Assia calls Patricia Mendelson and Tarn, telling them that Plath died, and on February 16, Tarn writes about the aftermath: "all the women," which Tarn places in quotation marks, presumably to indicate these are Assia's words, blame Assia for Plath's suicide because Plath told (what Tarn calls terrible) stories to a group of women. By March 12, Assia presents herself to Tarn as indecisive in her love triangle involving Hughes and Wevill and as someone who has no one to talk to about such matters, other than him. She thanks Tarn for being an excellent counselor. For his part, Tarn sums up Assia as "really fantastically naïve," despite retaining "her critical acumen in part." In June 1963, Tarn picks up on the very aspects of Assia's personal life that made her life from that time until the end of her life very challenging: he assesses that she is isolated and feeling like an outsider without the abilities to cope with what is happening to her (Nathaniel Tarn Papers).

Martin Baker put together a memoir, dedicating a chapter to Assia, his good friend and colleague, and to Shura, whom he had met and photographed. The only memoirist to write about the little girl in a sustained fashion, Baker captures Shura's zest for life and her personality. Baker and Assia met in 1966, when he was twenty-four and she was thirty-nine; they worked at Ogilvy and Mather as writers. Assia, from his first impressions, was "fabulous, mysterious and contrary" ("Assia Gutmann," 95), as well as "urbane, beautiful and wise" and an "archetypal earth mother" (97). They struck up a solid friendship and working relationship, with Assia serving as an informal mentor to him and to Chris Roose and Chris Wilkins. Indeed, their friendship and working relationship were so strong that Baker shared his ideas about a book he titled *Wellington the Tin Solider* with Assia, who, in turn, shared it with Hughes. Hughes offered to contribute text to the book; both he and Assia were supportive of the project.[7] This is an example of a collaborative project Hughes was willing to undertake with Assia and her colleague. Assia "seemed rather iconoclastic" overall, Baker recounts. She was not unfriendly, but he interpreted her as remote and individualistic (98). Baker's first impressions of Hughes were these: "a taciturn, Byronic figure. He spent the evening, ignoring Assia, surrounded by acolytes" (100). He adds, "In all the time that I knew her, Assia never spoke in a derogatory way of Ted Hughes or Sylvia Plath" (100). Over the last three years of Assia's life, Baker became aware of her "depressive personality" and "worrying insecurity" (100). By this point, Hughes was already established as a "mythical literary figure" (101); the copywriters at Ogilvy and Mather read his work and were influenced by it.

Assia and Baker's friendship extended itself outside of the office in social visits and excursions but also in artistic pursuits. For instance, Assia trusted Baker and confided in him about her poetry translations and how she felt about them. Recalls Baker:

> In 1968, while visiting Assia at her new flat, on Clapham Common, South London, Assia showed me some translations that she was making of poems by Yehuda Amichai. She explained that she was having difficulty in finding the appropriate English equivalent of some of the Hebrew expressions. Her

anxiety was tangible and yet the finished book, published by Cape Goliard, shows only her diligence and sensitivity. Assia's translations are lyrical examples of an unforced genius. She focuses the reader's attention to the substance and delicate nuances of the original words and meaning, never upon the translator's dexterity. In this she is translucent. (102)

This exchange should cancel any doubt as to whether Assia served as the primary English translator of Amichai's work in 1968. Thinking about these poetry translations, Baker wonders if Assia embarked on the book to establish herself as a rival to Plath (102). It might be impossible to corroborate this line of thinking one way or the other. What we do know: Assia's friendship with Baker was close, and she never mentioned Plath as a rival. Hughes, however, positions Assia and Plath as rivals in the poem "The Other" from *Capriccio*.

The joy of reading Baker's memoir derives from its acute observations and its witty, bright, and engaging language, with the best part being his centering of Shura. At four years old, Shura was "vivacious," with a "precocious intelligence" and boundless energy (102). Shura was much loved by Assia, who possessed a "genuine maternal instinct." As a result, Shura was "socially secure": "Assia loved her with an uncompromising devotion," writes Baker (102). His last memory of Shura is of her waving goodbye on the steps of Okeover Manor (103). We have Baker to thank for recording biographical facts and anecdotes brimming with life, and we have him to thank for recording the only extant videos of Assia in color. The videos capture her at English's Seafood Restaurant in Brighton and on a train, the occasion being a going-away celebration dinner for coworker Anne Semple in 1968.[8] Assia's "sensitivity about her appearance was quite apparent, at the age of forty-one, she seemed in mourning for her lost youth. Her weight was always of concern to her," notes Baker (105–6). In the video, Assia briefly and playfully covers her face with a plate, indicating that she did not wish to be filmed. Always aware of her appearance, Assia was "acutely fashion conscious" and "impeccably dressed" (106). As a person, Assia proved charming (106) and possessed "great charisma and sophistication" (107); she was not vulgar in the slightest way. At the ad agency, most of the female employees seemed to like her, Baker remarks (106–7).

During a lunch at the Neal Street Restaurant in 1968, Assia wanted to know if, should something happen to her, Baker and his wife would look after Shura. Not fathoming what Assia meant, Baker assured her everything would be fine. Assia then asked if Baker could secure a revolver on her behalf. Thinking Assia's request for a gun was a joke, Baker dismissed it (107). He was devastated to learn Assia took her own life and Shura's too in what he calls a "brutal" (102) and "barbaric act" months later (110). Right before leaving for her last, disastrous house-hunting trip with Hughes, Assia called Baker on the telephone, expressing concern that Shura might "create discord for Ted" (108). Years after Assia and Shura had passed away, Patricia Mendelsohn and Baker conversed about Assia, and Mendelsohn posed the question: "[H]ow could she leave Shura to the unknown, even with friends?" (109). To Mendelsohn, Assia and Shura were too tightly connected to be pulled apart. A "whirlwind of despair" swept Shura to death with her mother, Baker believes (109). At the end of his chapter on Assia, Baker gives us the last heartbreaking image of Shura at the funeral: "I don't remember very much through tears that I shed—the sight of the little white box, containing Shura, was as poignant and indelible an image of tragedy as I've ever known, as also was the figure of Lonya, Assia's father, who seemed quite bewildered and diminutive standing next to Ted Hughes" (110). His parting assessment of Assia: like her beloved netsuke, she embodied "tense perfection" and "generosity" (110). The tragedy is their deaths: untimely, unnecessary, and unjust.

In an interview with Harriet Rosenstein on March 21, 1974, that Jillian Becker shared with Clark, we learn that Plath's suicide prevented Hughes and Assia from developing a healthy relationship. Throughout the 1960s and the 1970s, even after her death, Assia continued to signify as evil, an object of scorn, and something to ridicule, rather than as a subject who might deserve a measure of empathy or pity amid the trauma and chaos that Plath's death ushered in: "Sylvia's death 'decided' her relationship with Ted as it had not been really decided before. . . . With Sylvia's death came (again) Romantic Inevitability—the black destiny to be lived out. She received, and bore, the responsibility for Sylvia's suicide. Ted was tragic; she was evil. . . . She accepted it—penance and identity all in one. . . . He would neither be with Assia nor release her" (Becker qtd. in Clark, *Red Comet* 915). Context matters as does positionality: how we respond to others reflects just as much on us and our biases and values as it does on the people we are judging within the grid of identity politics. Of note here is the easy exoneration of Hughes and the full culpability assigned to Assia. Assia was not married to Plath, and yet the responsibility lies with her. Gendered assumptions about who must be to blame and who deserves blame run amuck in interviews in the 1960s and 1970s because the values of that place and time called them into being. Public censure combined with the traumatic aftermath of suicide meant that Plath would haunt Assia for the rest of her life. To add to that tragic compound, Assia occupied more than one marginal identity, and, according to Bruce Perry, "Marginalization is a fundamental trauma" (220). Moreover, Assia's need to bond with Hughes was left unmet in a satisfactory way (for her). Ruth Fainlight, a close friend of Assia, explains, "[Assia] just didn't understand the possibility of living without a man. She wasn't quipped to" (Fainlight qtd. in Clark, *Red Comet* 917). Hughes never would propose marriage to Assia, and he could not create a stable family unit and life in a shared home for more than a few months at a time with her. The longest they were happy was during their sojourn in Ireland from February to May in 1966.

    Interviewees and memoirists compose portraits of a person that are contingent on their closeness to the subject and whether the relationship was positive or not. In other words, their responses will reflect the nature of their relationship to a subject. Lucas Myers considered Assia and Hughes friends, and his memoir illustrates the bias. I must say that it is refreshing to read or listen to accounts regarding Assia by her friends rather than enemies or by people who really did not know her very well because we have far more of the latter than the former in print. Like Plath, Assia "was good company" and "born to conduct a literary and artistic salon" (*Crow Steered* 127). Myers remembers her as "a very vulnerable person" (128), no less so because she "felt as though Sylvia were haunting her" (129). Clarifies Myers, "I don't think she meant that a ghost visited her at night but that the posthumous presence of Sylvia loomed over all her associations and poured over her thoughts" (129). In this way, Plath's life and death permeated Assia's life, and later, death, which resembled Plath's own to some extent. Assia suffered greatly in the years after Plath died. Shunned by others, Assia could not secure a safe place.[9] England, whether in the city of London or in the countryside, did not offer a safe haven for her. Even Hughes's parents went out of their way to make Assia feel ostracized, ensuring that she felt she did not belong.[10] It got to the point, in fact, that "Assia was the one who was shipped off" when the joint living situation at Court Green became unbearable for the adults living there—Hughes, Assia, and Hughes's parents—despite Hughes having "[n]o complaints about Assia, who was gallantly putting things into shape [at Court Green]" (Feinstein 157). Myers recounts that Hughes told him that Assia's accent was the "enemy" from Hughes's father's perspective; Myers notes, "These two survivors [Assia and William Hughes] of world wars did not see that they trod common ground" (132). Additionally, Olwyn Hughes told Myers that Edith Hughes, Hughes's mother, frowned upon Assia's three marriages, "the sort of behavior [that] was unheard of in Hebden Bridge," and the objections were to Assia's marital status and history (133). Wanting to comprehend Assia's suicide, Hughes assigned part of the responsibility to his parents because of their poor treatment of her; "he could not help blaming his parents, who had been so horrible to her," Bate pronounces, "for the downward spiral that led to her death" (278). Hughes found himself living through nothing short of trauma—Bate's word—in 1969 (283).

After Assia had died in relatively the same manner as Plath, Hughes wrote to Myers that he was at fault for both suicides. Writes Myers, Hughes blamed himself "in Sylvia's case because of his 'insane decisions' and in Assia's case because of his 'insane indecision'" (133). Hughes obviously felt safe in sharing his personal thoughts and feelings with Myers, and Myers's take on the situation, in hindsight, was that Hughes would settle with Assia in Scotland before 1970 came to pass: "I did not recognize," writes Myers, "that she might think it was impossible to wait. It seems likely to me now that she was not in an ordinary state of mind when she committed suicide and that her isolation in London had driven her off a central balance" (135).[11] If Myers could circle back to his observation of Assia as a vulnerable person, he might come to the conclusion that Judith Butler arrives at in *The Force of Nonviolence*: "What happens is not the miraculous or heroic transformation of vulnerability into strength, but the articulation of a demand that only a supported life can persist *as a life*" (194). She adds, "If any of us are to survive, to flourish, even to attempt to lead a good life, it will be a life lived with others—a [life] that is no life without those others. I will not lose this 'I' who I am under such conditions; rather, if I am lucky, and the world is right, whoever I am will be steadily sustained and transformed by my connections with others, the forms of contact by which I am altered and sustained" (199–200). As I trace in *Reclaiming Assia Wevill*, Assia did not achieve her dream of securing what I call in that book a good life; structurally vulnerable in several areas of her life, she felt bereft and, as Myers acknowledges, isolated in a major cosmopolitan city, which must have made the contrast between isolation and connection stark and even more unbearable.

The purchase of Rosenstein's research materials by Emory University in 2019[12] meant, for the first time, researchers could access what the people who knew Assia, Hughes, and Plath had to say in their own words and in rather unadulterated fashion, with the obvious exception of the influence of the interviewer. Historically, Assia constituted a subject not to be broached in literary studies, and what we discover, ironically, is a wealth of information that leads us to reconsider and, perhaps, refigure Assia and her relationship with Hughes. We are given a fuller picture, a panoramic one, that requires us to resurvey the landscape of what we thought we knew in Hughes studies in connection with Assia and Hughes himself, while also discovering or being reminded of how Plath plays a prominent role in the biographical narratives we are reconstructing. Specifically, the interviews invite us to consider how the people closest to Assia with respect to time and place viewed her, and Rosenstein managed to talk to people who were close to Assia and Hughes and who interacted with them personally. These recordings exist today as digital files transferred from cassette tapes, and they hold the promise of helping us to reassess our own assumptions about our subjects and stories we have long held to be true. Notably, Rosenstein's own assumptions—and those of her interlocutors—come across in startling, intriguing, and, sometimes, disappointing fashion. The interviews often display the historical context of the early 1970s: the attitudes toward Assia and Plath reflect the very dangerous and damaging sexism and misogyny both faced. Left unchecked or unacknowledged, we leave ourselves doomed to propagate the same harmful rhetoric and attendant stories.

The motivation driving the interviews was a Plath biography that Rosenstein had hoped to write and publish; the biography was never published, but the interviews last as a tribute to the impulse underwriting the biographical pursuit: a search for information that will fuel interpretations of significant lives.[13] The overarching objective of any genuine biographical project or scholarly one is to produce and safeguard truths, and as daunting as this objective is with respect to the fragmented record we have in connection with Assia's life in particular, it remains an objective worth pursuing. Understanding her life, especially in connection with Hughes and Plath, may allow us to survey twentieth-century poetry and its influence in nuanced fashion and offer us figurative measuring sticks and mirrors: we can see how far we have come and what we value as we metacognitively reflect upon and interpret their lives and work and what we find in them.

In *Reclaiming Assia Wevill*, my scholarly study of Assia in connection with Plath and Hughes, I concentrated on what emerges in scholarship and creative representations treating Assia. Our reactions to her, I maintain, suggest more about us than they do about her. In that book, I consider the texts and artifacts we have that build the narratives we circulate and the stories we tell about her. Assia's life stories have certainly been manipulated, most obviously after her death, when her presence and the impact she made on Hughes's life tended toward erasure. This textual erasure is mirrored in the way that her actual physical presence was obliterated. The wishes she articulated in her unfinished and unsigned last will (*Collected Writings* 266–67), went unfulfilled, and rather than being buried with a headstone, as she wished, she was cremated and secretly disposed of, presumably with Shura. In his interpretations of Hughes's poems and archival notes, Steve Ely posits that Hughes buried Assia and Shura secretly under a sycamore tree near Hughes's Lumb Bank home (63). Plath had achieved yet more—a marked grave, a resting place, a memorial site—that Assia wanted but could not secure or attain (Koren and Negev 220).[14] In private writing that he never intended anyone to read, Hughes allows that there are only two people in the entire world who know where to find Assia or where to send their thoughts to her; he refrains from mentioning who they are, though he is clearly one of them ("Capriccio, circa 1967–8 Nov. 1993" 166). Assia's sister Celia Chaikin passed away in 2019 without ever knowing what happened to her sister's and niece's remains.

The Rosenstein interviews, almost one hundred of them in number, contribute in mighty ways to fleshing out Assia's biographical story and adding to Hughes's and Plath's. For these reasons and more, they are valuable. With Assia, we can restore the complexity of her humanity, not a small feat when we recall that she has been painted as a femme fatale for more than half a century—when she was made visible. Consequently, we can now access intimate interviews with a bevy of people involved in the Plath–Hughes–Assia Wevill triangle, and the revelations impart facts, details, and perspectives that previously were not available to us in archives or publications. Moreover, these interviews took place within five years of Assia's death, making them timely and important as memories were vivid and clear. Among the noteworthy interviewees are Suzette Macedo; Edward Lucie-Smith; Faye Weldon; an unnamed and, therefore, unknown woman who knew Assia; Ruth Fainlight; Elizabeth Compton Sigmund; and Richard Murphy. To emphasize their decidedly subjective takes on Assia, Plath, and Hughes, I will feature discussions of them in piecemeal fashion rather than synthesizing or organizing what they have to say by theme or topic so as to better delineate in as complex a fashion as possible how Assia appeared to her friends. The Rosenstein interviews will be drawn upon throughout the chapters of this book; they will not be limited to this chapter, although this chapter is dedicated to them.

Suzette Macedo befriended both Plath and Assia; Macedo was important to Assia in particular. In a letter to Clarissa Roche, Olwyn Hughes calls

Macedo Assia's closest friend (copy of correspondence), although letters between Assia and Patricia Mendelson suggest that Assia had more than one close friend, with Mendelson being the closest. For her part, Macedo comes across as a particularly interesting interviewee because she functioned as a confidante to both Plath and Assia. During the course of her conversation with Rosenstein, Macedo provides details no one else Rosenstein interviews could. Describing Assia as "completely distraught" and "in complete despair" after living with Ted Hughes at Court Green,[15] Macedo states that Assia feared Olwyn Hughes, whom she suspected as having an agenda to defame Plath. Per Macedo, Olwyn is implicated as a factor in the unhappiness of Plath and Assia. Everyone and everything seem to wind up "going to pieces" at Court Green (Macedo, interview recording, November 27). In her interview on November 27, circa 1973, Macedo refers to Plath and Assia throughout, interweaving details and stories about them and their secrets in a manner that underscores how similar in many respects the two women are—or, to be more precise, how similar their situations were as separated women who were bringing up young children as the heads of their household at a time when those aspects would be considered triple jeopardy (that is, single women were figured as abandoned women; single mothers were even rarer than single women; and women serving as heads of their households were rarer still).[16]

Though similarities exist between Plath and Assia, neither woman could see them, nor could their friends. In describing Assia as a person, Macedo declares her friend to be a "feminine woman in the most extreme": she was, in Macedo's account, "extraordinary" and "enchanting." With her long, varnished nails, beautiful clothes, and memorable voice, Assia presented as a very feminine but also "artificial" woman; Macedo recalls Assia's false eyelashes and her embodiment of "a woman of mystery." Macedo asserts that Plath was obsessed with femininity and Assia was very feminine; Plath "must have realized" that she could never rival Assia in performances of femininity (interview recording, November 27). Rosenstein discloses in an interview with Murphy that Plath felt herself abandoned for "a marvelously beautiful woman" (interview recording, April 19, 1974, part 1). It is interesting to observe that Macedo, a friend of Assia, comments on her friend's thick legs and thick ankles, despite there being no apparent reason for doing so, except to paint a full picture of what Assia was like physically. In this depiction, then, we see that Assia's appearance always garners commentary, even from those close to her and from people who did not wish to see her denigrated. The femme fatale distinction—wherein Assia's physical beauty and related qualities are enumerated and then lauded or scorned—is quite entrenched in discussions about who Assia was and what she represents after her death. Her physical features repeatedly stand out as one of the most—if not the most—defining characteristics about her.[17]

While considering the difficulties Assia (and Plath) faced, Macedo repeats a claim Assia made about Ted Hughes being "violent."[18] To Elaine Feinstein, Macedo recounts seeing Assia the day following violent sex and that Assia "was ashen and seemed to have genuinely found Ted's passion alarming" (*Ted Hughes* 126). These are unsavory details and not meant to be sensational; rather, they are the exact words and details of a close friend who agreed to be interviewed about Assia, who knew her and to whom she confided. Assia may have embellished, but I follow William Trevor, who maintains that Assia "exaggerated" in stories she told him "only in the interests of what she saw as a greater veracity" (118). The sexual experience Assia described as rape must have been traumatic for her. Asserts Macedo, "Assia was frightened of Ted" (interview recording, November 27). She continues, "She wasn't a very sexual woman. She wasn't at all." Indeed, Macedo adds, "The actual physical contact frightened her." While Assia was very passive sexually, explains Macedo, Hughes was "very violent" sexually; he was a "beast" (interview recording, November 27). Assia never wanted to see Hughes again after they slept together for the first time; he was a "maniac," and she was "terrified." She described "black sweat coming down his face," presumably to bring the scene to life for her friend. It was a memory Assia surely never forgot, and Macedo most certainly did not (interview recording, November 27). Following this recounting, Rosenstein comments that Hughes tore the sink off the wall in a hotel room. Clark records that Plath confided in Clarissa Roche, telling her that Hughes "had beaten her and caused her miscarriage, and that he had pulled a sink out of a hotel room wall when he was with Assia" (*Red Comet* 817). How Assia describes her sexual relationship with Hughes is horrifying.

Rather than bury these details, it is important for us to acknowledge them for what they are: the words of a woman who understood herself as victimized, who was frightened of her lover and yet continued in an intimate relationship with him all the same, as countless women around the world do. In exposing these dynamics or drawing attention to them, we take seriously the victim and what she experienced in these pages *and* in the stories we encounter outside of this book. Instead of dismissing everything out of hand, we can accept what Assia reportedly said, believed, and experienced about this ugly and traumatic event, while keeping open the possibility that there may be even more layers to her story and Hughes's, which will necessarily mutually inform each other.

Emotional violence wreaks havoc, too, and Plath told Macedo that Hughes wanted her to take him back. He dismissed Assia to Plath, saying he was simply "masturbating with a moonbeam" in relation to Assia (Macedo, interview recording, November 27). But Hughes was "malicious," argues Macedo: he played Plath and Assia against each other in real life. He gave reports to Plath about Assia and vice versa. In his poetry, we catch glimpses of this dynamic in "Rules of the Game" from *Capriccio* (renamed "The Other" in *Collected Poems*) and "Dreamers" from *Birthday Letters*. Additionally, Plath and Assia both despised Hughes's radio play *Difficulties of a Bridegroom*, which aired in early 1963. Per Macedo, Assia thought Hughes was "manic" when he gifted her roses with "blood money," a scene depicted in his play. Assia was horrified with that scene, and so was Plath.

According to Macedo, Assia's fascination, envy, and horror concerning Plath's life, work, and death respectively took the shape of a poem that Assia wrote about Plath, that Hughes may possess, Macedo says. We know, from Tarn, that Assia was mesmerized by Plath, to the extent that she contemplated the prospect of writing a biography about her (Nathaniel Tarn Papers). As with so much else, many of Assia's written texts, drawings, and other artifacts are lost to time or not publicly available. Be that as it may, what we do have and what surfaces from time to time is quite miraculous when we consider the contexts within which Assia was living and working. The unavailable poem about Plath by Assia is a case in point: we would learn much from such a poem. Most likely we would be treated to details about Plath's life and Assia's perspectives about the same. Such information would further bolster the biographical enterprise and amplify literary scholarship in life and letters. Materials that we suspect are no longer extant may surface in the future. For example, in editing *The Collected Writings of Assia Wevill*, Peter K. Steinberg and I learned that the Estate of Aurelia Plath located a bundle of letters that Assia had written to Aurelia Plath, Plath's mother, after 1963, apparently confiding in her. These letters lay lost in Warren Plath's basement for decades and have since resurfaced and are in private hands at the time of the writing of this book.

Though Assia feared Olwyn Hughes at times,[19] she did not fear Suzette Macedo or her husband in the least. The same holds true for Suzette Macedo with respect to Assia. In her portrayal of her friend, Macedo emphasizes that she loved Assia very much and that she was very fond of her. Assia was not an angel; she "thoroughly enjoyed mischief," acknowledges Macedo (interview recording, November 27). She was fun to be around, telling stories to entertain whomever might be in her audience (Macedo, interview recording, November 27). It can be difficult to reconcile these lighthearted qualities with what we know: Assia made life-threatening decisions that we absolutely cannot condone. And yet, we can acknowledge that she also struggled with mental illness, as she documents in her March 11, 1967, letter to her sister (*Collected Writings* 116–18), while also coming across as someone immensely likable to her friends, who left their impressions and reminiscences for posterity, understanding that they contributed to correcting, bolstering, extending, and reshaping the biographical stories we tell about Assia, Hughes, and Plath.

Edward Lucie-Smith believes that Plath did not trust him because he was close to Assia; she saw him as "Assia's ally." (It will be clear why Plath would not have trusted Lucie-Smith, given his comments about her in his July 28 [circa early 1970s] interview by Rosenstein.) Furthermore, he says he could not like Plath either—he admired her, but "that was something different"; seemingly, if one liked Assia and Hughes, it was impossible to like Plath, too ("couldn't like all three"), according to Lucie-Smith (Lucie-Smith, interview recording, July 28). While Macedo picks up on Assia's constructed image, Lucie-Smith remarks upon Plath's cultivated exterior: she was always "on," maintaining "a well-organized facade." Unlike Assia, Plath "wasn't particularly well-dressed or fashionable," appearing as a country girl with braids, tending to bees, and she struck one as "curiously unfeminine" at that time of her life, according to Lucie-Smith. He avers that Assia once told him that she felt bad about "competing with Sylvia" because Plath possessed "so little knowledge of the weapons" of femininity that were employed.[20]

In a different interview, Rosenstein voices her belief that Plath's "sense of her own womanliness was never terribly strong" (Murphy, interview recording, April 19, 1974, part 1). We should take into account Plath's situation as a mother of two young children and a freelance writer; she was a woman who actively worked what is known in gender studies as the "double day of work" because she attended to domestic duties, too (Shaw and Lee 465), and essentially worked all the time, even with Hughes's pitching in to help with the children or around the house.[21] It is little wonder that Plath was "swallowed" up by work and young children, especially after her separation from Hughes. Plath also had to contend with what Lucie-Smith understands as Hughes's overwhelming masculinity and masculinist attitude.

In contrast to feminine Assia, whom he calls sexually successful and responsive, Lucie-Smith paints Plath as "castrating." Fueling feminist backlash, Lucie-Smith assesses Plath as a feminist, to which Rosenstein disagrees (Lucie-Smith, interview recording, July 28). And yet, Lucie-Smith may also have been thinking about Plath's appearance at a PEN party at the end of her life, where partygoers wondered how Plath would live without Hughes. He describes Plath as doing her best to communicate that she did not leave Hughes because of Assia but because she desired an "independent existence." Plath was really overwhelmed by domestic work (read: not by Assia), Lucie-Smith concludes. He is probably right about this issue, though Hughes and Assia's extramarital affair certainly served as the catalyst that further pried the marriage apart.

After comparing and contrasting Assia with Plath, the conversation turns to Lucie-Smith comparing and contrasting Plath with Hughes. Because Lucie-Smith views Plath as a very unfeminine woman, he argues that Plath must have been ostensibly comforted by the hypermasculine Hughes (per Lucie-Smith's line of reasoning) because the big contrast would have suggested that Plath was more feminine than she actually was. In an unpleasant moment, Lucie-Smith says that it is very easy to see why Plath wanted Hughes as her partner but not why he would want to be with her. However, Lucie-Smith concedes that Hughes discerned something in Plath that was extraordinary and that they were destined for each other because of their "exceptional gifts." But then he states how a sizable number of people loathed Plath during her lifetime; evidently, Lucie-Smith would not identify as an ally of Plath, due to his strong friendship with Assia. Here we see the strength of friendships and allegiances or alliances, and we would do well to identify those when we can throughout the biographical pursuit as those make an impact on how we interpret and come to understand subjects and issues that resonate.

Probably his animosity toward Plath stems from his belief that Plath "killed Assia in the end" because Assia struggled with her jealousy of Plath and an obsession with her as a great poet. In his admission that he knew Assia very well, Lucie-Smith claims that "Assia's [life story] is a bit more [of a] horrifying story still" after comparison with Plath's, presumably because of the death of Shura and what many perceived as a copycat suicide. The heightened tragedy of it all: Shura occupied the center of Assia's life, according to Lucie-Smith (interview recording, July 28), and so her subsequent death is not one that Assia would have taken lightly. Indeed, Assia contemplated how to provide for Shura, should she herself not live to care for her daughter (*Collected Writings* 117–18), and ruminated on "the criminality [of filicide] perpetrated on my little Shuri—these thoughts stopped me at the last sane moment" (155).

Like every other person interviewed about Assia, Lucie-Smith weighs in on his friend's appearance. As "a great beauty," Assia nevertheless had the figure with proportions that drew consternation from many; she was heavyset. Among her desirable physical qualities, Lucie-Smith lists Assia's hair, her skin, and her eyes, the most beautiful eyes he could remember seeing. Overall, her effect was very feminine and womanly, he says (interview recording, July 28). Further in the interview, he elaborates on her elegance and her talent; she proved herself as a writer at a top advertising agency.

Fay Weldon did not know Plath, but she was close to Assia. Assia confided in Weldon that a Plath poem about a cold moon was about her,[22] but Plath was very wrong, asserts Weldon, because Assia "was a warm-hearted person" (interview recording). Assia's reactions and responses were normal in an abnormal situation, Weldon maintains: of course, Assia would fixate on Plath, partly because of the blame assigned to Assia and partly for other reasons, notwithstanding Assia's admiration for Plath as a poet. People admired Assia's beauty, and other people's opinions mattered to Assia; she wanted affection. Dubbing Assia "poor girl," Weldon explains that Nazis murdered Assia's family in concentration camps; she was desperate and embodied the "survivor thing gone wrong." Weldon is likely referencing survivor's guilt, a condition in which a person experiences guilt because that person survived a life-threatening situation or crisis when someone else did not. Consequently, Assia's death, as Weldon interprets it, results from Plath's death; it is a "direct consequence." Rosenstein winds up calling Assia a "selfish cow" in her conversation with Weldon, after venturing to suggest that Plath and Assia sound alike in their concern about the judgment of others. Generally, the easy move is to revictimize the victim in traumatic situations, to blame her and hold her responsible for all that is traumatic and wrong in her life. Assia accepts blame in her May 19, 1963, journal entry,[23] but we fall into a deadly trap when we expect women to bear the brunt of ugly situations and punish them verbally, socially, or otherwise.

Little details that contribute to a composite picture of Assia are embedded in other interviews Rosenstein conducted in the early 1970s, shortly after Assia and Shura died in 1969. Assia's aspirations to a grander life than the one she managed to have can be seen in the observation that she "was ashamed to be seen" in the "shambles" of a car Hughes borrowed from the Merwins (Merwin). In terms of literary history, that addition to Assia's characterization merits little attention, perhaps, except to underscore Assia's desire for elegance and grandeur that are gestured to in Plath's and Hughes's poems about her. What is startling: Rosenstein speculates in one of her interviews with Elizabeth Compton Sigmund that Assia stole Plath's first editions of other writers from her padlocked study; Sigmund agrees such an act may have occurred. Furthermore, Assia also took Plath's manuscripts, including a lost novel, to gain insight into Plath or, in Rosenstein's words, "to understand the woman" she believed she "murdered." We know that Assia read Plath's unfinished novel about Hughes, David Wevill, Plath, and herself—titled *The Interminable Loaf*, then *Doubletake*, and, finally, *Double Exposure* (Clark, *Red Comet* 736)[24]—and that Assia covertly sent Plath manuscripts to her sister in Canada as insurance for Shura[25] because Celia Chaikin was meant to be Shura's guardian if she survived Assia. What Rosenstein and Sigmund could not know because they were not confidantes of Assia is that Assia was always thinking of Shura's future, as her letters and journals indicate. Shura was Hughes's daughter, and as Assia did not receive child support from him, Assia attempted to secure Shura's future financially through means available to Hughes, with the theft of Plath's manuscripts. However, we know much more in hindsight with the surfacing of these letters and other writing than Assia's and Plath's contemporaries could have known. Thus, Rosenstein goes on to say that Assia is "obsessed" with Plath and desired to know more about her and so took the manuscripts. Allegedly, according to Rosenstein, Assia called up a bookseller to unload Plath's manuscripts shortly before she died. Plath's pilfered manuscripts were easily stored in a big trunk Assia owned (Sigmund, interview recording, part 4). To stave off hagiography (not the intention of this book) with respect to Assia, we only need to turn to Sigmund. The nicest sentiments that Sigmund can express in connection with the woman whom she believed contributed to her friend's suicide is a sweeping characterization of Assia as a "Russian Jewess" who was "very beautiful" and "frightening." Sigmund believed that Assia was an "embarrassment" to Hughes, which may have factored into his neglect of Shura, whom he "never took any notice of," in Sigmund's words. An illustration of this lack of concern is given in a little story Sigmund relates about Shura outside the gate, presumably at Court Green, crying, while Assia was in bed, also upset (interview recording, part 4). Hughes did not cater to Assia or Shura in this tale; he is noticeably absent in it. Merwin may have made Assia out to be a snob, with her dislike of dilapidated cars, but Rosenstein and Sigmund establish her as a murderer, who may have been so depressed that she was unable to get out of bed on some days, and as someone who brought embarrassment to Hughes through scandal.

As someone hostile to Assia's memory—because she perceived herself on Plath's side—Sigmund unintentionally, perhaps, compares and contrasts Plath and Assia. After speculating that Assia must be tidier than Hughes, Sigmund talks about how very "tidy" Plath was. For Sigmund, Assia is forever tied to the memory of Plath in inextricable fashion: "I couldn't see Assia," confesses Sigmund, "without seeing all the things she had done." Assia's crimes, from Sigmund's point of view, involve intentionally pursuing Hughes in calculated fashion (interview recording, part 4); she believed that Assia timed the fated telephone call to Court Green to coincide with Aurelia Plath's visit, thereby embarrassing Plath and pushing the marriage to the breaking point (interview recording, part 3). How Assia would know Plath's mother and/or Plath would be present when she called is unclear. Without clarification, Sigmund declares, "Assia was as horrid a comedown" as Plath would ever encounter. This statement pits woman against woman, figuratively marking Assia as the lowly, base, horrid, villainous contender in the battle and Plath as the lofty tragic heroine. Missing is any call or acknowledgment of accountability for the marriage on either Hughes's or Plath's behalf. Grudgingly, Sigmund muses, "If Assia had mastered anything, it was the spurious art of womanhood" (interview recording, part 3). In other words, Assia—whose femininity is touted in other interviews—can only be equated with an invalid womanhood, as less than a real or true or good woman, per Sigmund's view.

Missing from Rosenstein's multiple interviews with Sigmund is a sense of empathy for Assia,[26] who suffered greatly in her relationship with Hughes following Plath's suicide. Rather than Hughes's failure to follow through on his promises,[27] Sigmund and Rosenstein place the fault on Assia for a "failure to claim" Hughes for herself. They posit that having children with Hughes was Assia's way to capture him, but they disparage such a move, despite faulting her earlier for appearing infertile. Declaims Rosenstein, "I couldn't imagine if I were Assia having that baby [the one Assia aborted immediately after Plath died]." She adds in a whisper that she would have killed herself if she were carrying Hughes's baby in the wake of Plath's suicide. Of course, Assia dies by suicide six years later, so these words are in poor taste. But they underscore the animosity from other women toward Assia, an unconventional woman who tried to live according to the conventional script of the heterosexual marriage plot. She was hated for trying to fit into the script and hated for failing simultaneously. She could not win then, and until we reexamine the details and perspectives on her life, we are not likely to give much grace to other women struggling with limited options: life narratives informed and circumscribed by gender. Sigmund believed Assia wanted everything Plath had, as did Hughes (interview recording, part 2), but this assumption is faulty in assuming that Assia had much choice. Especially in her time, as Carolyn Heilbrun argues in *Writing a Woman's Life,* there existed very few narratives from which women could choose.

Richard Murphy occupies an interesting position in that he was Hughes's friend first and foremost, but he knew Plath and had met Assia. In an interview with Rosenstein that took place approximately five years after Assia and Shura died, Murphy describes Assia as "a very beautiful girl who didn't want to get involved . . . with babies." He remembers Assia replied, "It's not my fault" within the context of conversations about Plath's suicide, and yet, in language never before attributed to him or published, Murphy conjectures that Assia did feel guilty, as Murphy did: "we all felt that, but who more than Assia?" "I think," surmises Murphy, Assia "was haunted by a sense of guilt. The tragic myth [of Plath's suicide] caught hold of Assia," especially because she sensed that she was deserted and alone (interview recording, April 19, 1974, part 3). In the interview, Murphy offers the idea that Assia died by suicide—she "did what she did"—because she was caught up in this myth. When Rosenstein counters that Assia killed herself out of rage, Murphy returns, "She was a haunted person." Apparently harboring more sympathy for Assia than

Rosenstein can, Murphy changes the subject to Shura and his impressions of the little girl and her mother. Shura, he muses, was "very intelligent" and "very bright." Upon meeting the woman who would become her mother, Murphy embroiders upon Assia's beauty: a "wonderfully beautiful woman with the most marvelous bust and jet black hair," looking like the "whore of Babylon." Following Murphy's description, Rosenstein exclaims, "I'm in love with Assia, though I've never met her!" (Murphy, interview recording, April 19, 1974, part 3). The problematic recitation of these threadbare characterizations regarding Assia is best realized in Murphy's interview with Rosenstein. Neither person—one who met Assia and one who did not—can conceptualize or apprehend Assia as a complex person rather than a stereotype or archetype. Both are fixed on her body, its sexual attractiveness, and Assia's putative sexuality. Despite admittedly not knowing Assia's name until Plath's death, Murphy pronounces, "Assia was the perfect mistress . . . born for the role," to which he adds that she would have made a wonderful courtesan—in other words, a sex worker in the aristocracy—and Rosenstein heartily agrees (interview recording, April 19, 1974, part 3). The stigma sex work carries to this day should show us what little respect Murphy and Rosenstein accord Assia as a person. By employing gendered slurs, such as "whore," and focusing their attention on Assia's shortcomings while inventing another life for her entirely, they misrepresent the life they are trying to uncover. Olwyn Hughes strove to rebut Rosenstein (and everyone else at various times) about Assia when she argued against Rosenstein's interpretation of "Lesbos," a Plath poem Rosenstein incorrectly believed to be about Assia. It could not be about Assia, Olwyn Hughes argued, because Assia "had good taste" and kept her kitchen clean (Murphy, interview recording, April 19, 1974, part 3). Even here, in a defense, Assia is located in a domestic economy, serving others, albeit this time she is complimented for her sensibilities.

It can be difficult to imagine other interpretations, let alone apply them, when we are inundated with the same threadbare story. We end up internalizing and espousing that story and the patriarchal values without realizing what we are doing because of the frequency with which the narrative circulates and how the values resonate with us in patriarchal societies. And such stories are seductive, as they must be: the dominant narratives in patriarchal societies must be able to convince and persuade because they safeguard and reinforce power. The stories only have purchase when we buy into them, but because they are so ubiquitous and "natural," they are very seductive, and we accept them unawares. We can see the ramifications in Winifred Davies's interview. Like Sigmund, she knew and liked Plath; Davies served as Plath's midwife and friend in Devon. Her critique of Plath is gendered, although not hostile. Plath was perceived as a difficult person, admits Davies. She was inflexible, "wanted too much," and desired everything to be perfect. The "wanting too much" will strike us as dated and gendered, although still understandable even though more than forty years have likely elapsed since this circa 1970s interview (Davies, interview recording, undated, part 1). Truly, Plath wanted it all.[28] That mindset is attacked in *The Bell Jar* as being too audacious for 1950s America, as conveyed in the fig tree parable.[29] For Davies, as for Sigmund, Assia is the root cause of Plath's dying. Conversely, Davies absolves Hughes of any responsibility for Plath's well-being. She adopts a "boys will be boys" rhetoric. In response to Rosenstein's prompt, asking what was wrong with Hughes, Davies says, "Nothing wrong with him—he just had tremendous sex appeal." In this arc, we can discern plainly the power imbalances. Held up as being exceptional, Hughes can behave as he likes and maintain his position as hero of his own life story and in that of others. The problems reside with the women, who fight among themselves, in Davies's conventional storytelling. She recounts that Plath told her that Assia wanted Hughes because David Wevill could not give Assia children, and Plath thought that Assia wanted her own children with Hughes as well as Plath's children with him. Rosenstein interjects to argue that Assia did not want children, due to her fear of ruining her figure, in Rosenstein's phrasing (interview recording, undated, part 1). We know Plath was aware of Assia's concerns about her body, which are documented in Plath's poems and in the first biography written about Assia. Whichever version of the account we accept, neither Plath nor Assia emerges as a hero(ine). Plath, the jealous mother and wife, dies an untimely death, and Assia, selfish and superficial, is painted as a contributing factor.

In *Reclaiming Assia Wevill*, I chart how Assia's body is intensely scrutinized. For me, the most memorable comment is this one: Assia, one unidentified "friend" remembers, had "hips like the rear end of a 158 bus" (Alexander 265). In twenty-first-century parlance, we would classify this as a body-shaming move on the part of her putative friend. Assia harbored shame apparently about her pre- and post-maternity body. Before Shura, Assia writes, "I'm just like Marilyn Monroe in the shape of a hot-water bottle" (Assia qtd. in Koren and Negev 120). Fainlight relates the following in an interview with Feinstein: Assia "'was terribly unhappy.... She was fatter than she had been—a beautiful middle-aged woman. And she knew it. And she felt humiliated by it'" (Fainlight qtd. in Feinstein 166). Throughout the twentieth century, fat has been designated a problem, as "carcinogenic" even (Wolf 226). Ultimately, what Naomi Wolf calls "the beauty myth" is bound up in a "belief system that keeps male dominance intact"; beauty functions as currency and a false, constructed fiction that "is an expression of power relations" (12). It is an error, Tressie McMillan Cottom posits, for women, especially women of color, to take up space; boys and men can take up space, and white girls can "shine," she remarks. Assia is not always couched as a white woman; Hughes cast her as a Black woman in one notable letter (*Letters of Ted Hughes* 696–701), which will be taken up as an item of discussion in chapter 4. Others, such as Emma Tennant, refer to her as a dark muse (105).

In her work, Cottom directs our attention to how we dismiss and disparage "thick," or big, women: "When I would not or could not shrink, people made sure I knew I had erred.... Thick where I should have been thin, more when I should have been less.... I learned that even I had limits when—in my pursuit of the life of the mind—my thinking was deemed too thick" (7). If this type of thinking dominates now, decades after Assia lived and died, we can imagine how much more virulent and unchecked such punishments for living in a not-thin (and, for Cottom, nonwhite) body must have been when the inroads of third-wave feminism and body positivity were not part of mainstream discourse. What body-shaming accomplishes is dismissal of a person: body and mind, as Cottom points out. And fat and beauty cannot coexist in the way beauty is conventionally configured: "fat and beauty are antithetical" (Cottom 46). If beauty is the currency of the realm, then it behooves women to figure out how to navigate the costs in a "global system where beauty is the only legitimate capital allowed women without legal, political, and economic challenge. That last bit is important. Beauty is not *good* capital. It compounds the oppression of gender" (56). Be that as it may, Cottom reflects, it is still valuable (56).

When Assia perceived her beauty was fading, she must have believed that Hughes would lose his attraction to her.[30] However, the situation was more complicated than Assia gaining weight and her hair turning gray. Wolf elaborates, "Aging in women is 'unbeautiful' since women grow more powerful with time. . . . Most urgently, women's identity must be premised upon our 'beauty' so that we will remain vulnerable to outside approval, carrying the vital sensitive organ of self-esteem exposed to the air" (14). The double standard is evident; Wolf points out that because "men are worth more and need not try as hard," their appearance does not factor into the equation of worth (49). No one castigates Hughes for gaining weight or laments the appearance of his gray hair. And yet, women, too, notice and enforce the beauty myth because we all are expected to do so. Elaine Feinstein shares what she learned from an interview with Sigmund, who was a neighbor of Plath, Hughes, and Assia when they lived at Court Green: "Meeting Assia on a North Tawton street, [Sigmund] saw that she looked much stouter than she had, and that there was a tinge of grey in her hair. Elizabeth's eldest daughter also reported that she had been in the village chemist buying henna while Ted was there, and that he had said, 'You should use Seawitch—that's what Assia uses.' Elizabeth intended me to condemn Ted's casual revelation, but the effect was to remind me painfully how an awareness of such village gossip would reinforce Assia's sense of isolation" (*Ted Hughes* 160). These interviews are important: they illuminate what the interviewer, the interviewee, and the author writing about them hold to be significant, interesting, or substantial to the argument being forwarded. What stands out to me about this exchange are two aspects: the emphasis on a certain standard of beauty and Feinstein's analysis of Assia's isolation. Isolation would only have fueled Assia's sense of precarity and vulnerability.[31] Onno van der Hart summarizes the "essence of trauma" as "the lack of support, of help, of comfort; being utterly left alone with the experience and having no one listening" ("The Haunted Self" 202).

John Horder, Plath's general physician, insisted on what, at first, might seem a different interpretation of the love triangle and its three figures but devolves into more traditional victim blaming of a woman. In his 1970 interview with Rosenstein, Horder identifies Assia as a person in a tragic situation. "The fact," adds Horder, "that he [Hughes] is a good poet doesn't make up for what happened." Horder assumes that Hughes left Plath for Assia, and Rosenstein attempts to refute this reading. According to Rosenstein, who received her information secondhand, Hughes, disillusioned with Plath, had been having affairs the last three years of his marriage, and Assia was only the latest one, per information Plath passed on to her therapist. There is no other record of Hughes being unfaithful to Plath before Assia, which leaves timelines ill-defined. "Who knows really what was involved in the breakup?" asks Rosenstein rhetorically (Horder). She is right.

One story that persists: who should ultimately accept responsibility for the tragedies of the love triangle. After Rosenstein says it is "curious" that Plath was upset with Assia and *not* Hughes, Horder (and his wife) respond that it is not curious at all because Assia took Hughes away from Plath. All agency is removed from Hughes by the end of the interview in this rhetorical move, despite Horder earlier suggesting Hughes should accept some accountability—for what, exactly, is not clear. Maybe a new direction for us to consider: with a trauma-informed perspective, might we do away with victim blaming altogether and accept that everyone suffered to varying degrees, with drastically different outcomes? To me, that is a much more interesting narrative, one that permits us to fine-tune characterizations and surface important issues that have heretofore gone unnoticed or understudied.

Approximately ten years after Plath died, Rosenstein ventures a summation of how Plath perceived Assia, continuing to link the two women in fleshing out Assia's profile over time. Plath, Rosenstein believes, saw

Assia as "quite lovely" but not as bright as she, and for whom Hughes displayed a "very driven kind of lust" (Helder Macedo, interview recording, December 1, 1973, side A). Plath and Assia remain linked after their deaths because of their relationships with Hughes, and what they shared, from the perspective of John Avery, a neighbor who also worked at a hardware store that Plath frequented in North Tawton. What they shared most of all, he believes, was the status of outsider in rural England. In her conversation with Avery, Rosenstein concludes that Plath and Assia must have been very unhappy in North Tawton, coming from London, and Avery agrees. In fact, Avery takes up the topic of their respective suicides after Rosenstein asks him what locals thought about their deaths. Avery expands on his principal point: people were not surprised because "they [Plath and Assia] were the complete opposites" from people in North Tawton, and the two women's lifestyles proved that how they lived (whatever that might mean) was "not the right way to live." "It was bound to happen to them," continues Avery shockingly, "because they lived in a world of their own" (interview recording). This interview likely took place shortly after Assia died as Carol Hughes is referred to as Carol Orchard, who works as a nurse. Thus, the memories of Plath and of Assia, especially, would be recent in this interview.

Avery addresses his take on Plath and Assia extensively. As for Plath, he casts her as a "wonderful woman . . . who stood out" and was "pleasant." However, it "takes a long time for people to be accepted" in Devon, Avery concedes, and people "would snub her." In contrast to the way that Avery will paint Assia, Plath comes across as reserved and less open than her counterpart. In speaking with Plath, "you knew she was something," marveled Avery. Additionally, Plath appeared fashionable, even if her clothes were considered unusual in North Tawton, and easygoing. People liked her, Avery says, while Hughes was "very arrogant" and "lived a strange life." Like Hughes, Assia does not fare well overall in Avery's recollections. Among his reminiscences, Assia stands out as "loud mouthed, very open . . . outspoken"; "she knew everything," he remarks. After he admits that he did not find Assia beautiful, Avery judges, at Rosenstein's prompting (she actually asks him who he thought was prettier) that Assia would win the imaginary beauty contest because Assia put effort into her appearance, and Plath did not to the same extent (Avery). This type of pitting woman against woman in a mythic beauty contest demonstrates the toxicity and tenacity of the beauty myth, as Wolf delineates it. The symbolic and concrete violence dealt women is staggering, Wolf argues. It takes a toll on psychological health, as well as draining energy, time, and resources away from women, none of which Plath or Assia, with small children to care for and careers to manage, could afford to see diminished or exhausted. Unfortunately, we still assess women's appearance as some sort of marker of their inherent worthiness, so it holds that, in 1973, one of the details that Alan Jenkins remembers is Plath telling him, "Ted doesn't think I have the right bone structure"—or something along those lines (Jenkins and Jenkins).

Assia experienced a difficult time adjusting to life in rural England. According to Rosenstein, "Assia started to freak out in Devon" (Klein, interview recording, undated, part 1). The causes for Assia's distress, per Rosenstein: Assia, as an aspiring writer could not manage to write ("but she could translate quite well," Rosenstein qualifies), and she needed to live in an urban environment. These problems—writer's block, rural isolation—are not unique to Assia and are reasonable, especially considering Assia's aspirations and the company she kept and her own background. Assia serves as an interesting case study because we can track what people value in how they respond to her life and work, and her life gives us plenty of material.

In terms of women's work, she occupied both sides of what today we call the "mommy wars": she learned to care for "bonus" children in addition to a biological child, and she moved back and forth between the identities and roles of a professional working woman with a career in a male-dominated field and that of the unpaid, taken-for-granted traditional homemaker. She worked at several different advertising agencies, receiving acclaim and accolades in the industry for her work, but she left her advertising career in London to work as a caretaker of Hughes and his extended family, including his children and, at times, his parents, in London, rural England, and rural Ireland, serving at Hughes's pleasure.

She did not choose where she and Hughes lived or what her working conditions entailed: Hughes dictated those.[32] I see these factors as mitigating ones: they should shape how we interpret a woman's life and work. Our interpretations have large implications for how we come to value women's lives and work, affecting how we vote, teach, write about, speak about, and treat women and what they produce in terms of products and services. Thus, it is unsettling to come across the dominant view of Assia, captured by Rosenstein as she sums up Assia's portrait in the last decade of her life for Klein: Assia "became sadder and hugely fat" while in Devon. "She left Ted" in Devon because she could not take it. She needed an "elegant house," where she could be a hostess (Klein, interview recording, undated, part 1). There is nothing wrong with wanting an elegant house or being a hostess. Indeed, Plath wanted both and thought she achieved these goals when she secured Court Green and, later, when she relocated to London, where she hoped to run a literary salon.[33] The verbal portrait Rosenstein sketches for us is meant to dismiss and denigrate Assia as letting herself go physically[34] and wanting too much in terms of lifestyle. She fails at making herself a pretty object and in not being content with a gendered, circumscribed lot in life. We are to infer from such statements that we would like Assia better—and she would be happier—if she were more decorative and less ambitious. Such women can never be agents of their own lives or truly powerful. And if they are—if they are actively living their lives and accomplishing great things in a man's world, as Plath did—they are tagged a "greedy, competitive woman," as Rosenstein classifies Plath, criticizing her for what Rosenstein calls her "get what you can to make up for what you don't have" philosophy (Steiner, interview recording, part 2). Following this line of reasoning, there resided a "terrible meanness" in Plath, Rosenstein expounds: she was willing to use people (Steiner, interview recording, part 1).

As noted throughout this study, competing interpretations of Plath and Assia emerge from a variety of sources. For example, with respect to Plath, Jenkins, who lived in Belstone, close to where Plath went horseback riding, believes that Plath was a "country person": see what happened in London with her suicide, he argues. She loved Ireland and the English countryside: "of course she enjoyed the country in every way," he says. She kept bees, and Nan Jenkins lent Plath a smock for her beekeeping (Jenkins and Jenkins). Alan Jenkins's account is in direct contrast to Avery's portrayal of Plath as a city girl who could not assimilate to life in Devon. And, in contrast to the posthumous stereotype of Plath as a depressed person obsessed with death, Alan Jenkins affirms, "She was a very gay and happy person. . . . [But] who wouldn't be affected by being left with two small children. . . . She did feel the circumstances very much." The idea of Plath being in love with death is "bunk," Jenkins declares (interview recording). Plath's relocation to London proved disastrous, Jenkins counters, because she was even lonelier there than she had been in North Tawton. Marcia Stern, a friend of Plath, echoes in a different interview that she only encountered Plath depressed in connection with "ill health" (interview recording, undated, part 2). Elinor Klein, who met Plath at Smith College, describes Plath as "totally lovely." Asserts Klein, "I never felt I was talking to a doomed person" (interview recording, undated, part 2). These friends of Plath are exceptions to the master narrative. On the whole, Rosenstein observes, people only remember and write about the morbid things about Plath, ignoring what is positive. I would add that tends to be true about Assia as well.

The adage "one cannot judge a book by its cover" holds true for Plath and Assia: no woman is all one thing or another. Jon Rosenthal first met Plath at a fraternity party in Amherst College in the 1950s, where Plath had been pointed out as a suicide survivor. Rosenthal admits that he expected she would appear maladjusted, and yet she struck him as quite "radiant" (interview recording). Only two weeks before she died, Plath talked about how she had secured a "marvelous doctor" and presented herself in January 1963 as "making a go" of her circumstances. She was "in very good spirits," claims Paul Roche, and Plath always seemed "balanced." If anything, Plath maintained an "apple pie quality" about her (Paul Roche, interview recording, November 21, side B).

When we tell patriarchal stories, we reinforce patriarchal values. No matter how perfect a woman might seem, no matter how closely she might adhere to cultural expectations of desirable femininity, she will find herself undermined. By nature and definition, patriarchal societies do not support, nurture, or safeguard women. Even Plath—the proverbial "golden girl" (Clarissa Roche, interview recording, November 1973, part 4) and academia's "darling" (Paul Roche, interview recording, November 21, side A)—cannot escape getting metaphorically cut down. When Roche and Rosenstein debate whether, in Rosenstein's choice words, Plath was indeed an "awful, frigid bitch"[35] or whether Assia was a "hot-blooded, warm-blooded sexy babe," they mark the false dichotomy between these two women and gesture to the trap encountered by successful, attractive, ambitious women (Clarissa Roche, interview recording, November 20, 1973, part 3).

No matter how beautiful or successful Plath and Assia were, they both suffered in their romantic attachments to a powerful man: Hughes. Assia's personal relationship with Hughes showed itself to be precarious in many ways (as will be discussed further in chapter 3). Now, I will highlight what we learn from never-before-cited audio recordings of interviews with respect to Plath and abuse she endured. Though Hughes treated Plath better and remembered her more fondly than Assia in his writing from the late twentieth century, decades after both women had died, his physical treatment of Plath while she was living deserves censure, no matter how generous or kind to Plath he was otherwise. Plath delineates domestic violence in her relationship with Hughes; we see it documented in her journal and in letters to her therapist.[36] "Ted was violent," Roche avers to Rosenstein (Clarissa Roche, interview recording, November 20, 1973, part 3). Plath confided in Roche about the intimate partner violence she suffered, about Hughes "beating" her. "He didn't really nearly kill her," says Roche; she thinks Plath was exaggerating about the degree of physical severity. What he did do, explains Roche, is "beat up" Plath, leaving her with bruises. "She spoke as if it were a common occurrence," offers Roche, "but if you really ask her about it, it was once or twice." Rosenstein believes what Roche tells her, elaborating that what Roche shares aligns with what Rosenstein herself knows about both Plath and Hughes. Roche reveals that she directly asked Plath why she stayed with Hughes if he was violent, and Plath's answer dovetails with everything we know about responses from victims in domestic violence situations. Tellingly, Plath maintains hope that Hughes will change; she conveys her optimism that intimate partner violence will not happen again. This mindset is very much in keeping with how survivors manage situations in which the people they love most in the world hurt them and in which perpetrators vow not to do it again. Knowing what she knows, Roche objects, "It never crossed my mind that [Hughes] was an attractive man." Roche saw bruises on Plath, she states, and she attributed them to Hughes's actions (interview recording, November 20, 1973, part 3). Also intimate with Hughes, Emma Tennant corroborates what is said in interviews by other people who knew Hughes and Plath in her own memoir. As Tennant explains in the 1977 section, with hindsight, "Hughes may be dangerous; but the threat he poses is harder to define than, say, Lord Byron's must have been" (93). A bit later in the memoir, Tennant's words about herself, Plath, and Hughes might apply equally well to Assia and Hughes: "I am the stand-in, the surrogate for the woman who did know everything and could write anything but lost the love she was unable to live without" (104).

In a very balanced account, Marcia Stern shares what she knows about Hughes and Plath, who were "intense people" (interview recording, undated, side A). Hughes "could be devastatingly charming" with his "booming laughter." He regaled friends with "marvelous stories" and "could entertain a room full of people." As socially graceful and interpersonally gifted as he undoubtedly could be, he, by turns, could be difficult: "he could really tune off and out" and subsist in a "black funk," Stern remembers. Additionally, Hughes appeared to have a "great volatileness," and Stern's impression of Hughes was that he could be "very cruel" and "destructive verbally." If Hughes "whacked [Plath] around," it was because that cruelty "seemed part of him," comments Stern.[37] Such a scenario breeds "trauma," to use Stern's word, which she reflects she can see more in retrospect than she could at the time. Similar to what would happen to Assia, Stern explains that Hughes left Plath with very little; he had taken parts of her away metaphorically. Plath "really didn't kill herself; she was already dead in a mysterious way," Stern insists (interview recording, undated, side A).

In many cases, intimate partner violence and sexual assault pivot on control and power rather than on interpersonal attraction or sexual desire. Elizabeth Compton Sigmund recalls a disturbing story about Hughes, control, and power. In Sigmund's story, Hughes and Sigmund are in Sigmund's home, where a party is taking place. Drunk, Hughes attempts to force Sigmund to go on a walk with him. She refuses—a child of hers is crying—but Hughes has backed her up against a wall. She feels trapped in her own home. Though he "doesn't want" Sigmund, as she phrases it, she recognizes that what is transpiring is Hughes asserting his will to overpower her. As she experiences it, he wants to force her to do his will. He eventually leaves her alone when he finds that he cannot make her go on the walk with him (interview recording, part 2, side B). The first guideline in gendered violence support networks is to believe the victim. Nevertheless, our tendency is to not believe women, to find fault with them for the gendered violence they experience or to discount their stories altogether. The interviews Rosenstein conducted with Plath's, Hughes's, and Assia's contemporaries, preserved for future generations, record details, facts, and stories that newly illuminate the people and narratives we think we know. These "new" findings are important even if they unsettle us. Perhaps we should attend to them even more closely if we find them disconcerting, to explore and determine why that is the case. Also, we should attend to the revelations that compel us to form affinities toward people and their stories. Only then will we be able to build more complete packaged narratives about who our heroes and villains are (if we need them) and why we have positioned them as such.

Hughes and Assia are complex figures in interviews and related reminiscences. Both made deplorable decisions and took deplorable actions in different situations. This book is not designed to punish or exonerate either of them. It is equally easy to demonize one or both, but both were real people. To this end, Nathaniel Minton records in his memoir that Hughes "was gentle and kind, which later detractors have always tried to deny. I am of course referring to those who tried to demonise him after Sylvia Plath's tragic death" (15). Minton met Hughes at Cambridge, when he was nineteen and Hughes was probably twenty-four. Milton remembers Hughes cutting "a powerful, warm, charismatic figure, with a life-enhancing laugh," and already known as a "very good poet" (9). Hughes and Minton enjoyed a lifelong friendship (11), and as Hughes's personal friend, it cannot be surprising that Minton assigns the responsibility of the affair between Hughes (who instigated it) to Assia primarily, making her the agent: Assia "had burst into Ted's life and swept him off his feet," writes Minton (27). Be that as it may, Minton moves on to take a more sympathetic view of Assia after he starts his residential psychiatric training in a hospital in Greater London in the early 1960s. Upon first meeting her, Minton notes that she seems superficially poised, but four months after Plath's death, Minton recollects:

> I remember giving Ted and Assia a lift. Ted was sitting in the front and Assia in the back. Suddenly Assia began to shout "I am going to kill myself, I am going to kill myself." I was by now a young trainee psychiatrist and managed to drive slowly, keeping calm. Assia eventually calmed down herself. Ted may have told her to be quiet. I feel this incident confirms that Assia was emotionally disturbed immediately after Sylvia's death and probably remained traumatized by it for the rest of her own short life. She had already begun to identify with Sylvia and with Sylvia's suicidal behaviour, which probably drove her to eventually kill herself, together with their young daughter, six years later. Sylvia had cast her shadow from beyond the grave. (29)

> Published accounts in Assia's biography quote her work colleagues saying that Assia showed no feeling about Sylvia's death and was emotionally unmoved by it. I know this to be untrue and perhaps I should have met the biographers, who in fairness approached me, but I was not in the mood to talk to them. (30)

I quote these passages because they show an evenhandedness when addressing the characters of Hughes and Assia (especially) from someone who knew them both and was trained in psychiatry, though he did not treat Assia, and we should be careful taking his statements as a diagnosis.

Typically, Assia is not the recipient of such kindness in written accounts, although there are exceptions. Martin Baker and William Trevor are two such exceptions, as they recount their impressions and interactions of Assia forthrightly *and* affectionately. Mostly, however, writers tend not to realize that she suffered from the trauma of Plath's suicide and the instability and toxicity of her own relationship with Hughes.[38] Many ironies stand out: Assia clearly signaled she needed help, years before it was too late for her to receive it, and yet, as Minton acknowledges, others portray her as unfeeling and unaffected, suggesting a cold and calculating nature and making her into a perpetrator rather than a victim. Another irony: Minton explains that Hughes confided in him that "he wanted to spend the rest of his days with [Assia]" (31). Assia laments that her life cannot continue if she cannot secure Hughes as a husband for her and a father for Shura in her circa January 1969 suicide letter to her father. Assia's biographers remark that Assia never sent that letter: it was found in her flat.[39] Bate records that two envelopes, one addressed to Hughes and the other to Assia's father, were discovered by her bed at the scene (*Ted Hughes* 275). She must have hoped that the conditions of her life would improve, and she could not bring herself to send that letter after she wrote it in January.

Another well-rounded and evenhanded treatment of Assia shows up in Fainlight's May 2016 interview with Clark. Fainlight, too, mentions Assia's suicidal ideations, and she sketches her shift in perspective from knowing about Assia as a stereotype to actually knowing her as a person. As Fainlight expresses it, "Everything was awful . . . [for Assia in 1968]. She said afterward she was going to kill herself at Christmas, but because I had invited her and was so nice, she didn't do it for a few months. Of course I didn't know that. . . . I felt so sorry for Assia. When I met her she was the demon woman, but I didn't sustain that. Then I got to know her, and I liked her. She moved me. She moved me very much" (qtd. in Clark, *Red Comet* 916). Feeling as if she and Shura had no place to go during a holiday season exacerbated an already bad situation for Assia, Fainlight believed, and the reality of who Assia was won Fainlight's friendship, leaving poignant memories forty-eight years later.

There are many perspectives to bring together when attempting to plot someone on a grid of who they might have been, and of the hundreds of first-person accounts I have reviewed about Assia (primarily) and Hughes (secondarily), I think Minton's accounts of *both* Hughes and Assia could be the most successful as snapshots. Here are examples, the first treating Assia:

> I have a vivid memory of sitting with Assia. We looked at each other, but did not speak. The communication was entirely non-verbal. I was struck by Assia's beauty and spirituality. Assia's gaze directed at me expressed fear, almost terror. I did not know whether she was experiencing all the terrible uncertainties of the next few years and her difficulties to come with Ted. She seemed alone, wanting help and support, which I was unable to give her. . . . Someone had told me she had attended some group analytical therapy sessions at the Tavistock Clinic and I thought, probably wrongly, that she had gained psychoanalytical insights into her life situation. (33)

As for Hughes, Minton reflects on him in August 1969, when Hughes attended Minton's wedding:

> He was charming, although he looked depressed. Assia had died earlier that year. . . . Ted was full of guilt because he had not done more to try to prevent [Assia's] death, which may have been more inevitable than he realized. I have suggested that Sylvia had an impact on Assia's fragile psyche. . . . Assia, as far as I know, was not even in touch with any part of the health care system. (35–36)

> He knew about tragedy. He was not a cruel uncaring man without feeling, but a deeply suffering and tormented man with a poignant range of feeling. (36)

Emma Tennant interprets the deaths of Plath, "Ted's pale American muse," and Assia, "his dark lady," as the basis from which the mythology forms, a "mythology from which he will, despite all his efforts, never be able to escape" (105). From my vantage point, an outsider who is able to not only look over and listen through more than a half century's worth of material and who has worked extraordinarily closely with Assia's own writing and life through my coeditorship of *The Collected Writings of Assia Wevill* and who has written the largest section of my second book, a book about Assia Wevill, Sylvia Plath, and Ted Hughes, about Hughes, truer words than Minton's were never said about Assia than these: "Both Sylvia and Assia belonged to genuine tragedy" (36). Perhaps for me, that is the hook: the tragedy deserves to be examined and unraveled, so we can learn from it. It is sensational when gifted, beautiful women with bright futures suffer untimely, needless deaths, with trauma reverberating in their wake. My own interest and stake in trauma studies revolve around justice and belonging: who is this world designed for, and what can be done about it? In the next chapter, we will focus on Assia, with the issues and discussions presented in this chapter serving as a context.

II

THEIR LIVES
AND THEIR WORDS

3

ASSIA

If the European masculine literary establishment, in the form of Richard Murphy and Al Alvarez, could view Sylvia Plath in 1974, when she was an accomplished and posthumously famous poet, as a "gushing woman" (in the words of Murphy) who earned "pats on the head" (as Murphy interpreted Alvarez's patronizing of Plath in his review of *Ariel*), then Assia Wevill never had a chance at acceptance, let alone belonging. When Murphy made these patronizing remarks, he was an established poet, and as a white man who benefited from privilege, he clearly did not understand privilege and ability in the ways we do today, as we gather from the interview he gave to Harriet Rosenstein. Plath, Murphy maintains, was good enough not to be considered a female poet (interview recording, April 19, 1974, part 1). Surely, he intended this comment to be a backhanded compliment, but condescension toward women writers permeates it. Ironically, Murphy claims he felt intruded upon by Plath: she staged an "invasion" of his homeland and his poetic subject, given that she wanted to write about Ireland in her own poetry and had the ability to do so, what with publishing in the *New Yorker* (interview recording, April 19, 1974, part 1). Ted Hughes, too, was jealous of Plath's work, submits Winifred Davies, though she cannot remember whether it was Plath herself or Assia who confided in her about that (interview recording, 1970, part 2). To add to this discussion, W. S. Merwin confesses to Rosenstein that Plath wrote her best work in his study, and he was resentful of this scenario because he viewed Plath as a lesser talent than Hughes. Merwin implies that Hughes and his work should have been prioritized when it came to resources, over and above Plath and her writing. He thought Plath had designs on Hughes; she wanted to make him a "nanny," notwithstanding she was the "lesser talent" (interview recording). Suzette Macedo explains that mid-twentieth-century women, such as Plath and herself, had to apologize to the boys if they were first in the class, asking for forgiveness, and they had to work on being "sexy and nice": Macedo clarifies that this scenario was true for Plath, who identified "problems with femininity and being clever" (Suzette Macedo and Helder Macedo, interview recording, December 1, 1973, parts 3 and 4, side B). Paul Roche further elucidates the hostile environment for women, specifically in England at the time Plath and Assia were living there: "England was a man's country, not a woman's country," observes Roche. "The woman had to make allowances" because the country—its systems and culture—were not designed for her, he adds (interview recording, November 21, side A). This is the atmosphere in which Plath and Assia struggled to be taken seriously as writers, albeit in different genres.[1]

Intersectionality, a critical race studies metaphor that enables us to envision what privilege and oppression look like as well as to track their effects, remains pertinent to examinations of women's lives and work. Citing Kimberlé Crenshaw, Patricia Hill Collins explains, "Using intersectionality as a metaphor provides new angles of vision on each system of power" (28). She urges us to consider how social justice is at the heart of intersectionality, despite being valued as a secondary concern within academic scholarship. Not only, then, is social justice divorced from intersectionality and scholarship where it can have impact and ignite change, but this splitting or absence "fosters a division between truth and power within intersectionality" (47). Collins references racial minorities and women as "subordinated groups" who needed to produce "oppositional or resistant knowledge that was grounded in their own experiences and that challenged prevailing interpretations of them" (24). Audre Lorde states that women nurturing each other is a redemptive act in a patriarchal society; that act ushers in "real power" ("The Master's Tools" 111). Such a sisterhood emboldens, protects, and nurtures. Everyone has challenges, but people with certain constellations of identities have particular ones in particular settings.

Intersectionality provides a lens with which we can examine our subjectivity and positioning within the grid of identity politics. In other words, intersectionality uncovers and clarifies the convergences of identities and privileges or the lack thereof, offering us a concept or lens that, when applied, fosters awareness and mindfulness of our locations within systems of power and privilege. Intersectional feminism, such as that espoused by Crenshaw, invites us to consider how we function within oppressive environments and how people who do not share our identities fare ("Kimberlé Crenshaw Discusses"). As Lorde explains it—in a way that illuminates Assia's experience as a middle-aged woman and ethnic minority[2]—some women experience far more precarity than others: "Those of us who stand outside the circle of this society's definition of acceptable women [such as those women who are poor, queer, nonwhite or perceived as such, and older, per Lorde's list] . . . know that *survival is not an academic skill*. It is learning how to stand alone, unpopular and sometimes reviled, and how to make common cause with those others identified as outside the structures in order to define and seek a world in which we can all flourish" ("The Master's Tools" 112). Assia would never find acceptance, let alone approval, from a masculine establishment that would grudgingly and continually remark upon and praise her for her physical appearance when she was younger, only to find fault with her, by turns, for that purported dangerous allure, on the one hand, and what was considered her fading beauty by the time she reached her forties, on the other.[3] Rather, Hughes's *Capriccio* poem "The Pit and the Stones" captures Assia's social persecution and Hughes's too because of his association with her. Ultimately, Assia discovered that, as Lorde catalogues, unacceptable women face exclusion: they do not belong. They are ostracized and sometimes hated, forgoing community unless they can identify and bond with other unacceptable people. We would do well to heed Lorde's admonition in her talk "Learning from the 60s": "Sometimes we could not bear the face of each other's differences because of what we feared those differences might say about ourselves. As if everybody can't eventually be too Black, too white, too man, too woman. But any future vision which can encompass all of us, by definition, must be complex and expanding, not easy to achieve" (136). Intersectionality helps us to understand Assia's life in ways that would otherwise be foreclosed, and this chapter strives to open up her life and critical conversations about it by setting in motion new narratives, steeped in uncovered information and new analyses.

Regarding her achievements, Assia accomplished astonishing feats, despite staggering odds (and despite sexist and misogynistic detractions). To that point, Assia laments to Keith Gems on January 30, 1944, after having read Mark Twain's *The Adventures of Tom Sawyer* (1876) and *The Adventures of Huckleberry Finn* (1885), that the "great fun" of the novels "makes one regret having been born a girl," presumably because the two male characters, although boys, enjoy enormous freedom and agency compared to any girl in literature or in Assia's own world. Assia determines in the same letter, "Still I am going to get my freedom through evolution" (*Collected Writings* 20). Years later, Assia vows to herself in a journal entry, dated August 12, 1963: "I shall will myself to write. I shall will to read with more concentration" (178). Reading and writing are the means to unlock empowerment, and Assia also unlocked achievements. On her résumé, rediscovered in an archive and published in *The Collected Writings of Assia Wevill*, we see that Assia selects what she presumes will be of most interest to Eric Walter White, in her aim of securing a job at the BBC, on September 11, 1968. Among the highlights are Assia's groundbreaking film and television commercials. "I named and wrote the script for a 90 sec. cinema commercial called *Seawitch*, which at the time, 1966, caused a mild commotion in the trade. Another 90 sec. commercial, *Woodnymph*, won the 2nd prize in Cannes, 1967," she relates (152). In his review of *Poems* for the *Chicago Tribune*, showcasing the Amichai poems Assia translated, Chad Walsh calls the book a "linguistic miracle," ranking it as the best book of poetry of the seven he reviewed for the article. *Kirkus Reviews* refers to the book as "an accomplished rendition from the Hebrew by Assia Gutmann." In a review for *The Guardian*, P. J. Kavanagh writes, "The translations of [Amichai's] *Selected Poems* by Assia Gutmann are so stunning, such good poems in

English, that it seems absurd to treat them as translations at all" (6). Truly, by any professional standard, what Assia achieved is outstanding, and her translations of Amichai's poetry retain their critical importance.[4] However, Naomi Wolf cautions us to remember, "Women of all classes know that achievement is considered ugly and punished accordingly" (30). In Assia's case, the punishment is a forgetting and a subsequent erasure.

Mary Catherine Bateson, in her study of women's lives and the pursuit of biography in *Composing a Life*, attests to the gendered expectations for women at midcentury: as a result of socialization and limited opportunities (and pay), women were expected to adjust their lives to the men in them. She advocates a new model for measuring women's lives and achievements: a patchwork (14–15). A patchwork paradigm to midcentury women's lives and achievements, personal and professional, would go a long way in establishing coherence and clarity with respect to such narratives. In this way, "we can discern in women honoring multiple commitments a new level of productivity and new possibilities of learning" (166).[5] In Assia's case, she began her career as a copywriter in advertising in 1960 (*Collected Writings* 98): working at paid employment allowed her some financial security. She moved to Fitzroy Road in London, Court Green in Devon, and two homes in Ireland, and, with a detour to Court Green, back to new lodging in London, all within the time frame of six years. During that time, she worked in advertising; as a nanny; and then as a stay-at-home mom before returning to advertising *and* taking up artistic projects, such as translating. What we should know about this patchwork: Assia accepted living where Hughes wanted (and where he wanted her to live when he determined he no longer wanted to live with her) on his timeline so that he could work peacefully and productively and live his life on his terms. Tailoring her labor inside and outside the home to him, Assia worked as a caretaker of Hughes and his children (and his parents) and as a copywriter and artist in various media in rapid succession. Her career choices hinged on Hughes and his decisions about his own career.

I understand that "victim" (or "survivor") is a fraught term. Victims only ever seem innocent when they eschew the term themselves, and even then, the victim should be removed from the present and ensconced in the past in order to be palatable (Mardorossian 30–31). Victims encounter disapproval, distrust, and condemnation routinely (30) because, as I suspect, others do not want to have to be implicated in the messiness and ugliness of traumatic experiences.[6] Carine M. Mardorossian delineates how Britian and the United States share in the mechanics of delegitimizing victims and victimhood (31). I think of both Plath and Assia as victims—they are victims of trauma and of suicide—rather than survivors; survivorship suggests that a victim has triumphed over the trauma or has moved on in some measure. With the traumatic experience of electroshock therapy weighing on her, Plath could not move past it at the end of her life, and with the traumatic feeling of having lost everything in the years following Plath's suicide, Assia, too, could not escape from thinking that her life was over. As Bessel van der Kolk argues, trauma permeates bodies, and bodies keep the score; an unbearable heaviness accompanies remembering (*The Body Keeps the Score* 189). And the culture one is immersed in plays a role in traumatic outcomes. According to van der Kolk, "Culture shapes the expression of traumatic stress" (189), meaning that how and what Plath or Assia could or would communicate about trauma would be culturally mediated. For instance, Assia, as lonely and isolated as she was, may not have known where to go or to whom to turn when her relationship with Hughes seemed to blow up, as detailed in "The Error" and "Flame" from *Capriccio*.[7] We must remember that feeling "terror and helplessness" are the result of facing traumatic events and reliving them (van der Kolk 194). Furthermore, traumatic memories are dissociated: they cannot take the form of a proper story or autobiography (196). Consequently, victims cannot make sense of their traumatic experience(s), but understanding the trauma story is important, even necessary for many, when it comes to healing. For trauma is that which feels ruinous and ever present (197), and as van der Kolk articulates, "The essence of trauma is that it is overwhelming, unbelievable, and unbearable" (197).

You will notice that I broach the topic of suicide early in this chapter, rather than leave it to the end, so that we can address it forthrightly *and* investigate other important topics. Suicide remains the traumatic event that serves as one ending in Plath's and Assia's biographical stories; sometimes their stories include discussions of their afterlives or legacies, and, when that happens, we move beyond suicide as the last word. In speaking about his friend Plath, whom he met at the BBC Broadcasting House in 1961, per his recollections, Marvin Kane describes her suicide as a "final rejection of life, circumstances. . . . The final retreat" (interview recording). Referring to Plath, Lisa Levy, once a scholarship student at Smith alongside Plath, argues that she "can't really say [Plath] brought it on herself when no one was able to help her. . . . [People] who kill themselves have no happiness" (interview recording). Likewise, Assia addresses suicide in her last letter to her father, circa January 1969: "The prospect before me is so bleak, that to have lived my full life-span would have entailed more misery than I could possibly endure" (*Collected Writings* 155). Her life is "hell," and she interprets her life as marred by "exile and disaster" (155). Belonging is a fundamental human need, and Assia believed she never belonged anywhere.[8] She also worried immeasurably about her future and Shura's before arriving at the conclusion that the future was not worth living for. According to Assia,

> It is the life alone, dependent on an au pair to look after my little Shuratchka properly—dependent on the sort of people for whom I work—a very bad, 3rd rate agency who would fire me in case of illness. No husband. No father for Shura.
>
> I've often thought of this—but the pain it would give you, and the criminality perpetrated on my little Shuri—these thoughts often stopped me at the last sane moment, in the past.
>
> I have lived on the dream of living with Ted—and this had gone kaput. The reasons are immaterial. There could never be another man. Never. . . .
>
> And I couldn't leave little Shura by herself. She's too old to be adopted. (155–56)

In confusion and sorrow, Assia's father, Lonya Gutmann, told Assia's younger sister, Celia Chaikin, "I can't understand it. People were killed in Bergen-Belsen, and here's a woman who kills herself because of her love for a man" (Gutmann qtd. in Koren and Negev 210). Fay Weldon offers context for understanding Assia: "The times were against Assia, as against Sylvia. Both talented women died of love, not depression, let alone suicidal tendencies. In those pre-Feminist days, women saw their lives in terms of being loved or not loved by a man. It was terrible to be abandoned, death was better than rejection" (qtd. in Koren and Negev 218). Elaine Feinstein also corroborates Assia's understanding that an unpartnered life equated a life of failure for women at midcentury: "In those days, indeed, to be alone as a woman represented a profound failure, and men were reluctant to take on any woman who already had a child" (167). Feinstein documents how Weldon "observed that by now Ted was 'incredibly dismissive' of [Assia]. . . . It was as if she was second-rate" (167). In 1966, while in Ireland, Assia signed her name "Assia Wevill-Hughes" in correspondence to a friend (Koren and Negev 155), highlighting her desire to formalize her partnership and merge her life with Hughes's. In 1967, she received a postcard, sent to "Mrs. Assia Hughes" (Koren and Negev 167), surely to her delight. Although she and Shura spent Christmas 1967 with Ted, Olwyn, Frieda, and Nicholas Hughes, by Christmas 1968, she was lonely and spent the holiday with friends, bringing Shura with her, and talking of Shura, money, and loneliness (Feinstein 169). Three months later, on March 23, 1969, Assia and Shura died.[9] Their funeral followed on March 31, 1969 (171). "Fatally," writes Jonathan Bate, Hughes "misjudged the extent" of Assia's "vulnerability." Assess Koren and Negev, "Alone was Assia's most dreaded scenario" (111).

As research shows, mental illness is not contagious, and yet "there's a strong body of evidence that suicide is still contagious" (Sanger-Katz). What seems to be especially triggering to people who tend to already be vulnerable to suicidal ideations is the publicity surrounding a suicide. Younger people succumb to the contagion more readily, the research suggests, but it is clear that "one death can set off others." Suicide outbreaks or clusters are serious social problems, due to the "particularly strong effect from celebrity suicides" (Sanger-Katz).[10] Best practices in journalism avoid the following in connection with suicide coverage: depicting the death as a means of escape; disclosing the means of suicide; and engaging in repetitive or prominent coverage. Unfortunately, Assia could not adhere to any of these evidence-based best practices. She knew Plath was troubled, and Hughes informed her that an adverse effect to the antidepressant Plath was taking at the time was the catalyst that fomented the situation. Naturally, Assia knew how Plath died, and as Plath's literary star skyrocketed after the media revealed her death by suicide, everyone associated with Plath became inundated by the news and the impact it made.[11] To add to this calculus, Assia herself suffered from a history of mental illness and previous suicide attempts, and, while her family escaped murder by Nazis in fascist Germany in the 1930s, her extended family did not.[12] Diane Middlebrook calls Assia's death and that of Shura "appalling" (233), as indeed they were, precisely because they could have been avoided, as Hughes himself concludes in a letter to Assia's sister.[13] To Plath's mother, Hughes writes, in a letter dated April 14, 1969, "This last horror [the untimely and simultaneous deaths of Assia and Shura] has maybe taught me one thing. Sylvia's death threw my whole nature negative. I now see the senseless cost of that, for others as well as myself and I must in some way set everything behind me if I'm to carry on at all" (*Letters of Ted Hughes* 291). In other words, Hughes presumably recognizes the contagious nature of trauma and suicide here and the need to extricate oneself and others affected by it from the constant presence of the threat and its ramifications.

With such a traumatic event, people want to assign responsibility for it, to make the event understandable and, perhaps, to distance it from themselves. What is unfortunate but telling about Plath's suicide is the evergreen desire to lay blame on someone, typically Hughes or Assia. Even when other factors are introduced, Assia is not absolved of responsibility; she must be held to account because of her inability to accommodate herself to suitable conventional gendered expectations. As a woman too beautiful and too grasping (read: she wanted too much), she must be thoroughly bad and irredeemable, despite any evidence to the contrary. Here is a case in point. Julia Matcham, who disliked and disapproved of Assia intensely, records the following anecdote, which she shared in a letter to Elizabeth Compton Sigmund, Plath's friend and neighbor, on January 17, 1987: "When later, Sylvia committed suicide, Assia's attitude shocked me in it's [sic] self deceiving jettisoning of responsibility. According to Assia,

Sylvia had been to some doctor in London for tranquilisers or sleeping pills which he should!nt [sic] have supplied to a depressive of suicidal tendencies. And that, conveniently, was that! I was'nt [sic] a passive recipient of this information, and argued with her more and more aggressively as I could see that she was'nt [sic] going to lose a wink of sleep over it" (correspondence, Box 1, Folder 21, Item 42). Hughes deserves to be exonerated "from all responsibility for three dead bodies," asserts Matcham (correspondence). Arguing to the contrary, Linda Wagner-Martin writes Sigmund on January 23, 1987, a few days after Matcham, about Hughes's constructed image of "poor Ted, married to this crazy American, kind of a Zelda Fitzgerald person." Wagner-Martin pronounces her assessment, from the information she had gathered in writing a biography of Plath: "There seems to be a real misunderstanding in England about Ted's role in Sylvia's life and death, and about his character since . . . since he never married Assia—am I right there?—no one knows that she committed suicide, with their daughter" (correspondence). In an extant draft of her will, Assia details that she wanted to be buried with a headstone, and she would have been horrified to know Hughes directed that she and Shura should be cremated *and* that he took possession of the urns and subsequently sought either what Koren and Negev dub "a furtive burial" at Lumb Bank or a secret scattering of her ashes (211). Either way, Hughes was hiding Assia, making her final resting place a secret—and it remained a secret to her family and friends, many of whom are now no longer alive. Hughes was neither the executor of Assia's estate nor a family member or the person closest to her in a legal sense; he had no legal right or standing with respect to Assia's person or estate. In fact, Assia's father, who died in 1969, and her sister, who died in 2019, never learned what happened to Assia's and Shura's remains. Chaikin, who could not attend Assia and Shura's funeral, would never be able to pay her respects to them at a burial or memorial site. Assia and Shura had effectively disappeared.[14]

Hughes certainly could not give Assia what she needed. Another romantic partner, Brenda Hedden, recollected how Hughes confronted a crisis: "In the crisis he would be absent . . . passive, secretive or devious when he could not be absent; then callous even ruthless when he was forced to face the issue" (correspondence). For her part, Assia writes about Hughes as follows on November 31, 1966: "I have these fits of huge love and admiration for him—but it is still 2 parts that and one part memory of Ruthless" (*Collected Writings* 189). Like attracts like, Matcham implies, as she characterizes Assia thus: "Assia has an original, entertaining mind but her ideas were always highly coloured by (in my opinion) an exaggerated romanticism, which in its rather tenuous relationship to reality allowed her free reign to be quite ruthless in the pursuit of anything that she wanted, without the burden of bad concience [sic]. Obviously this stood in the way of any real friendship with women, but I observed it to be quite hypnotically attractive to many men" (correspondence).

Much as Plath's journals showcase her voice and life, Assia's journal writing, as well as her letters, evidence a person different from what she has been made out to be, which cannot be surprising as, like Plath, she has become a character in a myth. In his foreword to the early excised edition of Plath's collected journals, Hughes writes, "This is her autobiography, far from complete, but complex and accurate, where she strove to see herself honestly and fought her way through the unmaking and making of herself" (xiii). Here, Hughes alerts us to the values of personal writing, not necessarily marked for publication. In her own writing, Assia apparently seeks to make sense of her life; her interactions with Hughes; and Plath's daunting professional and personal legacies and influence. Truly, Assia wrestles with the making and unmaking of herself in letters, journal entries, miscellaneous notes, and I would contend, in poems, too. As an early editor of Plath's journals, Frances McCullough became very familiar with Plath's journal writing and reasons that such writing has "the usual function of such documents [of life writing]—to chart a life, to pique memory, to confirm inner life and perhaps to dispel the doubt that one exists at all" (ix). These scintillating insights help us in framing Assia's writing: she documents her life and that of other artistic luminaries; she attempts to call up and reflect on memories; she engages in a kind of soul searching to determine what she is thinking and how she is feeling; and she writes to insist on her presence, despite forces that were already at work to erase her. As Al Alvarez states in an interview with Carl Rollyson,

"What you have to understand is that Olwyn and Ted had a very Soviet view of history, that you could just airbrush people out" (150).[15] As a result, scholars are still piecing together narratives concerning Assia—and Plath and Hughes as well.

Letters and journals are central to the genre of autobiographical writing (Marcus, *Autobiography* 110). In 2021, Assia's letters, journals, original poems and translations of poems, as well as miscellaneous texts, were published. Assia comes across as engaging and forthcoming in her letters. In fact, in a missive to her, dated February 9, 1964, Hughes writes, "If [our relationship] were to live on your letters, it would prosper—they ring sincere, or I'm a fool" (*Letters of Ted Hughes* 229–30). Readers and critics eagerly received the book: at one point, it was ranked first for new releases in gender studies ebooks on Amazon's website, and it received the 2022 Susan Koppelman Award for the Best Anthology, Multi-Authored, or Edited Book in Feminist Studies in Popular and American Culture on behalf of the Popular Culture Association. Clearly, there exists a popular and an academic audience for Assia's writing. In her work on autobiography, Laura Marcus points out that such writing is popular and central to the work of literary critics, and it straddles the divide between popular and academic readerships. The appeal of life-writing lies in what it promises: "an understanding of the ways in which lives have been lived" and forays into "the most fundamental accounts of what it means to be a self in the world" (*Autobiography* 1). Additionally, autobiographical writing may feature the impulse to bear witness and testify in connection with traumatic episodes and events, and the author may even feel "an obligation" to do so (*Autobiography* 24).

As her letters and journals show, Assia loved Hughes and his children with Plath. Hughes loved Assia, too, in his own way. Middlebrook interprets the relationship: "They never married, but there is good reason to believe that Hughes loved Assia deeply, even after his first infatuation ended. They were more or less a couple for almost exactly the same amount of time that Hughes and Plath were a couple, a little over six years. . . . Still, Assia couldn't hope to compete with Plath for Hughes's esteem" (231). The problem? As Hughes confided in Lucas Myers, "I've withdrawn all investments of distress and agitation, and become a monster of suiting myself" (Hughes qtd. in Middlebrook 232). In fact, Hughes sometimes blamed himself for the deaths of Assia and Shura. As Middlebrook phrases it, Hughes, when feeling utterly despondent, "thought that intimacy with him had been deadly to all of them," and he faulted himself for letting "my lovelies drift & die" (Hughes qtd. in Middlebrook 234).

Assia's life writing provides the documents necessary to construct her version of stories told about her. By May 23, 1963, Hughes fired the nanny and decided Assia would "look after the children henceforth," as she expresses it (*Collected Writings* 167).[16] Even when Assia was uncertain or angry at Hughes, she remained devoted to his children, as she writes in her May 24 and May 25, 1963, journal entries. Assia's summation of Frieda and Nicholas Hughes is succinct: "Children docile and touching" (169). On November 29, 1966, Assia occupies herself with the following: "Hair washing. Supper for 6, 7, bath, pity, love, story. Cup of milk" (187). By this time, she has welcomed her biological daughter with Hughes, Shura, to their blended family. Assia loved Frieda and Nicholas Hughes, as the draft of her 1968 will evidences: "To Nicholas Farrar Hughes, since he is too young for possessions, I will all my most tender love. To Frieda Rebecca Hughes, I will also my love and all the lace, ribbons and silks she can find, as well as a fine gold chain" (267). As for Shura, Assia intended to leave all her estate to her, should she survive her mother. Echoing what Assia has to say about the children she cared for, Winifred Davies reported that Assia promised that she would always stay with the children. "I think," Davies relates, "the children were quite fond of Assia" (interview recording, undated, part 1). Following her untimely death by suicide, Assia's absence in the lives of the children who were once hers to nurture could have been likened to an abandonment and a traumatic repetition of loss. She would have been the second mother figure to disappear from the lives of Frieda and Nicholas Hughes.[17] Shura was mourned, too, by Ted Hughes in his private writing, as touched upon in the next chapter, and by Frieda Hughes in her poetry. It makes the situation all the more tragic that Shura loved her father. As Assia observed about her August 8, 1968, trip to Germany with Hughes and Shura, Shura "responds to him with complete but slightly impertinent adoration" (192).

In her autobiographical poem "Assia Gutmann," collected in *Out of the Ashes* (2018), Frieda Hughes confesses how she now perceives her sometimes caregiver and her father's partner. As a young child, the speaker could not fathom Assia's disregard of her. The poem attributes it to the fact that Frieda resembles Plath:

> . . . I'd no idea
> How my mother's face reflected
> In the polished coals of her eyes,
> So that she saw right through me,
> Not to the inner workings of my mind,
> But to the wall behind. (185)

Assia could never understand her, Frieda maintains in the poem:

> I open a book of Jewish poetry
> And there's her maiden name,
> Translating as she never
> Translated me. . . . (1–4)

In a strange twist of fate, I own this very book of Jewish poetry, what was Frieda Hughes's copy. Up for auction with Bonhams as part of lot 339, item 21, on March 21, 2018, *Selected Poems* (1968) by Yehuda Amichai, translated by Assia Gutmann, came into my possession when I purchased it from the seller who had initially purchased it from the Bonhams auction. A tiny slip of paper contains the following in Frieda's handwriting: "PB 1968 / Amichai / Gutmann." Other than this tiny slip of paper, no annotations or other marks were made. To me, the paper slip puts into relief the material reality that Hughes did not mark up or annotate Assia's translations—she did not translate her writing, turn it into personal meaning for her in the margins, for instance—just as Assia could not translate or make sense of Frieda's traumatic responses to the death and displacement of her biological mother.[18] The only other memory Hughes seemingly exposes in "Assia Gutmann" pertains to Assia's proclivity to nap taking, tied to Assia's anxiety about growing older: "she slept in her airline mask / In the afternoons, as if / Youth could be got back again" (185). In this vein, Frieda Hughes takes after her father, who ruminates on Assia's unusual beauty and fear of losing it as a result of advancing age in his own writing, as in the poems "Dreamers" from *Birthday Letters* or "Fanaticism" from *Capriccio* respectively.

The British Library holds materials related to the *Capriccio* poems, and in drafts of "The Locket," Hughes considers Assia's beauty a drug that kept her awake, meaning that it kept her alive, as her yawning and sleepiness are associated both with death and the symbolic locket she wears ("Capriccio, circa 1967–8 Nov. 1993" 26–29). In a series of notes to himself, also housed at the British Library, Hughes assesses Assia as being undone by her beauty; her appearance was lethal to her, and she was infatuated with how she looked. When her beauty began to fade, nature, Hughes asserts, offered nothing to substitute for it, and Assia killed herself rather than be ashamed by what she perceived as her less-than-beautiful appearance (166). By other accounts, Assia worried not only about getting old but about the lack of power she would have as a result. According to Yehuda Koren and Eilat Negev, Assia "told her boss, Angela Landels, that she wanted to die young, 'because growing old, with one's skin wrinkled and hanging down, losing one's feminine potency, was ghastly." She "would talk about having a facelift in virtually the same breath as she did about dying" (Koren and Negev 84). Assia herself dispatches the phrase "the grotesque shapes of middle age" in a January 16, 1969, journal entry.

Of course, the archetype of an evil stepmother runs rampant through fairytales, but it materializes in lived experiences, too. The following account by Maggie Nelson underscores the structural vulnerability of stepmothers:

> When you are a stepparent, no matter how wonderful you are, no matter how much love you have to give, no matter how mature or wise or successful or smart or responsible you are, you are structurally vulnerable to being hated or resented, and there is precious little you can do about it, save endure, and commit to planting seeds [of] sanity and good spirit in the face

of whatever shitstorms come your way. And don't expect to get any kudos from culture, either: parents are Hallmark-sacrosanct, but stepparents are interlopers, self-servers, poachers, pollutants, and child molesters. (21)

Assia's situation was very complicated: she stepped into a stepparenting role (as did other women later on) at Hughes's request, a request made immediately after Frieda and Nicholas Hughes lost their mother at very young ages. If we consider that stepmothers are almost universally reviled in cultural stories and that suicide can result in unfathomable trauma for those still living, then we can honor the difficult feelings people experiencing that situation would harbor. Certainly, the archetype of the evil stepmother reinforces unfair and harmful stereotypes about women more generally. Also, it seems an injustice for those outside the situation and looking in to demonize Assia for performing the role of a mother; she could never be or replace Plath, and she knew this truth firsthand. In a May 19, 1963, journal entry, Assia invokes Plath's presence as one that comes between Hughes and herself, even after Plath's death: "Sylvia, my predecessor between our heads at night." She continues, explaining that she never feels she measures up to Plath: "she had a million times the talent, 1000 times the will, 100 times the Greed and passion that I have. I should never have looked into Pandora's box, but now that I have I am forced to wear her love-widow's sacking without any of her compensations" (*Collected Writings* 163). Later in 1963, Assia writes about how she is "immersed now in the Hughes' monumentality. *Hers* and his. The weak mistress, forever in the burning shadow of their mysterious seven years. I'm getting weaker and weaker. I have no will. No talent. A slight, decorative intelligence. . . . No husband" (165). On November 31, 1966, Assia makes note of her thoughts after reading Plath's journals: "Once again a strong sensation of her repugnant live presence. '. . . work at femininity' in a list of resolutions and things to buy, including a bathrobe, slippers and nightgown. Were the elbows really sharp? the hands enormous and knuckled? Or is this my imaginary shape-giving to the muscular brain, my envy of her splendid brilliance" (188). At the end of her life, Assia references the "terrible talk" she has with Hughes, in which he tells her that Plath will remain a barrier between them. His words as Assia records them: "It's Sylvia—it's because of her" (Hughes qtd. in Wevill, *Collected Writings* 195). Assia responds, "I can't answer that. No more than if it were a court-sentence. It says die—die, soon" (195).

Conventionally, with stories about women, we elide or diminish evidence of violence, especially gendered violence. It is in our interest to ask ourselves what kind of explanations we construct and why: what do we tell ourselves so that we can move past information, evidence, or signs that call us to witness? Should we decide to stand in solidarity with victims and survivors of gendered violence and trauma, we will need to accept the victim's story and believe her, which will necessitate a different kind of story than what is likely the dominant one. In advocacy efforts associated with domestic and intimate partner violence awareness, prevention, and education, the motto is "start by believing." We can start by believing Assia—and Plath. And their friends: Marcia Stern informed Rosenstein that she knew Hughes slapped Plath to get her to come to her senses (interview recording, undated, part 2). Rather than dismissing the claim or the behavior (which is worse?!), we would do better to understand what is being said and figure out how to help the victim or connect her with resources. In one of her interviews, Rosenstein raises the problem of domestic and intimate partner violence, only to diminish its violence and impact: "Maybe he [Hughes] hit her a couple of times or something. That's not important. What's the secret? What are they [Olwyn and Ted Hughes] trying to protect? I don't understand. . . . I'm not trying to elevate Sylvia Plath," says Rosenstein (Murphy, interview recording, April 19, 1974, part 3). We could spend the rest of this book unpacking these statements. First, what victim would ever come forward with her story if she knew she would be met with this type of attitude and response? In two sentences, a young woman dispatches the abuse of another young woman. The betrayal, the potential trauma of the impact of being hit by the person one loves most in the world is elided in favor of white male privilege. To find these kinds of statements and attitudes embedded in biographical enterprises about Plath of all people—a heralded "golden girl" of her generation and now a literary icon—is sobering. If Plath cannot be elevated, cannot assume center stage, in her own biography, then women are never going to find equality, let alone equity, in literature, letters, or culture. If we continue to favor patriarchal stories that literally and figuratively harm women, we will have to suffer the consequences. When it comes to victimization, we want our victims to exhibit a "morally blameless existence" (Alcoff 170); only then does the victim deserve our help, sympathy, and the like. Such a fallacy is exacerbated by gender, wherein we tend to blame women for their own victimization. Instead, we should recognize that perpetrators are at fault. "Abusive behavior is a choice," explains Stephanie Cunningham, a specialist in healthy relationships and a preventionist at Turning Point Domestic Violence Services. People, she elaborates, can learn how not to be abusive.

In *Down Girl: The Logic of Misogyny*, Kate Manne focuses on privilege and how it protects "the men who are the most privileged" (xv), men like Ted Hughes: white, straight, and cisgender throughout his life and with socioeconomic privilege and social status later in his life. Such men come to expect women to nurture, comfort, and care for them and their children, as well as provide sexual, emotional, and reproductive labor (xv). The entitlement can run so strong that privileged and entitled men may expect that women owe them: in other words, an entitled man will feel he is owed a woman's services and what she can offer (xv). For women who occupy multiple intersecting identities of oppression, they "may face injustice that is best understood as dehumanization" (Manne xvii), which we see in much of Hughes's *Capriccio*. Poems that dehumanize Assia include "The Locket" (associated with a demon); "The Mythographers," (associated with demonic and immortal characters who wield superpowers); "Systole Diastole" (represented as a lioness and the ghost of the lioness); "Possession" (associated with demons and a ghost); and "Smell of Burning" (represented as a tree but also as a person).

Moral criticism or accusation of wrongdoing will send the type of entitled man Manne calls out into overdrive; he will "seek payback, revenge, retribution" (xxi). What powerful and dominant men will do is seize control of narratives and, therefore, control how the women in them are portrayed: all of this, Manne points out, boils down to control and violence (10–11). As a result, Manne defines misogyny as that which serves to "uphold patriarchal order, understood as one strand among various similar systems of domination," and it visits "hostile or adverse social consequences" on women and girls (13). Sexism, as Manne understands it, "justifies and rationalizes a patriarchal social order," whereas misogyny "polices and enforces its governing norms and expectations" (20). Misogyny takes many forms, including acts associated with vilifying, demonizing, sexualizing, silencing, shaming, condescending, and blaming (68)—all, as I show in *Reclaiming Assia Wevill*, activated in the sequence of poems Hughes wrote about Assia in *Capriccio*. Misogyny also strives to discredit accomplished women: "excellence in a woman may have the opposite effect on some people, resulting in her being a polarizing figure. In other words, women may be penalized for being too qualified, too competent. People may be 'taken aback,' and unwittingly engage in post hoc rationalization to make sense of their inchoate feelings of suspicion or consternation" (102). The scenario Manne paints helps us to grasp why, despite all evidence to the contrary, some detractors continue to stand their ground that Hughes was the primary translator, even though he did not know Hebrew and did not translate the poems in *Selected Poems* or *Poems* by his own admission. He did make small suggestions regarding the English translations she produced, as any reviewer of any writer's work would do. The way to determine whether misogyny is present is not to ask the male or masculine agent about his take but to turn to the women or feminine subject or target audience for her experience of the situation (60). Otherwise, all privilege and rights are always accorded to the most powerful, which will protect men in a patriarchal system and which will always cast doubt on and erase the feminized victim (178–79). Treatment like that is a form of violence: symbolic, emotional, and physical (193). As Catharine Stimpson underscores in "Beginning Again and Again," there is a pattern of dehumanizing others through language because language is powerful.

In considering the power of language in connection with victimization, we will revisit an incident that was discussed in the previous chapter. In chapter 2, we concentrated on piecing together narratives from other people's perspectives, and this particular instance also connects to Sylvia Plath, who suffered from intimate partner violence in her relationship with Hughes. In this chapter, the focus is on Assia's words as they reach us across time, somewhat mediated. Assia once told her friend Nathaniel Tarn that Hughes raped her; she says it happened on July 13, 1962, during a planned sexual tryst that did not go the way Assia anticipated. Instead of romance, she informed Tarn that the sexual encounter with Hughes was "violent" and "animal," and she suffered a rupture. She "turns against [Hughes] and goes quite cold." Hours later, Assia disclosed to her husband that she was raped (Nathaniel Tarn Papers). A week after the violent sex, Assia also informed Celia Taylor, the wife of David Wevill's department head at the advertising firm at which he worked, that Hughes had raped her (Koren and Negev 99). Much later, Richard Larschan recalls reading letters to Plath's mother from Assia, after Plath had died; in them, as Koren and Negev cite, Assia "complained to Aurelia Plath that Ted was brutalizing her, with 'frequent mentions of emotional and physical abuse, some of it, I seem to recollect, sexual," written in an "anguished tone," Larschan remembers (Koren and Negev and Larschan qtd. in Koren and Negev 183–83). In retrospect, Brenda Hedden confided to Assia's biographers, "when they were together, he did terrible things" (Hedden qtd. in Koren and Negev 221). Manne clarifies how a disclosure like Assia's may be an act of agency in laying claim to the moral narrative and making others aware of "the reality of the injury." This act of telling "can matter, quite properly, to people who have been victimized" (223). It also matters because "claiming victimhood effectively involves placing oneself at the *center of the story,*" a fraught move in that the victim "is liable to be perceived as at once self-dramatizing and self-important" (225). As a result of gender ranking and a desire to preserve gender hierarchy and the status quo in a male-dominated society, Western culture tends not to believe victims in the first place (Manne 237), so victimized women who reveal what happens to them face an uphill battle. As the authors of a 2021 United Kingdom report on false allegations of rape maintain, "Disclosing an experience of sexual violence takes enormous courage, and a skeptical response can seriously compound an already profound harm and increase someone's reluctance to engage with the justice system" (Rape Crisis Scotland). What emerges from transatlantic studies is identical: 97 percent of victims are telling the truth. The 2021 report from the United Kingdom cites the rate of false allegations concerning rape "at around 3%" in England, Scotland, and Wales. According to the report, "this [statistic for false reporting] is no higher than any other crime" (Rape Crisis Scotland). From data collected in the United States, we know, per the FBI, that the rate of false reporting for rape is less than 3 percent, mirroring the percentage of false reporting for other violent crimes in the United States (Shaw and Lee 545). What Manne dubs "himpathy" filters how we interpret what victims reveal and whether we even want to believe them (196). Himpathy is "the excessive sympathy sometimes shown toward male perpetrators of sexual violence" (197). Notwithstanding the trauma they inflict, our sympathy is channeled to male perpetrators, and "we sympathize with him first, effectively making him into the victim of his own crimes," transforming the actual victim into the villain in the stories we tell (201)! A common power move in cases of victimization of women is to erase women entirely from the narrative, as if they do not exist (202). Perpetrators and those who control narratives are not necessarily monsters but "socially situated, morally multifaceted, and sometimes talented" human beings (211).[19] On the other hand, victims are not perfect.[20] But the bottom line of misogyny is this: "It has always been [about] killing girls and women, literally and metaphorically—especially those who step out of line" (281).

There were many warning signs of toxicity in Hughes and Assia's relationship, captured in their letters. In referencing Assia's letters in this chapter, we discover warning signs as early as August 15, 1962 (or thereabouts). Taunting Hughes to bring a manifesto and a razor blade to celebrate his birthday, Assia describes a small injury a bottle opener has left on her wrist. She also asks him where he has "banished" her (*Collected Writings* 102). In her January 22, 1964, letter to Hughes, she angrily tells him that she will not see him again: "I'm surprised at the anger I feel towards you. I'm convinced you've mayhemmed my life. You've left me with a rubbishy life—with nothing to salvage. Absolutely nothing" (109).

As her journals document, Assia struggled with increasingly poor mental health episodes. Her living situation—residing with Hughes and his children with Plath in the flat Plath died in—surely did not help matters. One night, in spring 1963, Assia experiences what appears to be a panic attack, what she calls "a panic fear" (164), as she gazes at Hughes's nude body next to hers in the dark. She wonders whether he is a "Negress eater, the killer," startling words when we consider how Hughes depicts Assia as Black and persecuted in his letter about his poem "Shibboleth" (discussed in chapter 4). The next day, following her bout with panic, Assia displays thinking that we would code as suicidal ideation as she forms a plan to kill herself in such a way that no one can help her (166–67). With the publication of *The Modern Poets: An American-British Anthology* (1963), featuring poems and photographs of Plath and Hughes, Assia is triggered: she feels "near wild hysteria all morning. Sylvia growing in him, enormous, magnificent. I shrinking daily, both nibble at me. They eat me" (168). The day after—clearly, Assia's journal served her as a mechanism to share what she was going through and to process it—she fears she is "Trapped. trapped. trapped [sic]. Joanna [whose identity remains unknown] came—says I must go away; can't let them trap me like this" (169). She hopes that loving Hughes will "make *me* whole," and that is one of the saddest revelations of her extant journals (171). Perceiving herself as broken and desiring wholeness—healing and health—Assia signals her despair and gestures to the trauma informing her life after Plath's suicide, which proved to be traumatic for Hughes, too. Following Plath's death on February 11, 1963, Assia divulges that it is not until around June 12, 1963, that she and Hughes "lived in peace for 5 days now—the longest (it seems) since Sylvia died" (176). However, by August 8, 1968, Assia is in despair about Hughes's interactions with her: "He uses the word *sentimental* frequently, whenever he refers to love between people. He condemns [sic] himself. Us, whenever he says it. What he *seems* to say is that feeling, matters of the heart, matters of *my* heart, matters of his heart that were, are unworthy of life. Unimportant" (191). Come September 6, 1968, about a month later, Assia sounds like she is in distress about Hughes's infidelities: "It is only inevitably [sic] that the life I have lead [sic] should end like this. That I should be sup planted (*sub*-planted!) by others. I was endowed with too many minor qualities, but with neither the will nor huge intelligence to bring them a life of their own" (193). The next paragraph she writes after this disclosure in her journal exhibits signs of suicidal ideation.

The March 11, 1967, letter that Assia writes to Chaikin is most concerning because Assia directly informs her sister that she is "literally suicidally depressed" and "clearly ill." As Assia explains, "The last four years have been a strain simply too hard to bear" (*Collected Writings* 117). The last four years for Assia included Plath's suicide, the breakdown of her marriage with David Wevill, and a peripatetic existence: following Hughes and living with him in Ireland (February–May 1966) and Devon, England (February 1966–spring 1967). In this letter, she makes plans for the future care of Shura, enlisting her sister as Shura's guardian in the event of her death. Chaikin read a letter full of warning signs. Clearly, Assia had invested a great amount of energy and thought into shoring up a future for her daughter; she carefully describes where Shura's two trunks are, states that there is a check for $1,200 made out for Shura's fare to Canada, and gives directives concerning how to invest money for Shura, after bequeathing all her worldly possessions to her little girl under the care of her sister. Struggling in a hostile environment and functioning as a single mother, Assia writes that she is doing her best to battle with her poor mental health, experiencing respite from the struggle at times. Her quality of life is most obviously affected by her living situation, which she sketches for her sister in this letter. She sends an honest, heartrending letter to Chaikin, confiding in her in a way she could to no one else, as isolated as she was in Devon with Hughes and his extended family and without any friends. Specifically, Assia names the strain and tension between Hughes's parents and her and Shura as taking a toll; she and Shura are relegated to lunch alone, for instance. In addition to the family tension, Assia names "the isolation, the hostility and to me, fine contempt of Ted's friends here" as "sometimes unendurable" (117). The bright spot for Assia is Shura: "She is all I have. I adore her, as only I adored Mutti [our mother]" (117). "I see little of Ted," writes Assia; he spends his time writing ("He is hiding in the hut writing" [123]), lunches with his father, and plays snooker with his father and Trevor and Brenda Hedden, the latter with whom he had an affair, when he is not otherwise eking time out for Assia and Shura in the Court Green library. For someone who loved books and posh settings, the library would not have suited Assia. As she relates to her friends in Israel, Yehuda Amichai and Hana Sokolov-Amichai, from Court Green on August 19, 1967, "I am in the library thinking very intensely of you, and the rats are scrabbling amongst Ted's papers" (123).

Ultimately, the living situation at Court Green, filled with people who openly showed their hostility to one another on a daily basis, proved untenable. To her close friend Patricia Mendelson, Assia focuses on the upheavals and attendant distress in her life and Shura's in a letter, dated September 12, 1967:

> Things here have reached a pitch of mild disaster, culminating in a feverish rush to London of mine to try and find a job within 3 days. Through some kind of miracle, I *did* find one—waiting for the contract to be signed/ [sic]. The idea being that I spend weekends here, and work for four days in London. That seemed the only working compromise. Ted is exhausted with the war between parents and me, and I seem to be the most expendable factor. Terrible on the children. Insufferable for Shura. She wept throughout the two nights of my absence almost throughout. [. . .]
>
> I feel unendurably sad. (125–26)

Despite the best of intentions, the plan to spend so much time together in the English countryside as a family never materialized. Rather, distance exacerbated an already troubled relationship. Assia's telephone did not ring (Koren and Negev 193), and Hughes did not often answer the phone when Assia tried to call him (195). It was during this sequence of events that Assia confided to her colleague Chris Wilkins "that she couldn't stand the state of things as they were, and if it didn't change, she would kill herself" (Wilkins qtd. in Koren and Negev 197). To Hughes, Assia writes in a July 9, 1968, letter, "How I want us to live together, the 5 of us, to make a family again. . . . These long absences feel so dangerous—they show me that I *could* live without you, but once I make contact with you again, the total independence seems worthless" (148–49). Beseechingly, Assia tells him, "We're *meant* to be together. And the children need both of us. And we need both of us, and it's worth the effort" (149). Dubbing him an "island," Assia acknowledges that Hughes is not physically or emotionally available to her in most cases. What Assia does not acknowledge is that most of her relationship with Hughes has been in pursuit of a unified family in one household, and what she could not know until March 1969 is that it would never happen. In an undated letter to Mendelson, written sometime after the fall of 1967, Assia laments, "It's them bloody artists what bash up womens' [sic] souls" (127). Assia knew by January 11, 1968, that she and Shura would never live at Court Green again, as long as Hughes's parents continued to reside there (134). She continued to feel vulnerable and sad, as her February 2, 1968, letter to Hughes shows. Calling it "miraculous" that "we have somehow survived," she admits that "this week was excellent proof to me—I don't know what it looks like to you" (134–35). The letter closes with Assia realizing, after finding photographs from their time in Cleggan in her bureau drawer, that it has been two years since their happy months living in Ireland. Since then, according to Assia, "There isn't a single, safe anniversary between us" (136).

In late March 1968, Assia implores Hughes for validation of their relationship: she loves him but does not know if he loves her: "I still have ABSOLUTE HOPES that we can build a happy, loving life together. I know that I can still love you fully with all my faculties and my body and my life—my darling Ted" (138). She knows that she "will flourish under you, and care for you and give you everything I have" (138). Hughes wielded the most power in their relationship, Assia recognizes. She begs him twice in the relatively short letter to let her know if he wants to continue the relationship. Most of all, she wants their relationship to be reciprocal: "Love me back—and if you can't, then say so and let me go with whatever peace I can salvage," she writes in closing (138).

It is telling of Hughes's attachment to Assia that he kept her beseeching, loving letters and handmade cards; he chose not to destroy them, as private as he wished to be. In particular, he kept a card from 1968 in which Assia lists attributes of his that she finds valuable. She names "his spirit fiery and splendid" and calls him one of God's "best creatures." Hughes is "rare and marvelous," and God "spent so much love in creating him," Assia avows. She wishes financial wealth for him, so he will no longer worry about money, and asks God to heal him and make him whole again. In invoking God, she asks that Hughes "forget our awful tribulations of the last year" and "to forgive me my pride and its consequences." Finally, she asks, "if it's the last thing I ever ask you God, send him back to me loving and sweet as he was before our sorrows" (*Collected Writings* 139).

All during this turmoil, Assia proceeded to translate Amichai's poems from Hebrew to English, rendering his poetry into English for the first time. In reading Assia's letters to Amichai and his to her, it is evident that she not only worked as the primary translator, seeking feedback, but also as a coselector of the poems to be translated in consultation with him. For instance, Assia writes the following to Amichai, highlighting the process they used: "Anyway, would you like to send me 20 poems from your new book, or from your old book, as you like, with a rough English translation. Or, more practically, send me 5 poems at a time. I would like to see the Hebrew originals first, though, because that's where the real magic lies, which stimulates me" (130). She writes about this process on November 21, 1967, at the time that she is "translating the other 21 poems" for the Penguin edition of Amichai's poetry, which she did not live to see published (131). As the primary translator, Assia informs Amichai on March 6, 1968, "I have begun, am in the midst, in full steam of translating what I like best in your newest batches" (136). Her role as coselector of the poems to be translated is evidenced in this letter: "I think they're terrific—infinitely more varied, and with fine steel backbones, and I enjoy doing them. I have received your November batch. Some I began translating and found they lost too much, so rather than quarrel with the words I abandoned them—promiscuously thinking I'll find lots more magic mushrooms . . . which so far, I have done" (136–37). On May 29, she writes, "I have finished translating 22 of the new poems. I translated many more, but some of them simply didn't work in English, and I abandoned them" (144). In another instance, she recommends, in a June 18, 1968, letter, that a poem that did not make the current book project could be a part of a future collection (146). She did seek feedback from Hughes about how the English versions sounded, but his contributions were very minimal, mostly because he was not fluent in Hebrew. He read the translations and offered suggestions for tweaks (145, 147–48). Assia's letters to Amichai—namely the ones dated August 19, 1967, October 31, 1967, May 8, 1968, May 29, 1968, and June 25, 1968—demonstrate the dynamics at work in the translation project as described above, and other letters she wrote show how well-versed she is in Israeli poetry more broadly, as her November 21, 1967, letter to Amichai indicates. However, this poetry project, a significant literary event that resulted in two books and that Hughes encouraged and nurtured, did not lend itself to harmonious relations between Hughes and Assia. On January 4, 1968, Assia tells Aurelia Plath, Plath's mother, that she "must perhaps think of living without [Hughes] completely" because the "degree of brutality" she suffered in the relationship "would slowly dement me" (132). And yet, Assia signed her name and Hughes's on the last Christmas card she ever sent to Yehuda Amichai and Hana Sokolov-Amichai in December 1968 (154). She was still hoping, holding on, and trying to have faith that the relationship would work.

Not only was Assia dealing with a toxic interpersonal relationship, but her work situation presented itself as dire too. Friends of hers had been fired, and she relates to Amichai and Sokolov-Amichai on January 11, 1968, that "in the past 6 weeks 27 people have been fired. The survivors are treated to little cocktail parties in the evenings, where our brains are then further picked" (*Collected Writings* 133). Assia desperately needed to keep her job: Hughes did not contribute to Shura's support, as he did for his children with Plath. Assia's concern is palpable: "A feeling of last ditch panic seems to fill the whole of England, and advertising always feels it most immediately and most acutely. We've been working like slaves until 9, ten o'clock at night all in order to grab some £1,000,000 account from another agency—but the sensation is that if you don't do it, you're out" (133). Regretfully, Assia informs Amichai that she would love to continue to translate the other half of the Penguin book as soon as "the office panic stops." Obviously, her toxic work situation prevented her from spending the time she desired with Shura or engaging in self-care activities. To put her situation in perspective, Assia was struggling to survive professionally and financially in a pressurized and competitive work environment, in addition to wrestling with poor mental health and navigating an unsupportive partnership with Hughes. Surely, we can see how the workload alone would feel stressful, and when combined with a lack of support and worries about the welfare of her daughter, money, and loneliness, Assia was dealing with an overwhelming situation. According to Assia's first biographers, "In a profession that had become more aggressive and flashy, with most copywriters in their twenties, her experience and age were working against her. She had the rent to pay, a daughter to bring up—and she was well aware that Ted was not going to support them" (Koren and Negev 181–82). All of this is quite ironic, given how talented and versatile Assia was. By the end of May 1968, Assia had achieved notable successes and accrued a variety of work experiences: jewelry maker, teacher, secretary, antiques dealer, peer reviewer of poetry, artist, translator, funded film director, copywriter of award-winning and acclaimed commercials and print advertisements, and graphic designer (because, at this point, she was working with Cape Golliard on the cover design of *Selected Poems*).

As a person, Assia is compared and contrasted with Plath. Conflicting accounts help us to see that one interpretation cannot accommodate all facts, details, and plot developments in a story. According to Rosenstein, Plath thought of herself as a child, and this perception contrasts with how Plath viewed Assia; Rosenstein argues that Plath considered Assia a beautiful woman, and their mutual friends saw Assia's confidence and Plath's lack of it as contributing factors to how both women are perceived (Helder Macedo, interview recording, December 1, 1973, side B). Indeed, Helder Macedo asserts that Assia was "the most beautiful woman in London," and she seemed entitled: she would make her guests wait thirty to sixty minutes before she would descend, presumably stairs, to meet her guests. Mindful of her image and her presentation, Assia took care in dressing; Suzette notes that Assia dressed to impress. As we know from Plath's letters, Plath, too, cared about her image and how she was perceived. Perhaps the pressure Plath placed on herself to excel in all arenas made her feel socially awkward. Suzette Macedo tells Rosenstein that Plath found social occasions difficult because she was very insecure; Plath viewed herself as ungainly and awkward and would, consequently, "ingratiate" herself with others. "Social graces didn't come naturally to her," says Macedo. "Her way of bridging the gap was to be super nice," she concludes (Helder Macedo, interview recording, December 1, 1973, side B). In contrast to Plath and her perceived childlike, unwomanly presentation, Helder Macedo declares, "To be a woman is to be Assia." This line of thinking is "propaganda," declares Macedo, with Plath believing it and Assia almost doing so (interview recording, December 1, 1973, side B). In a journal entry dated January 28, 1959, Plath records the following: "Symbolic: get over instinct to be dowdy lip-biting little girl. Get bathrobe and slippers and nightgown & work on femininity" (467). Of all Plath's journal entries, this is the one that Assia highlights in her own journal in a 1966 entry. Plath's journal entry prompts Assia to ruminate on Plath's "muscular brain" and "splendid brilliance," in turn (*Collected Writings* 188). Rather than affirming Plath's insecurities, Assia channels them into compliments for her counterpart. However, from the summer of 1962 until 1963, Plath would not have characterized Assia so favorably.

Understandably, Plath harbored animosity. On more than one occasion, she verbalized resentment toward Assia rather than Hughes (Horder). Plath's view of Assia is one that makes sense to us, and her treatment of Assia does not surprise.[21] On their end, the Hughes family made life very difficult for Assia—and Shura—for reasons that are more challenging to understand. Assia assumed that Plath must have had a much easier time than she herself did in attempting to blend into Hughes's extended family. And she was right to some degree: she and Hughes had to sleep apart when they visited the family home in Heptonstall, with Assia staying in Olwyn's bedroom (*Collected Writings* 172). As she sketches it, "I sit near the window in this tiny child's, maid's, unwanted-guest room. Feeling fully unwanted, a quarter my size, stunted, not knowing what I should assert." She adds, "I feel absolutely alien to [Hughes,] to them all" (173). Yet, Clarissa Roche reports that Plath described the family in terms like "gross" and "mean," noting "vulgarity" and "uncouthness," too. They were similarly intolerant of Plath, says Roche, "leaving her to fend for herself" (interview recording, November 30, 1973, part 1). Assia seemingly suffered much more from it, given that she had no legal standing or otherwise with Hughes from the perspective of his family, which will be discussed in the following chapter. That official sanction to her relationship would have meant everything to Assia. Notwithstanding the family they created, support from Hughes's extended family was always lacking, and some friends took a while to reach the point where they could support Hughes and Assia individually and together. Even relatively early in their relationship, in early June 1963, Assia guesses that Hughes will never actually serve as a ballast for her. She writes, "T is a long night of nightmares. Whatever the consequences for me, T. is unconcerned. He forces me to look out for myself" (175). Except for the sojourn to Ireland, Hughes and Assia would never live happily together with their children. At Court Green in late 1966, upon their return from Ireland, the situation—Hughes's parents are also living with them—"is difficult, almost impossible," shares Assia in a letter to Patricia Mendelson and Nathaniel Tarn (115).

One of Assia's loudest antagonists was Hilda Farrar, Hughes's aunt. In her letters, archived at the British Library in London, she declaims her views (and displeasure) to Olwyn Hughes with myriad examples. In an undated letter, likely from 1963, Farrar conveys the dislike Ruth Fainlight initially showed Assia in the wake of Plath's suicide. (Assia and Fainlight eventually became close friends.) Farrar informs Olwyn Hughes that Fainlight and her husband snubbed Assia, ignoring her and not inviting her to lunch, although they invited Hughes. Unsurprisingly, Farrar went out of her way to point out the insults to Assia, asking her how she could stand them. Assia reportedly answered that she believed time would improve the situation. In her letter to Olwyn Hughes, Farrar argues she does not think the hostility will pass, and she states that she does not want to see Assia again. In another letter to Olwyn Hughes, dated only Wednesday and addressed from Plath's former flat at 23 Fitzroy Road, Farrar sounds very annoyed. Calling Assia "a reincarnated Cleopatra" whom she could not bear the sight of, Farrar admits that she tells Assia to go away and leave Ted Hughes alone. Assia ignores her, and Ted Hughes admonishes Farrar to mind her own business. To Farrar's great annoyance, Assia appears each evening, "messing about in the kitchen with foreign foods." In other circumstances, Assia would present as a "novelty," Farrar writes. Her major concern lies in Hughes being "simply bewitched" by Assia. "I have told him," laments Farrar, "he has only left one bondage for another, and she will turn into a devil one day." Xenophobia cuts across Farrar's remarks, as does misogyny and maybe racism, too, depending on whether Assia's Jewish ethnicity is interpreted as racial by Hilda Farrar (as it was by Ted Hughes, it seems). Making Assia out to be a magical devil who entraps Hughes is not a positive endorsement by Farrar, and rhetorically, the aim of the letter seems to be to convince Olwyn Hughes to side with her rather than with Hughes himself or Assia. Assia's take on Farrar: "I can't stop to be for her sake," she writes in a May 20, 1963, letter to Olwyn Hughes. In response to what he detects his aunt is doing, Hughes also writes to Olwyn in an undated letter, probably from 1963, noting Farrar's "panic" about Hughes's choices and about Assia in particular. Farrar shows "pure terror at the sight of Assia," pronounces Hughes. In a different, undated letter to Olwyn Hughes, we learn that Ted Hughes is having a hard time securing a suitable nanny; the current one finds Assia to be competition because the nanny perceives her as glamorous when the nanny desires to be the most glamourous woman in the flat. It is a problem because Hughes reveals Assia lives with him now and is gradually assuming responsibility for running the home.

Concerning Assia's family unit and her sense of home, Shura deserves special mention because Assia loved her dearly. Shura transformed Assia. When Shura (full name: Alexandra Tatiana Elise Wevill) was born on March 3, 1965, Assia writes ecstatically in a March 13, 1965, letter to Lucas Myers that Shura was "very touching" (110). Assia "was a woman who changed very much," acknowledges Richard Murphy (interview recording, April 19, 1974, part 2). In a December 1965 letter to Patricia Mendelson, Assia apologizes for how indifferent she had been to her friend upon the birth of Mendelson's daughter. Motherhood has changed her: "I am ashamed now, to think how ignominiously indifferent I was to Andrea's infancy, and how I let you apologize for your doting. I was a stupid, seriously flawed bitch-woman" (114). In this same letter, Assia details how she desires to purchase pretty things for Shura and how proud she is that

Shura ate "real bread and butter and egg, for the first time" and perfectly too (114). Her love and devotion to Shura are palpable in her letters.

From the extensive study I have engaged in with respect to Assia—over the course of three books now—it is clear to me that Assia viewed Shura as an extension of herself in a cruel and uncaring world, one without a safety net or adequate support system for women and children. She could not leave her unprotected child alone, left to a life of misery. I do not believe that Assia killed herself and Shura in Medea-like fashion to spite Ted Hughes.[22] The evidence simply is not forthcoming to support the interpretation of Assia as a contemporary Medea. There is speculation that she wanted to hurt him with her death, but there exists the same speculation about Plath. For instance, in taking up for his friend, Murphy maintains that Plath's suicide was intended "to kill Ted slowly" (interview recording, April 19, 1974, part 2). Given that everything Murphy knows would come from Hughes, we must remember that there are more than two sides to any story involving Plath, Hughes, and Assia.[23] There are at least three.

Assia loved Hughes and wanted to be his partner. She captures her awe and admiration of him in 1963: "The whole man glitters. The whole man is ferocious with such intelligence and magic I am afraid to occupy the space next to him" (*Collected Writings* 170). For Assia, Hughes "*has* genius, easily and innocently. He *is* magnificent. He doesn't cultivate it. He is easy, easy superb" (171). Even with those admissions, Assia cast herself as "bewitched by this huge creative, who's touched off dreadful, magic things in me, I may never know what to do with" (174). Three years later, her admiration and love (and insecurity) are even more intense: "His superb legs and thighs—the beautiful Anatomical Man. One of God's best creations. Is God squandering him on me? He carries so many perfections that I would in all truth not begrudge him an affair or two with other women—as long as he remains loyal to me. I would suffer bitterly—but this in all truth is the only due thanks I could give him for all his grace." The journal entry ends: "He is one of God's best creatures. Ever. Ever" (189). Perhaps unsurprisingly, Assia wanted to collaborate with him on projects or in areas in which her expertise or abilities would be of use. The premium Assia places on collaboration can best be understood through Bateson's observation: "In heterosexual couples, collaboration is valuable because the women's goals are not automatically reduced to second rank, even if her contribution often is" (82). Together, Assia and Hughes discussed and/or worked collaboratively on the following: film scripts (Koren and Negev 107); at least two book projects; one, drafts of Hughes's poems about a deck of cards, *A Full House*,[24] is archived at Emory without Assia's drawings, which appear not to exist any longer, and the second book dealt with animals and plants, of which Assia created miniature paintings to accompany Hughes's poems (Koren and Negev 149); and, of course, the translations of Amichai's poems from Hebrew to English. The idea to translate Amichai's poetry originated with Hughes, who urged Amichai to appoint Assia—whom Hughes referred to as "my wife" on May 7, 1967 (Hughes qtd. in Koren and Negev 166)—in the role, given the years she lived in Israel, her familiarity with Hebrew, and her closeness to Hughes.

We are most fortunate to have any of Assia's writing extant, and similarly, we are lucky to have Hughes's about Assia. He never intended for anyone other than himself to read his private musings and writing about Assia. Koren and Negev give an overview of the systematic way in which Hughes expunged her from his life and work.

> When Ted Hughes's archive at Emory University in Atlanta, Georgia was made available to the public in 2000, it was devoid of Assia's presence in his life: of the numerous letters that they exchanged, of all the notes, drawings, and photos, none existed. Hughes admitted that he went over each piece of paper, and sorted them himself before packing and shipping the eighty-six crates to the United States, exercising self-containment. In 2003, his widow, Carol Hughes, sold to Emory six thousand volumes from his library and all of a sudden Assia surfaced. About eighty of the books either belonged to Assia, or were presents to Hughes from her. (134)

Assia's personal library assumes an important place, then, in the recovery and reconstructive efforts associated with piecing together her life and Hughes's.

In the writing of this book, I have attempted to read everything Assia wrote that has not been lost to time, and I have incorporated what warrants inclusion. I have been mindful that some readers have amassed considerable knowledge about Assia, whereas other readers will know very little. Balancing this divide, I strove to take care in presenting what fascinates me or what I deem essential in understanding Assia's life and how it intersects with Hughes's and, to a lesser degree, Plath's. As a result, I paged through books once owned by Assia, looking for inscriptions or marginalia. Unlike Plath, Assia tended not to write in her books, so when she did, it became especially noteworthy. In acquiring Plath's copy of *The Art of Loving,* Assia adds her name under Plath's, with "Sept. '63." Plath had inscribed the book with her address and dated it November 9, 1962, indicating that she started reading the book after she and Hughes separated. Assia may have begun reading the book, hoping to find help or answers to her own fragile and difficult relationship with Hughes. While Assia did not contribute marginalia to *The Art of Loving,* she did mark lines on pages 19, 30, 37, and 97. Mostly, she emphasized sentences or passages about the psychology of and bodies affected by the following: independency, dependency, power over another person, the man as a child who will act out masculinity in sex and through sadism, and mental illness. To be forthcoming, I hoped very much that she might have read and recorded her thoughts about Thomas Hardy's novel *Tess of the d'Urbervilles,* about a woman suffering a traumatic outcome. However, her copy, inscribed "Assia Wevill / 1 9 6 7" appears unread. Also from 1967 is Assia's playbill of *Oedipus,* adapted by Hughes, wherein he inscribed, "Asseeke sat in white, on this opening night, she was the best sight." When I paged through *Anna Karenina* by Leo Tolstoy, nothing stood out, except that Assia had written her name in it (without a date). The book *The Film Sense* by Serge Eisenstein from 1968 looks unread; it was a gift to Assia from Hughes and stands as a testament to their artistic sensibilities and their romantic partnership. Her 1968 translations of Amichai's poetry more firmly establishes the features of their relationship, as well as predicting the tragedy of it, rent by trauma, in brief lines, full of meaning.[25] In an inscription from May 31, 1968, Assia writes, "My dearest, lovely lost Ted from Asya [name transliterated from Hebrew]." On the previous page, she inscribed the poem "Reshut 7" by Ibn Gabirol, with the opening line ("Open the gate love rise and open the gate") and closing ones ("None can explain me / And I am ignorant").

Assia's penultimate journal entry, dated March 20, 1969, holds the keys to understanding her and her disastrous last acts on March 23. It opens: "I pretend to be alive and ask the lard-white landlady if she knew of a house for sale." Securing a home with Hughes functioned as a lifeline for Assia. At the writing of this entry, she is visiting Haworth, Yorkshire, with Hughes, who will participate in a poetry television program. Fearing that establishing a home together was not to be (and correct in that assessment, as the previous almost seven years seemed to show), Assia then goes to town to secure sleeping pills. Feeling "criminal" and "totally bankrupt," she worries about "My Shura" (*Collected Writings* 194). She also worries about her inability to write *Wellington the Tin Soldier* with Martin Baker (and Ted Hughes). Categorizing her mental state as a "sinking—further and further inwards," Assia needs an immediate intervention (194). She thinks about Frieda and Nicholas Hughes, whom Hughes says are "in average despair," as Assia records it, and she notes that he does not mention Shura. This is the entry wherein Assia discloses what transpired between Hughes and her at the Elm Hotel—where Hughes declares Plath will always factor into their relationship—and Assia ruminates on her own impending suicide. "He feels as though he has already buried me—that feels hideously accurate," writes Assia (195).

In the last recorded journal entry, March 21, it is more heartening to read, "I woke in optimism—it's receding in caution" (195). The last journal entry of her life surfaces resilience: despite traumatic losses, hardships, uncertainties, hurt feelings, panic, depression, and a plethora of other challenges, Assia articulates a noble desire to attempt to overcome. Perhaps part of her motivation lies in her love for Shura, documented in her letters and journals. Whatever her motivations may be and however she manages to tap into a reservoir of resilience and adaptability on this day and the one prior, Assia's journal writing proves that we might never really know a person the way we think we do. It also gestures to the systemic inequality and inequity embedded in the expectation that women bow down to men when it came to important decisions or status in their personal and work lives. In other words, as Assia's writing shows time and again, Assia could never choose for herself exactly: she waited to be chosen, and her hope ran out, as her last letter indicates. There are two important points to make about the very last sentence of Assia's last journal, however, which is this: "Ted is to pick me up this morning. He went to visit his mother in hospital yesterday—spent the night at the Beacon. 10^{30}, he said." One point: no punctuation ends the sentence; it is left open-ended, just as any interpretation of Assia's life must be as well. We can approach her as a subject and interpret what we find, and we should do so as Assia's life and work teach us about our world then and now. Her letters, journals, and poems offer unique perspectives, original insight, and creative contributions to arts and letters. What is also telling about this last sentence, the second point I would like to make, is that Assia, maybe unwittingly, ends with prioritizing Hughes's words. Conventionally, Hughes's words about Assia have been prioritized over her own, and so, in this chapter, one that foregrounds and centers her life and work, it is fitting to close with one of her original poems, likely about her relationship with Hughes from her point of view. The poem is addressed "For Teddy A Valentine" in its manuscript form. Here are the last four stanzas of Assia's original poem, "Once There Was a Large, Flat Stone":

> As the summer went on, the stalk flowered—it sprouted
> a lily, which sprouted a poppy, which sprouted a
> strawberry flower. When summer ended, this 3-flower
> flower dropped off, and when November came an oak
> kernel sat tight on the hollow wavering stalk, moving
> back and forth with the wind.
>
> One day, when the milkman rang the bell, waiting to
> be paid, he noticed the oak kernel, and because he
> didn't have much else to do, he pulled it out. But
> as he pulled, he heard a song which he hadn't heard

since he was a very young man, and it seemed to come from the stalk. He tugged once more, and the stalk came away, roots and all. But, at this end of the roots there dangled half a bright red heart.

The other half of the heart lay hugging the mossy stone, red and ragged—and he looked again, and saw that the icy white milk bottles were splattered with tiny drops of steaming blood.

Then he went back to his van, and thought about it all morning.
 (*Collected Writings* 225–26)

4

TED HUGHES

Hughes remains powerful, part of an establishment, even after his death in 1998. He set in motion narratives about Assia that we readily come across in work featuring her today.[1] Such status and influence (read: privilege) should encourage investigations and interrogations into Hughes's representations of women and minoritized people. In *Reclaiming Assia Wevill: Sylvia Plath, Ted Hughes, and the Literary Imagination*, I analyze and track the narratives that Hughes activated with respect to Assia, a feminine-presenting woman and, as I learned from her job résumé, someone who claimed her Jewish ethnic identity.[2] The values embedded or heralded in Hughes's narratives are sometimes covert and sometimes overt, but it behooves us to figure out what we are consuming, adopting, rejecting, or calling out or in.[3] To complicate matters, trauma permeates the lives and stories of Hughes, Assia, and Plath. Like Plath before her, Assia experienced great turmoil in a romantic relationship with Hughes. Furthermore, it seems that Assia was subjected to physical and emotional violence, not unlike Plath, during the course of her partnership with Hughes, and Assia also grappled with trauma in her personal life, albeit of a different nature than Plath's. All of this is not to deny that Hughes himself experienced trauma firsthand and at the hands of the women he loved. Rather, I intend to affirm that all parties suffered in the traumatic aftermaths of tragedies without minimizing responses.

One of the women on the faculty at Smith College in 1971 asked Harriet Rosenstein if Hughes actually loved Assia. That, Rosenstein responds, is an "impossible question" (Gibian and Smith College English Faculty).

For his part, Hughes writes to Celia Chaikin, Assia's sister, in a letter dated April 14, 1969, "Assia was my true wife and the best friend I ever had" (290). And during her lifetime, Hughes presented Assia with, in his words, the "First copy to be bound," of his *Wodwo*, inscribing the following to her: "To sweetest Assiake from Permanence [Ted Hughes]" and dating it October 23, 1967. At that point, Hughes wanted to declare his constancy to his partner. In this chapter and throughout this book, we encounter various takes on this question, and, in looking back at the relationship, we can determine how representations of it play their part in a larger cultural narrative about women, their worth, power, and politics.

Before we go further into stories about trauma, it is important to know that no one wants to remember it (van der Kolk, *The Body Keeps the Score* 196). Everyone wants "to live in a world that is safe, manageable, and predictable" (196). By contrast, the traumatic experience presents itself as unsafe, unmanageable, and unpredictable. We will find that we possess a "natural reluctance to confront" a traumatic reality (and a reticence, too), and courage is required to listen to (and tell, I would add) the trauma story (van der Kolk 196–97). For the dialectic of trauma involves denying or stonewalling horrible events and, paradoxically, needing to proclaim them. Hughes shows courage in facing up to traumatic remembering and working to overcome the reluctance and reticence associated with the articulation of traumatic events in his writing.

As others do, Hughes tends to mark the distinctions between Plath and Assia as if they were literary foils, as we see in *Capriccio* (1990) and *Birthday Letters* (1998), poetic sequences dedicated to Assia and Plath respectively. We see the literary foil device animated in poems, such as "Capriccios" and "The Other" from *Capriccio* and "Dreamers" from *Birthday Letters*. Regarding Assia, Hughes characterizes her as his "dark muse" to Daniel Huws in July 1962 (Huws 50), years before she becomes exactly that in *Capriccio*. In both *Capriccio* and *Birthday Letters*, Hughes acknowledges obliquely his pursuit of her. Although people like Julia Matcham are quick to point to Assia (her coworker) as the perpetrator of the disastrous affair (correspondence), Hughes mostly attributed the start of the affair to fate or to his desire for her, and his writing wrestles with that desire and the mixed emotions he felt following her horrific death and that of their child.

In the aftermath of Plath's suicide, Hughes's family took sides in the Plath-Assia divide, treating them like real-life literary foils. Hughes's parents and aunt railed against Assia. Nothing about her was appealing to them; her appearance, accent, marital history, nationality, and her status as Hughes's romantic interest in the wake of Plath's suicide poisoned her chances at acceptance.[4] Tensions ran high when Hughes brought Assia to visit his family home in the weeks after Plath died. As Hughes confides in a notebook from that time: "Hilda high & weeping, calling A[ssia] a hor [sic] and that kind of woman. . . . Pa & his reason: A[ssia] being with me after S[ylvia]'s death, the root of the scandal, quite correct. Hilda's irrational suspicion and antagonism against Assia . . . moral defendent [sic] of the family name, etc. . . . But how loyal she's [Assia] been and still seems to be—even against that lot. But it's easy for her to take [an] absolute stand against Hilda—for me not so" (Hughes qtd. in Clark, *Red Comet* 911). Hughes would not come to Assia's defense at the Hughes's family home, the Beacon in Heptonstall, in 1963 or at Court Green in North Tawton, where his parents joined him and Assia and their children, living as a blended family in 1966. Indeed, Keith Sagar, Hughes's friend, understood that Hughes conveyed to Assia that he could not marry her while his mother was alive; she disapproved of Assia that much and maintained a fidelity to Plath (Clark, *Red Comet* 915). In an undated letter to David Compton and Elizabeth Compton [later Sigmund], Hughes mentions that his parents fear his alliance with Assia has caused a scandal and ruined his respectability. Because Assia had married three times, his parents believed he could never secure a knighthood or have an audience with the queen, writes Hughes (Letters from Ted Hughes). Those fears were ill-founded and even ironic, as time would show. And yet, Hughes attributed the trauma of the news of Assia's suicide as the reason for his mother's subsequent death.

A year after Assia's and Shura's deaths, Hughes continued to suffer. After purchasing Lumb Bank, a house Hughes and Assia had looked at as a possible home base, Hughes thought about how Assia, with her talent in interior design, would have made the home beautiful, but, in her absence, it was dismal. As Jonathan Bate asserts, "The whole of England was bleak because of her absence, London 'unbearable.'" Since Assia and Shura had died, Hughes "had been trying to piece together his broken life" (*Ted Hughes* 286). To my mind, there exists no more fitting metaphor or language for trauma than that which refers to a life as fragmented and in shattered and broken pieces. Certainly, Hughes could not be understood to be healed and whole.

His traumatic responses to Plath's death would have shown Hughes how unsafe and, in fact, dangerous the world is. People who suffer from trauma come to view the world differently because they know firsthand how precarious existence can be.[5] As Stephen C. Enniss and Karen V. Kukil note, "In the weeks after Plath's death, Hughes confided to friends, 'That's the end of my life. The rest is posthumous' (Hughes to Leo and Ann Davidow Goodman, 8 May 1963, Smith)" (x). Even more revealing with respect to Assia and Shura are the lines Hughes composed around May 1969, about two months, give or take, after his partner and daughter died. Writes Hughes in a draft of poetic lines:

> I don't compose for a reader
> what stranger's momentary pleasure
> will pay me for ruining my life, and causing the deaths
> of those I have loved best
> and who loved me best, and who were my life[.]

He continues in this vein: "I am not composing poetry. I am trying to get out of the flames" (Enniss and Kukil 59). One of the common paradigms in trauma studies is the three-prong approach or pathway toward healing, as articulated by Judith Herman, which encompasses telling the trauma story, along with establishing safety and reestablishing connections between victims or survivors and their communities (3).[6] Securing a safe place is an important part, and Hughes must have felt safety was elusive in the 1960s as the trauma of Plath's suicide, Assia's suicide, and Shura's killing confronted him unexpectedly. Cathy Caruth theorizes that what makes an event especially traumatic is believing that one is alive only by accident (70–71), and a remorseful and trauma-stricken Hughes pens the above lines about being metaphorically burned by flames in response to the loss of Assia and Shura. In a private notebook, never meant to be published, Hughes reveals he suffers symptoms of trauma: recurring nightmares every night—Assia has not yet died and her death is preventable and a result of a misunderstanding, thereby rendering it an accident (Hughes, [Notebook 11]).

For his part, Hughes wrestled with crafting narratives and portrayals of Assia in order to heal from trauma and make sense of his own life, as I posit. He desired Assia in life and after her death, even though sometimes that desire turned to antipathy. This scenario calls to mind Janet Malcolm's description of the power of stories, namely journalism, mythology, and folklore: these "derive their power from their firm, undeviating sympathies and antipathies" (69). As Anne Stevenson confides to Malcolm, "Ted didn't demand that people be silent, but he asked me to keep what I said about Assia to a minimum, and I obeyed" (qtd. in Malcolm 103). Hughes desired above all else to control not only the narrative about Plath but about Assia and himself as well. Indeed, the narrative about Assia was so tightly controlled that she was essentially written out of literary history and culture, except as the mythological femme fatale, as I show in *Reclaiming Assia Wevill*.

Throughout his life, Hughes stayed preoccupied with Assia and with what he perceived to be her social class or, to be more precise, the trappings of it. Her accent galled him and attracted him, too. Elizabeth Compton Sigmund describes Plath as a "young, brilliant, aristocratic American" and says in an interview that Hughes's mother could not see Plath making the tea or otherwise helping or doing any of the housework in Yorkshire (interview recording, part 6). Social class and nationality matter, and while these intersecting identities offered Plath privileges, even in interpersonal circles, they proved to be far thornier and more complicated for Assia. The Hughes family never included Assia or made her feel welcome, whether in their home or hers. In fact, while they were content with her serving them and making them feel welcome at Court Green when she lived there with Hughes, they did not attempt to make her feel included in their extended family when they were living with her in close quarters, despite the fact that Shura was part of their biological family.[7] From Sigmund's point of view, the Hughes family's focus on social class was "not a personal thing," though it must have felt very personal to Assia.

What tracks as both a personal and systemic injustice is the manner in which Assia is racialized in order to justify or promote her denigration and abuse, whether symbolic or otherwise. The most obvious instance of this type of aggression can be found in Hughes's business writing. If Plath could not fit into life in Devon "because she was too blatantly an American" (Davies, interview recording, 1970, part 2), Assia would have stood out even more. In a November 19, 1997, letter to his English-to-German translators Jutta and Wolfgang Kaussen, Hughes exhibits unbridled racist and sexist attitudes, bound up in a colonialist project. The target of the exclusionary and symbolic colonialist violence is Assia. The point of the letter seems to be a setting up of the context of poems from *Capriccio* to be translated, namely "Shibboleth," "Folktale," and "Descent."

In the round, Hughes's letter to the Kaussens displays a lack of empathy for Assia as a person or subject. But it does show a heightened awareness of the minoritized identities she bore. The imagined characters populating "Shibboleth," for example, share in the "social banter of mutual cruelty, used almost as the norm for dinner party conversation" because they are socialized or "bred" into it (*Letters of Ted Hughes* 696). "Shibboleth" is a poem about putative passing (in this case, passing for a more privileged or different race, nationality, and social class). The English men in the poem discover that the Assia character is not English by birth; her accent betrays her act of passing for one of them; she cannot pass as a white English man with upper-crust social standing. To extrapolate, then, the racist and sexist, even misogynistic, overtures are the common sort, to be encountered by the middle class and "fringe-aristocracy," as Hughes dubs it (696). Very astutely, Hughes ventures, "It is a masculine thing, but their women imitate it" (696), and the people in the world Hughes sketches are the "English the world hates" (696). Even here, though, Hughes qualifies the entitled and cruel group: "At bottom, of course," he writes in the same letter, "They are often very good chaps" (696). And they are "often very good chaps" in spite, Hughes concedes, of their "violently racist and often quite anti-semitic [sic] attitudes" (696). As for the Assia figure, from which he draws directly from Assia's biography, Hughes characterizes her as

> an exotic and by fashionable standards very beautiful foreigner whose mother tongue was German but who now spoke (left Germany in 1935, though her mother was Prussian) an elocutioner's English rather more lofty than the élite English who sat around her (German behind English can sound super-echt English). True to type, all were disturbed by her. They were out of their depth with her, of course, and at some point their attentions turned nasty. She had no defences, being a born refugee: a jew [sic] born in Hitler's Germany (Father a Russian Jew); later, a German in Israel (Mother as I said Prussian); later, in Western Canada, a continental freak (married to an English ex-Army officer); later, cosmopolitan beauty and wife of a wandering Canadian student in the far East, eventually settling in England—but never forgetting for a moment that she was *on the run* and belonged nowhere. But a big personality. Passionate about Tolstoy. (696–97)

Part of the scene Hughes sketches he finds "very funny." For instance, the persecuted Assia character speaks in a very British manner, with flared nostrils and tones, and Hughes believes she must strike the racist party assembled as bizarre (697). Nonetheless, he renders the Assia character a victim:

> The 'game'—her—it now becomes clear, has been winged (hit on the wing), has fallen, and has been seized, and is now held, by one of the dogs. Held in that fashion—broken-winged (pinioned) and held trussed (pinioned), she is both held to be killed (as the game bird) but also held, arm-pinioned, for cruel interrogation, as a human alien. So she floatingly exists in my lines simultaneously as the wounded about to be killed bird held in the mouth of the dog, as all the hunters stare down, and as a foreign fugitive suddenly dragged upright, arms screwed up her back, to face these dusty

officers of the Raj on some North-West frontier. Double exposure of the two locations and events. It has now dawned on the whole table that they have here not only a disturbingly exotic woman who is *faking her English manners* (like a spy) but who is also actually a savage Tartar probably begotten by some big black geni [sic] out of the Arabian Nights. Hence the coup-de-grace—the Englishman's ultimate social skull-crusher: 'Lick of the tar-brush?'—a phrase from colonial days meaning 'tainted with native (Indian or African) blood.' (697–98)

I quote directly from this 1997 letter because I can neither make this up nor can I (or do I want to) imitate it by attempting to paraphrase it. One can see the intersection of racism and misogyny (rather than sexism, given the animating hate and violence) throughout the excerpts, as Hughes has carefully documented prevailing attitudes of a white socioeconomically privileged class. To me, it speaks volumes that Hughes, unaffected by the social forces depicted in the poem and in this letter, understands what Assia was up against: the force of the violence made itself known even to someone outside of it and, in fact, protected from it or benefiting by it. Assia's crime in the poem and the world of the letter: being a woman of color, per Hughes's interpretation. "She was racially mixed all right," he writes, before going on to mention the ancestry of his children, presumably with Assia and Plath (700). In "Descent," the Assia character—which Hughes equates to the actual person of Assia—assumes "a whole provisional persona, assumed under duress" (700).

A colonialist ideology runs amuck in Hughes's letter to his translators, as he recognizes.[8] Of course, colonialism is a global phenomenon, not limited to England or the United States. However, colonialism should not be underestimated in its power: "its transformative effects and legitimating claims may be playing more of a role in the formation of cross-cultural misogyny than Western feminists have understood" (Alcoff 153). Too, it is an example of structural power. And it follows that the people in power are not in power because of their sheer force of will: men are given and occupy positions of power because institutions grant them power and sanction said power (Talbot 161), and as such, the public sphere, historically, reads as "an exclusively male domain" (180). Even language becomes an institution involving struggle (230). Hughes's letter necessitates a discussion about race because it is overtly about race; here, race and colonialism intertwine in a discussion about Assia. Ijeoma Oluo argues that the "ultimate goal of racism was the profit and comfort of the white race, specifically, of rich white men"; racism "was never motivated by hatred of people of color" (32). Rather, the motivation underwriting it is money and quality of life. I would suggest that status plays a part in it, too, as Hughes's letter seemingly evidences. In short, racism is "racial prejudice backed by systems of power" (30). As Oluo summarizes, "We live in a society where race is one of the biggest indicators of your success in life. There are sizable racial divides in wealth, health, [and] life expectancy" (31). What Diane Middlebrook identifies as a predatory impulse in Hughes, present in both his sexual life and his creative one (171), emerges in Hughes's letter to his translators. It should be apparent, but to be explicit here, we need to point out the racism that is part and parcel of Hughes's letter. Explains Tessie McMillan Cottom, "Black girls and black women are problems. That is not the same thing as causing problems" (10). Assia's purported Blackness is a problem for Hughes in this letter; Assia herself did not cause the problems Hughes associates with Blackness. History shapes "who we are allowed to become" (Cottom 26), and we are all a product of those histories, whether we buy into or reject our socialization with its historical legacies. But history is not kind to the historically minoritized. The more success one has as a marginalized person, the more one can be considered a problem (Cottom 15), and this sentiment is embedded in Hughes's letter also. "In a modern society," writes Cottom, "who is allowed to speak with authority is a political act" (19). And, of course, racism and sexism frequently intertwine and/or parallel each other, so much so, that, even linguistically, the term "sexism" was coined as an analogy to "racism" (Talbot 31).

Real change can only begin when we acknowledge what privilege we have and where it intersects with the oppression of other people (Oluo 65). To take the steps to ignite change, we can pose two of the questions Oluo asks, questions relevant to this book:

How might race, gender, sexuality, ability, class, or sex impact this subject?

Am I shifting some focus and power away from the most privileged in the conversation? (80)

While these questions guide the thinking and design of this chapter, as well as chapter 3, it is up to readers to determine their own answers to Oluo's feminist, intersectional questions. I highlight them to make transparent what this study is attempting to do—fuel difficult conversations about Assia and Hughes—and what kind of conversations about identity politics it might enable. Furthermore, we might examine how Hughes racialized Plath, too, as Heather Clark depicts in the "Colonial Contexts" chapter of *The Grief of Influence: Sylvia Plath and Ted Hughes*.

My scholarship on Assia continues to be informed by feminism. I do not see how it can be otherwise: Assia's body was and is constantly under scrutiny. This attention is not unusual for women. Mary Talbot sums up a large body of scholarship thus: "The way women look is vitally important: the success of social relationships hangs on being desirable, and being desirable is all about visual impact" (137). Hughes records Assia's deep-seated fear about growing older and losing her much-heralded beauty in the *Capriccio* poem "Fanaticism," where the Assia character declares laughingly but seriously that she will kill herself after she turns forty years old. Her sister remarks upon it, too, in interviews with Assia's first biographers (Koren and Negev 180). Our tendency to address Assia's physicality reminds us that we also need feminism to complicate our interpretations and approaches.

Beauty and Blackness serve as physical markers of Assia's presence in Hughes's writing, with Blackness also functioning as visual and figurative markers that allude to her.[9] For example, Hughes's poetry collection *Crow* (1970), dedicated to the memories of Assia and Shura, creates a violent and dark world, one marked by the color black and gloominess, dismalness, and grimness. In the midst of processing Plath's traumatic death and his deteriorating relationship with Assia, Hughes wrote *Crow*. Assesses

Peter Porter, Assia "had always encouraged Hughes's writing—the best poems in *Wodwo* and *Crow* were written under her aegis." Hughes deemed the *Crow* poems as sufficiently appropriate in content and achievement to be dedicated to his partner and daughter after their untimely deaths; they were, in a sense, posthumous literary tributes. In language suited to the language of trauma, Hughes writes to Sagar on July 18, 1998, "This revival, in A's [Assia's] death, of S's [Sylvia's], and in my mother's death a big psychological melt-down with accidental complicating factors, knocked Crow off his perch. (I wrote the last of them a week before A's death—on my way to take her looking for a new home in Northumberland, returning from which, she died)" (*Letters of Ted Hughes* 719). This statement can be read in two ways. First, Assia's death triggered the traumatic recall of Plath's for Hughes, and the death of his mother heightened the traumatic response. It must have seemed that all his loved ones were dying, all around him. We know from trauma studies that repetition presents itself as a hallmark of the traumatic experience.[10] Second, the trauma of Plath's death can be read as an influencing factor in Assia's demise, a contagion effect of suicide. *Crow* shows Hughes processing the traumas of his life, the act of which he describes as liberating because the writing of the trauma stories enables healing. In fact, Hughes likens the energy he experienced composing *Crow* with the energy he felt in composing the confessional *Birthday Letters*. To Sagar, Hughes writes, in reflecting on his practice about a year before he died, "Once I'd determined to do it [write confessional poetry], & put them [the poems] together, & started repairing them wherever I could, & writing the few last ones, I suddenly had free energy" (*Letters of Ted Hughes* 720). Elsewhere, Hughes acknowledges a writer's block and the lack of energy and inarticulateness associated with trauma (read: that which cannot be said, that which is too excessive to be comprehended, let alone expressed with words), which compromised his abilities to write what he could have and to live fully.[11] In the letter to Sagar, Hughes correlates the writing out with the working through of the trauma stories, pathways which are necessary in the healing process because they involve reconstructing the trauma story and making sense of it in order to establish distance and healing. In processing his world,

Hughes relies on power dynamics, as epitomized by race, gender, and traumatic experiences, to depict the unsafe world that mirrored the very one in which he lived.

Among the poems that showcase Hughes's use of blackness are "Two Legends," "Crow's Fall," and "Crowcolour." With Plath's death fresh in his mind and on his heart, it is surely surprising to no one that *Crow* bears witness to the horror, loss, and suffering that is trauma. What is fascinating about this poetry collection is the manner in which it overtly addresses race and gender within the context or backdrop of trauma: in an unusual move for Hughes, intersectionality arises as a salient facet of his poetry. Opening the collection, "Two Legends" sets the tone of *Crow*. In the twenty-four-line poem, "black" appears sixteen times; it is the controlling image of the poem, all else feeds into it. Indeed, the topic of the poem is blackness, sustained and divided into two parts. The first defines blackness in terms of embodiment and lack. Every body part—eye, tongue, heart, liver, lungs, blood, bowels, muscles, nerves, brain, and soul—is catalogued as evidence of the blackness of the entity being described internally and externally. This first section presents blackness as that which is immutable and which, finally, cannot be associated with light or wholeness. To be black, according to the speaker, means to be without the light and its associations, despite the desire and striving to "pull out into the light" (line 9). "Unable to suck in light" (line 5), such blackness cannot and "could not / Pronounce its sun" (lines 13–14), failing in its attempts. Black can never blend with white in the world of *Crow*; the division between the two is rigid and seems insurmountable. The second part of the opening poem offers the crow as the image par excellence of blackness. While its flying might intimate liberatory impulses as a kind of symbolic action at the end of the poem, the crow remains associated with emptiness: "Bend in emptiness / over emptiness" (lines 22–23). The value, the worth of the black crow and, by extension, blackness is that it is alive, but admirable or redeeming qualities are missing in this opening poem.

"Crow's Fall" reads rather like an allegorical retelling of Icarus and his fall, caused by his own prideful journey and subsequent burning by the sun, a narrative that mirrors what the speaker of "Crow's Fall" relates. The poem opens with a white Crow who decides to attack the white sun because it is too white. Though the sun continues to be white ("But the sun brightened—/ It brightened. . . ." [lines 11–12]), Crow returns "charred black" after the violent attack. He announces he is the winner in the last lines of the poem: "'Up there,' he managed, / 'Where white is black and black is white, I won'" (lines 14–15). The theme of this poem might be summed up as "aggression and violence will occur and prevail in matters of color, namely whiteness and blackness." Another way of phrasing this is "race matters, and the power dynamics involved in racial constructions will agitate and explode in violent outburst and events with winners allegedly emerging." Crow proclaims himself the winner of the attack, and so he utters the final statement about it. Obviously, the poem serves as an allegory to racial strife, wherein winners and losers are named and situated, and power—taking the shape of brute physical force, as well as the symbolic violence of narrative control and authorship—permeates every aspect of the scenario. In the black and white cosmos of *Crow*, we come to understand that racial battles determine winners and losers: to be named the winner (whether or not one is actually victorious) is of the utmost importance. Saying so might make it so in Crow's world, affirming the potency of language more generally but specifically in matters related to race.

In "Crowcolour," the speaker directly appeals to race, reminding us that this collection situates blackness as a defining element. Figuring Crow as "much blacker / Than any negro / as a negro's eye-pupil" (lines 4–6), the speaker emphasizes the fact that race shapes and even dictates identity constructions in the world, then and now. Interestingly, the speaker reminds us that, in Crow's version of his Icarus tale, the sun is black ("Even, like the sun, / Blacker / Than any blindness" [lines 7–9]) in the last three lines of this short poem. It is imperative in Crow's (and the speaker's) world that he be the victor. The competing tensions of a character positioned as having a Black identity (and, therefore, a marginalized and disempowered identity traditionally in society and conventionally in literature and culture) *and* exhibiting the power to challenge, transgress, and win through violent means is curious and unexpected in *Crow*. It suggests that the existing order can be toppled in a rather Marxist fashion. Another poem in *Crow*, "Notes for a Little Play" exemplifies the violent revolution that will result: "The demolition is total" (line 10), asserts the speaker, amid imagery of violent upheaval and destruction.

As for how Hughes addresses and shapes gender as a subject in *Crow*, these poems offer material for much discussion: "Examination at the Womb-Door," "Crow's First Lesson," "Crow's Undersong," and "Revenge Fable."[12] In "Examination at the Womb-Door," the very title locates and situates the poem within the female body. The poetic examination entails questions and answers that suggest a Catholic catechism. Every question receives *"Death"* as an answer, with the exceptions of a few lines. The end-stopped lines emphasize the all-encompassing nature of death in the cosmos of *Crow*. The female body in the poem straddles the divide between life and death, as does the Crow character. For Hughes, this point must have been especially resonant while writing the poem and in retrospect, given Plath's, Assia's, and Shura's deaths. The memories of them stayed vivid and alive, as Hughes reinscribes them in his writing, but their deaths were of such a magnitude that Hughes spent his lifetime working through the subsequent trauma.

Other poems direct our attention to the ways in which gender forestalls happiness and gestures to or ushers in traumatic scenes. "Crow's First Lesson" depicts a woman's genitalia strangling a man, while God and Crow watch. God intervenes, struggling to part the woman and the man, while Crow furtively leaves the scene. The drama that makes up the bulk of the poem involves Crow finding itself unable to utter the word "Love," despite God's encouragement and insistence that it do so. Love between a man and a woman, the poem chronicles, is violent and death defying (if death can be staved off). "Crow's Undersong" appears to be a song about a woman associated with an underworld: unable to "come all the way" (1), the woman still makes the attempt because she has hope: "If there had been no hope she would not have come / And there would have been no crying in the city / (There would have been no city)" (lines 21–23). This otherworldly woman can barely manage in the speaker's world; among other grievances, the speaker holds her accountable for her inability to meet his gendered standards. The lines "She comes sluttish she cannot keep house" (line 13) and "She cannot count she cannot last" (line 15) address the woman's failings as a feminine woman in a world, like ours, that polices the gendered division of labor in the home and outside of it, while reckoning that the woman is not long for this world of human beings. Unable to represent herself, the woman must be represented by the masculine speaker: "She comes dumb she cannot manage words" (line 16). These gendered circumscriptions and restrictions resonate with Assia's own biographical story; after becoming entangled with Hughes, Assia deferred to him in decision making, living and working at the time and place he designated throughout their turbulent relationship. The detail about the woman's "favourite furs" (line 19) seems to be a nod to Assia, whom Hughes depicts in a fur hat and coat in poems in *Capriccio*.[13] Furthermore, the speaker avers the woman gives speeches ("and these are her speeches" [line 19]), and yet no speech is printed or forthcoming in the poem, and this erasure is reminiscent of the manner in which Assia herself had been erased from Hughes's biographical story.[14] The other detail that appears to reference Assia, especially with *Capriccio* in mind, is the following: "She has come amorous it is all she has come for" (line 20). Ever the femme fatale in Hughes's work, Assia's ghostly presence is conjured here in a collection of poems about death, power (imbued by racial and gendered dynamics), and trauma.

"Revenge Fable" ties up these gendered themes of woman as something to overcome, to destroy in its misogynistic lines and conceits. If a fable delivers a truthful lesson, the only truth to be uncovered here is that men and women are mortal enemies, even if the woman is a mother. The speaker of the poem explains that the story he will relate is about a man who "Could not get rid of his mother" (line 2), and he employs all violent means to do so: pounding, hacking, lying, investigating, incriminating, penalizing (lines 4–8), and "Forbidding, screaming and condemning, / Going for her with a knife" (lines 9–10). The man wins: "With all her babes in her arms, in ghostly weepings, / She died" (lines 15–16). "Revenge Fable" instructs us that it is not enough to symbolically silence a woman. She must be destroyed with gusto. Of course, the woman with the "ghostly weepings" who dies with "all her babes in her arms" reminds us of Plath's speaker in "Edge" (and of Assia and Shura later on), and "Revenge Fable" is clear about who the perpetrator and victim are in *Crow*. After the woman is vanquished, the man's "head fell off like a leaf" (17), insinuating that the tragedy is that he dies as a result of what has transpired.

We would be remiss to pass over the depiction of trauma in *Crow*, a collection that resounds with it. In his July 18, 1998, letter to Sagar, Hughes discusses writing about autobiographical trauma in covert fashion in connection with *Crow* (*Letters of Ted Hughes* 718–19). Of especial note in this regard are the poems "A Bedtime Story," "Truth Kills Everybody," and "Lovesong." "A Bedtime Story" qualifies the wholeness of the speaker from the very first stanza, putting forward a person who is only a shadow of himself: "Once upon a time there was a person / Almost a person" (lines 1–2). This person cannot use his faculties to the fullest. Unable to perfectly or fully see, hear, or think (lines 3–5), he finds that "Somehow his body, for instance, / Was intermittent" (lines 6–7). The speaker, then, delves into a scene involving the Grand Canyon in a manner very reminiscent of "Grand Canyon" in *Birthday Letters*. In the latter poem, the speaker emphasizes the intrusive nature of trauma with the onomatopoeic "PAUM!" appearing throughout the poem. That extralinguistic sound registers the unknowability the speaker wrestles with throughout the poem (and, indeed, *Birthday Letters* as a whole) as he tries to work through his own traumatic losses, which are underscored in the last two stanzas:

> Nothing is left. I never went back and you are dead.
> But at odd moments it comes,
> As if for the first time, like a hand grabbing
> And shaking me from light sleep,
> Through all these years, and after thirty years,
> Close, itself, ours as the voice of your daughter—
>
> PAUM! (lines 70–76)

The sense of reliving the trauma, of it being ever present, repetitive, and woven into the fabric of the speaker's psychology and emotional and physical responses is captured in the recognition of the daughter's voice, so similar to that of the dead mother and wife, as a trigger. The poem ends with the all-encompassing onomatopoeia because nothing else can be said or processed as the speaker is overcome with traumatic losses that feel present and unhealed. The Grand Canyon, with its deep cut that cannot be filled in and made whole, becomes the perfect image for a poem about trauma. Likewise, in "A Bedtime Story" from *Crow*, the speaker notices how the Grand Canyon spreads before him as if it had been cut open in a surgical operation (lines 14–15) and how he has "only half a face there" (line 16). Not a whole person from the first stanza onward, the speaker transforms into an inhuman creature in the long fourth stanza. Fittingly, Cathy Caruth's description of a traumatic response—"the threat is recognized as such by the mind *one moment too late*" (62)—is expressed by the speaker as "Somehow he was already too late" (line 39). The main character in this poem desperately wants to heal from the overarching traumatic event(s) that inflects his very identity as something not human and not whole. To that end, he attempts to write an autobiography (line 52), presumably to tell the trauma story, to recover from it, as his "head was a broken windowpane" (line 56). But he fails at doing so (line 57). The bedtime story related in "A Bedtime Story" is nothing short of a nightmare.

Other poems in *Crow* signal trauma as a major theme. "Truth Kills Everybody" portrays Crow as evincing superpowers in his struggle to control the world, attempting to limit or contain that which refuses to acquiesce. The last line shows the futility of a struggle with that which engulfs one (the truth?): "He was blasted to nothing." Hughes depicts Assia being blasted to nothing in the *Capriccio* poem "Flame," and in the uncollected poem "Do Not Pick Up the Telephone," the character who appears to be his proxy endures a similar fate. As an aside, the violent world of *Crow* is staunchly gendered in "Truth Kills Everybody." While Crow might be viewed as an antihero, he still assumes the center stage. The "screeching woman" (line 12) being strangled by Crow (and probably murdered by him, as the title suggests) garners two lines only.

"Lovesong" anticipates the *Capriccio* poem "Systole Diastole." A published version of "Lovesong," featured in the 1967–68 number of *Northwest*

Review, is held with manuscript versions of the *Capriccio* poems, housed in the box of Assia materials that are archived at the British Library in London. These poems share more than archival space: they present an all-consuming love that could consume the lives, metaphorically and literally, of the characters in the respective poems. Indeed, the woman in "Lovesong" throws glances that are likened to "ghosts in the corner with horrible secrets" (line 25), thereby associating the woman with ghosts and secrets perhaps too horrible to be revealed in the poem. Putatively a song about love ("He loved her and she loved him" [line 1]), "Lovesong" takes its cues about love from real-world relationships: the speaker acknowledges that the woman in the poem is predatory in the sense that she wants him all to herself ("She bit him she gnawed him she sucked / She wanted him complete inside her / Safe and sure forever and ever" [lines 4–6]; "Her embrace was an immense press / To print him into her bones" [lines 16–17]) and would nail him down if she could to keep him with her ("Her eyes wanted nothing to get away / Her looks nailed down his hands his wrists his elbows" [lines 8–9]). The woman induces or tricks the man into a romantic relationship ("Her love-tricks were the grinding of locks" [line 29]), one that threatens not only his sense of self but all that he holds dear, including his life: "Her laughs were an assassin's attempts" (line 23); "Their heads fell apart into sleep like the two halves / Of a lopped melon, but love is hard to stop" (lines 40–41); and, by morning, they wear each other's faces (line 44). The man wants to keep his love from what awaits ("He gripped her hard so that life / Should not drag her from that moment" [lines 10–11]) and wishes the future would cease (line 12), as the future does not look promising for this relationship or in the world of *Crow* writ large. As dismal as the future seems—so much so that the man would rather topple into an abyss with his lover (lines 13–15) than face the future—the man realizes he wields great power. His words resemble "occupying armies" (line 22), and his looks are likened to "bullets daggers of revenge" (line 24). Hughes's words about Assia (or women who could stand in for her) could not be described any better than as invading and occupying armies that take up and over her life story and rewrite it with "bullets daggers of revenge," stamped with Hughes's perspective or "looks."

The impulse or subtheme underwriting the revenge plot is trauma. What Assia did in taking her own life and that of Shura's as well as castigating Hughes for his faithlessness to her and their daughter proved traumatic to Hughes, as will be examined and discussed later in this chapter. In "Lovesong," the woman in the poem gives promises that "took the top off his skull" (line 33), and Assia's promises, made in times of great distress and duress, did just this in metaphorical fashion. If taking the top off one's skull does not kill one, it would most likely lead to traumatic responses and outcomes.

In dedicating *Crow* to Assia and Shura, Hughes linked them to the poetic world he created in that book. The word is dark and dismal; it is a racialized and gendered world, where violence, aggression, and death run rampant. It is a world in which power—as in, might—could be the only virtue. And even power cannot save heroes or antiheroes, as we see in the poems that pursue trauma as a theme or issue. Hughes wrote the *Crow* poems while Assia and Shura were alive and a part of his life. After they died, the poems became permanently linked to them as a tribute to their importance in Hughes's life. Asserts Edward Lucie-Smith, one should read the *Crow* poems "[i]f you want to know more about Assia." He believes that the blackness of Crow is an allusion to the blackness of Assia's hair (interview recording, July 28). Whether *Crow* specifically or broadly touches upon Assia, the book fleshes out the ways in which Hughes conceptualizes and wrestles with race, gender, and trauma, sometimes with poignant allusions to real-world counterparts. Understanding how Hughes approaches these subjects has everything to do with how we can interrogate and problematize his representations of Assia—and Plath.

Writing in an autobiographical vein proved freeing to Hughes.[15] In a letter to Seamus Heaney on New Year's Day in 1998, Hughes writes about the effect of publishing autobiographical poems, namely those in *Birthday Letters*, about Plath and their marriage: "publication came to seem not altogether a literary matter, more a physical operation that just might change the psychic odds crucially for me, and clear a route" (*Letters of Ted Hughes* 703). In a long letter to his son Nicholas Hughes, dated February 20, 1998, Hughes describes healing as "the sense of gigantic, upheaval transformation in my mind. . . . It's as though I have completely new different brains. I can think thoughts I never could think" (713). He adds in a letter to Marie and Seamus Heaney on June 17, 1998, "The weird effects of having got rid of it all . . . are still making themselves felt. Strange euphorias of what I can only call 'freedom' or a sense of self-determination, internally, that are quite new to me. . . . [A] pity I left that unburdening (even if it was mainly symbolic unburdening) so late! Strange business, confession" (718). In what is obviously a continued attempt through letter writing to process and understand the nature of trauma and healing from it, Hughes writes the following on July 18, 1998, to Sagar:

> I have wondered—some justification I think—if an all-out attempt [*insertion:* much much earlier] to complete a full account, in the manner of those [*Birthday Letters*], of that part of my life, would not have liberated me to deal with it on deeper, more creative levels—i.e. where the very worst things can be made positive, where the whole point of the operation is to turn deadly negatives into triumphant positives, in the total picture. On the autobiographical level, that can be difficult, because—if things cannot be got off that level, and onto the creative level . . . then they simply stay as if they were a recurrent stuck dream that simply goes on delivering its inescapable blow. (718)

He goes on to identify a "reluctance to deal with the episode directly" (718). A bit later in the same letter, he explains that Assia's suicide revived the trauma of Plath's suicide, all followed by the unexpected death of his mother, leading to a "big psychological melt-down" (719). Much earlier, in a March 11, 1970, letter to Yehuda Amichai and Hana Sokolov-Amichai, Hughes relates, "After Assia and Shura died I did not know how to write to anybody. I carried your letter around unopened. I carried her sister's and father's letters around unopened. I was just paralysed, and I'm still not much improved. I've been swallowed up" (303).

Hughes knew that writing could heal: his dedication to the craft of writing and his covert attempts to write himself out of trauma, even when he did not know how, are remarkable and exemplary. With *Capriccio*, a poetry sequence brimming with trauma as I map out and explicate, poem by poem, in almost fifty pages in *Reclaiming Assia Wevill*,[16] Hughes entered new territory. He was willing to write when "there was no programme," as he puts it in an October 13, 1996, letter to Leonard Baskin (688). Hughes's relationship with Assia "was the undeclared theme" of *Capriccio*, notes Lisa Baskin (*Letters of Ted Hughes* 689). Writing about trauma takes courage, and it also requires some measure of faith in the power of storytelling, both of which Hughes embodied from 1969 on. And he was right about the healing potential of writing. According to Laura Marcus, in her survey of autobiographical writing, "there has been an extension of psychoanalysis as the 'talking cure' (the term coined by one of Freud's earliest patients) to the concept of the 'writing cure,' or 'scriptotherapy,' which is underpinned by the belief that the 'writing out,' and 'writing through,' of difficult or traumatic experiences, and the composition of an integrated life-story, will have powerful therapeutic effects" (*Autobiography* 65). According to Sylvia Plath in her December 27, 1958, journal entry, writing offers a "way of ordering and reordering the chaos of experience" (*Unabridged Journals* 448). Hughes did not necessarily want to write about Plath and Assia; he had to do so. In a 1996 interview, Hughes volunteers the following: "[B]eing a writer, these things [related to tragedy] are chewed all the time, because you write about them and they disturb you, and they keep appearing and disappearing. They keep hanging on your neck and you deal with the emotions again and again, as if it's a broken record, stuck in the same monumental groove. And instead of letting go of the past and living for the future, you find your past in front of you. A monument, sitting on your head" (Koren and Negev 227). In articulating the necessity of writing about tragedy, such as the deaths of Plath, Assia, and Shura, Hughes also deftly captures what trauma does. It animates one's life, making the past present in recursive fashion. Trauma is a burden; one is stuck reliving it with the weight of the traumatic experience heavy and, sometimes, crushing.

As Jo Gill suggests, "[I]f Plath (or Wevill) do influence or otherwise haunt Hughes's writing, they do so not of their own volition, but as agents of some larger power" (61). Gill ventures that maybe a "pre-ordained script" is the larger power, from Hughes's perspective. I would argue that the role of trauma likely played an even larger role in the dialectic between traumatic resistance to telling the story and the traumatic need to act out and work through trauma, with the body (and mind) keeping the score, as Bessel van der Kolk would have it. In a letter to Lisa and Leonard Baskin, dated May 6, 1984, Hughes seemingly concurs: "Almost all art is an attempt by somebody unusually badly hit . . . who is also unusually ill-equipped to defend themselves internally against the wound. . . . In other words, all art is trying to become an anaesthetic and at the same time a healing session drawing up the magical healing electrics" (*Letters of Ted Hughes* 484–85). But he makes a distinction: art can lull one into "the anaesthetic tendencies, which displace the real confrontation that can only be solved by a real healing" (485). Healing from trauma is never guaranteed, and Hughes suffered terribly.

The examples given here emerge from published texts; now we will turn to writing that Hughes never intended to publish. Of particular interest to me are the miscellaneous pieces related to *Capriccio*, writing Hughes never meant to publish or make accessible to researchers. Because *Reclaiming Assia Wevill* showcases close readings, extensive analyses, and extended discussions of *Capriccio* and other published works, informed by biography and trauma studies, I will not treat that poetry collection here. *Reclaiming Assia Wevill* took as its premise the understanding that published words wield tremendous power and carry much import. This book picks up from where that one left off, demarcating the line between published and unpublished texts and considering both kinds. The archival documents housed at the British Library will now occupy us as we struggle to understand complex and complicated lives and the literary writing they generate.

The unpublished archival materials pertaining to Hughes's writing about Assia consist of unpolished drafts that, as of now, remain unpublished. Hughes "jotted down his key memories" (Bate, *Ted Hughes* 453) to prepare to revisit the traumatic story he needed to tell.[17] To treat or heal trauma, one must talk (or write) about it ("Apocalypse Terminable and Interminable" 274). The secret to survival "becomes a struggle to grasp what happened" (274), which is what Hughes undertakes through the cache of materials about Assia at the British Library and the newly acquired (as of 2023) notebook at Emory University. Until trauma can be processed and healing occurs, "the problem isn't just about surviving PTSD but the fact that the rest of your life, or much of your life, will be shaped by the burden of figuring out what you experienced" (284–85). The symptoms akin to PTSD, such as recurring nightmares and debilitating depression, that Hughes experienced in the wake of Assia's suicide and maternal filicide of their child may best be thought of as "a protest against something unacceptable" (288). Arthur Blank describes PTSD as "a processing deficiency disorder . . . namely that things happen to people that they don't have the capacity to integrate, digest, narrate, understand, comprehend, fit in with their world views, fit in with their views of themselves" (288). Shoshana Felman tells how she came to value the trauma story, that giving testimony "produced a sort of revolution in people, in their lives, in their destinies." Further, Felman observes, "It was a kind of instinctual response to record and to archive, to create an archive of history or of the memory of trauma" in the pursuit of grasping the truths of the traumatic experiences ("A Ghost in the House of Justice" 325).

In approaching the unpublished writing about Assia, we examine words that Hughes never intended to see the light of day. In perusing these writings—or the published writings that make up *Crow* or *Capriccio*—it is easy for us to become fixated on how much Hughes seems to dislike Assia, how much hate emanates from his words about her. Of course, these texts appeared after Assia died, and Hughes was trying to navigate his shock, trauma, and grief over the untimely and unexpected deaths of Assia and Shura—and Plath. In 1971, Leonard Baskin, who collaborated with Hughes on the art in *Capriccio*, emphasized that Hughes was "extremely devoted" to Assia (interview recording).[18] That devotion—or love in his fashion—meant that Hughes felt destroyed when Assia and Shura perished.

The British Library holds Hughes's unpublished writing, as well as drafts of his published *Capriccio* poems, in the archive. More than 230 pages are enclosed in a file box. Among the papers lies a numbered list, ideas for what become the *Capriccio* poems. The first one: Why, Hughes ponders, did he "interfere" with Assia, and why did she do what she did?

Presumably, the writing that follows addresses this question. Other points treat the nightmare of the Holocaust in Germany and some specific poems, such as "Snow" (which Hughes references as walking in the snow), "Opus 131," and "Shibboleth." After the first point, the only other one that really stands out to me is number 3; here, Hughes writes that he wants to attempt to "get my life back." If he was writing to get out of the flames, to make the traumatic experiences of his life make sense to him, then he would need to be able to meaningfully construct what happened to him to reclaim his life as a survivor of trauma rather than a victim suffering from it. Moving on to the other hundreds of unpublished pages Hughes wrote about Assia, my impressions of Hughes as both victim and survivor—as someone presently suffering at the time of the writing and someone who lived through terrible ordeals that could crush anyone—further humanized him. Coffee stains on one manuscript invoke the real-world materiality of the papers and Hughes's own life; obviously, he was a flesh-and-blood person, but his (and Plath's) mythological transposition of their lives into characters in myths they both wove blurs the person with the character. Handling manuscripts serves as a reminder of the person behind the literature. Another example of how the manuscripts underscore the once-living person who was doing the writing: Hughes wrote on the back of poetry submissions from school-aged children for many of the Assia manuscripts. Not only does this writing emphasize how he juggled professional responsibilities with the need to write his own material, but it suggests that the trauma was ever present, even during mundane activities like judging poetry contests when he would not likely have been triggered by memories of Assia. The drive to write about her and sometimes Shura persists through what was once secret material, spanning decades.

    Due to the emotionally wrenching nature of the writing, it is not surprising, perhaps, that Hughes's already difficult-to-read hand becomes frequently illegible. Sometimes the handwriting looks chaotic. The personal investment in this writing correlates with the intensity of it, but what I find important in this cache of papers are the lessons we can learn. What does trauma look like, for Hughes? What memories does he capture of Assia that were previously unknown to us? How does he approach her and Shura with himself positioned as writer and reader? (He is his own intended audience for some of these papers.) When confronted with giving up or going forward, Hughes chose to go forward, and there is an incredible resiliency braided into the day-to-day living and thinking, of which these papers offer the smallest snapshots.

Early on in the pile of numbered pages (numbered by the British Library as they were being processed and catalogued), we see Hughes equating Assia with blackness and fire in a draft of a poem. Everything went into the fire, and the speaker (Hughes or a mouthpiece for him) witnessed it. A page later, Hughes writes that the woman turns into a dead leaf. However, the trauma has not precluded Hughes from feeling anger and resentment toward Assia for the horror of her acts in killing herself and their daughter; instead, trauma functions as a prerequisite in some of the drafts of poems, allowing Hughes to dismiss the eyes of the woman he loved as alien and that of some demon or animal. As a good reminder, Hughes confesses the sharpness of details has been lost; this recognition receives its own stanza in one line on pages 8 and 9. The white space surrounding the line both times it appears suggests that very absence, details that, in Hughes's words, have gone out of focus. Art is created and manipulated (as are memories), and Hughes's writing about Assia occupies this liminal space of poetry and life writing.

Be that as it may, by page 14, in a different draft of a different poem, Hughes contemplates how he has already forgotten which dress Assia wore in a memory about her eating strawberries, and yet the "false" and "invented" memory or picture that the speaker continually replays in his head is relatively static and knowingly reconstructed. Usually, the speaker relays, Assia wears a certain dress and perfume, and the speaker peeps through a keyhole, seeing it all as it was and as it remains—firmly etched and feeling permanent, he confides. Nothing changes, and it all feels inaccessible, so much so that the speaker feels as if he had died instead, with the implication that the already-dead Assia carries the air of a living person more than the speaker in the world of the poem. One line, on page 16, stands out, linking and carrying on the themes of the drafts: he thought, reveals the speaker of this poem, that he was about to die. Many of the drafts of poems carry lines in Hughes's most difficult handwriting, making it impossible or nearly so to read; so much of the writing appears to be written under duress, which is certainly understandable, given the emotionally charged nature of the topic. That emotional stress and turmoil surely informs the content of the poem, as well as the actual appearance of it on the page.

In wrestling with Assia's untimely death, Hughes processes her history and that of world history in an attempt to contextualize Assia's unfathomable actions in her last moments. Calling her one of "Hitler's casualties" on page 42 of the drafts, Hughes keeps coming back to the image or symbolic action of a swastika striking her and knocking her out of the air as she is flying, leaving her fallen, on the ground for several iterations on pages 42, 45, and 47. The speaker remembers how she has many "hurts," and she allows him to touch and kiss them all. In a handwritten draft of a poem on page 51, Hughes incorporates Shura into the poetic world, having Assia hold her hand as they walk on a magic path and find a strange flower, which Assia plucks and gives to the speaker at the end. The flower turns to ashes in his hand. The imagery of these drafts marks the life-and-death scenarios constantly being reenacted, over and over again, mirroring the repetitive qualities of trauma.

Working through a draft of what became "The Error" (initially titled the "The Grey Cairn"), Hughes crosses out two lines, rhetorically asking the addressee, Assia in this case, why she did what she did. He crosses out another line about the Assia character sentencing herself, following the second iteration of asking her why she did it (without a clear pronoun antecedent, leaving the entire poem to answer for "it") in a poem about self-immolation in the wake of Plath's suicide. The draft indicates that Hughes wants to address Assia's traumatic experience of Plath's death in a poem, finally, about her own self-immolation, a kind of traumatic suicidal contagion, as configured in the poem.

The drafts of *Capriccio* poems Hughes worked through show his acting out and working through trauma. What the drafts demonstrate that the final products cannot are the negotiations Hughes made between revealing and concealing his autobiography and Assia's biography in poetry. The published version of "Flame" is less forthcoming than earlier drafts. For example, the typescript drafts of "Flame," spanning pages 142–44, supply information not widely known. At one point, Hughes assigned part of the responsibility for Assia's suicide to her past and/or her personality or inability to cope with what is to her dangerous news. In the published poem, the catalyst is a "signed bit of paper." In the drafts, the news is variously referred to as "the last signature of divorce had found you / and was waiting in your flat" and "signed papers" and "sealed contract." Now we know that, in fact, Assia received the signed divorce papers in the mail, a reminder that she was legally free to marry Hughes and, with the state of their relationship, as far as she could be from doing so. She would have received the final papers upon returning from a failed house-hunting trip with Hughes, during which he told her he could never fully commit to her because of Plath. The disastrous telephone conversation with Hughes took place immediately after she received the papers. The published version of "Flame" closes with these lines: "You barely had time to open the envelope / And grab for the telephone / Before it was all over" (lines 35–37).

Sometimes the discarded lines bring new information to light; sometimes they simply add poignancy. An instance of the latter is Hughes's lines in a draft of what seems to be "The Coat" on page 149; the Assia character hopes the ponyskin coat referenced looks stylish and glamorous. In a different text—this one on graph paper and comprising a numbered list of ideas for *Capriccio*—Hughes admits he kept the ponyskin coat; he could not throw it away (157). Another poem that did not make it to a final version or publication carries a line about the speaker knowing himself to be helpless (153). The conflict between disclosure and secrecy runs rampant in the box of materials about Assia at the British Library. The oppressiveness of trauma surely factored into what Hughes could bring himself to express and what he could not, but he was also conscious that who he was could be misconstrued if people knew about Assia and her relationship with him. Writes Hughes, "So—they—will have clear notion of me—you will not be known, shadowy, a name they will not know how much you were more real than me more real than them" (157). Hughes attempted to keep Assia in the shadows of his life, but even his archived writing testifies to the power, influence, and impact she had on both his life and his writing. Furthermore, his dreams of her puzzle him and muddy his life, he writes (162). The dreams must feature Shura, too, for one of the memories is dedicated to her; Hughes remembers her being little, getting up at night and climbing into what appears to be Assia's bed. He mentions, too, that she possesses a horrible horoscope. Much as Assia does, Shura haunts him: "Wherever I go is a little impetuous girl / Who is not" (165).

It is common knowledge now that, in 1962, Assia sent a blade of grass to Court Green (arguably a symbolic action and a play on words: he could court her as grass is green) in response to Hughes's advances on her at her workplace, all of which set off a domino reaction that resulted in tragedy for many people. "Chlorophyl," published in *Capriccio,* attests to this. In the beginning, Hughes pursued Assia and acted on her ambiguous acknowledgment of his romantic-sexual interest in her. Whether Hughes faults her blade of grass or the one he sends back, alongside of hers, is also ambiguous. In notes he penned about Assia, Hughes wonders whether a blade of grass destroyed five, six, or seven lives (166). As one of those destroyed lives, Assia is remembered by Hughes at Lumb Bank, close to where her final resting place seems to be. Addressing her, Hughes confesses that she did not imagine that she would lie forever under sycamore trees and be covered by ferns, with a view of the place she supposed she would live and be happy. She lies there now, happy or unhappy, with a view of the place that she thought would be her home with him, Hughes writes. Only two people know where to find her, confesses Hughes (166). He took the secret to his grave, after admitting it in his notes. His last point in this list is his belief that he spared Assia the horror of decomposing in a coffin; he had her cremated (against her wishes, it turns out). Hughes brings up Assia's beauty, a bit earlier in the list, arguing that she was infatuated with it, and her attractiveness was her undoing, once she perceived her beauty was fading and with nothing to replace it or to compensate her for its loss. She felt ashamed, Hughes relates. Her beauty, then, is lethal (166). Perhaps, for Hughes, his cremation of his partner and their daughter served to keep them permanently alive (as they were because they could never rot) in his memories. Subsequently, his putative secret burial of them kept them close to him and undisturbed. He remained in control in Assia's life and after her death.

Among the papers in the "A" (for Assia) box is a draft of a handwritten poem titled "Dream of A." The first stanza concerns itself with a dream about Assia, leading to other memories of her. In the dream, Assia looks and acts as if she were still alive; indeed, in the dream, detailed in the second stanza, she seems more alive and more beautiful now after death than she did while alive, Hughes writes. Furthermore, Assia desires the speaker, who is an obvious mouthpiece for Hughes, and engages in what Hughes calls "lovemaking" with him. Described as a masterpiece, full of love, beauty, and strength, the sex is too much for Earth to tolerate or allow (167). Following "Dream of A," which could be characterized as an erotic love poem, full of desire and strangeness, is an untitled draft of a poem, in which Hughes wonders whether Assia still loves him and if she is trying to make him love her even in death. While "Dream of A" concentrates on a dream, this poem states that someone (probably Hughes but Assia works here, too) is unable to wake up and be in the world. Hughes declares he does not care for Assia's calculations, that he prefers a life without her than dreams of her and/in death. He admonishes her several times, urging her to leave him alone and saying that he does not want her, now that she is in her element in the death realm. The poem closes with Hughes starkly ordering Assia to stay away from him (168). In a different poem, pages later, entitled "An Intruder into the Family Myth," Hughes imagines Assia, already dead, crawling out of a grave, and he beseeches her not to leave him. In fact, he says, she has saved him (210). Many lines down, if I am interpreting and transcribing accurately Hughes's handwriting, he admits Assia has not managed to save him, but he is happy all the same because he is dead alongside her (210).

A blue exercise book with a yellow "A" taped upside down is filled with handwritten drafts of poems and notes; this book is also part of the Assia box of Hughes materials at the British Library. In this book, we find Hughes depicting Assia as a risk taker, one who would gamble everything but beauty. Her chief concern, beauty becomes the thing she fears to lose, and so, she fears turning forty. Forty means the end, the finish (173). In addition to choosing to live an unsafe life, Assia is associated with boredom especially and drama and crisis to a lesser extent. What she winds up doing is ruining her life, Hughes assesses (175).

A separate blue-gray exercise book captures Hughes's diverse memories of Assia and Shura across years. The memories take the form of jottings, often unfinished and unpolished, with most quite elliptical as these would make sense to Hughes but exist without much context for other readers. In one of the early entries in the book, Hughes remembers what may have constituted his last visit to Assia in Clapham, including her bitterness and resignation to what Hughes said or what she thought he meant (213). Not surprisingly, Assia's Dior perfume makes the list as a memory. Also making the list is Hughes's pursuit of freedom. He references Plath, writing that liberating himself from her meant freeing himself from burden and tyranny. However, he counters that line of thinking by then asserting that he came around to viewing Plath and Susan Alliston as the means of escape from Assia, whom he was already trying to evade, he admits, in 1962 because he suspects that she takes up with other men. Her image at that time also dominates him, and he notes that Assia struggled with her self-confidence when it came to her body. Unsure about Assia's motives early on in their relationship, Hughes wonders whether she felt a competitiveness with Plath, rendering Hughes a prize of sorts. They do talk of Plath's poems, Hughes reveals, when everything in his life still felt redeemable to him (meaning Plath is presumably still alive) (214). In documenting his memories, Hughes records what is meaningful to him, and among these is a night of sex with Assia, replete with details about a memorable dress and strawberries. The sex, what Hughes calls "endless love," lasted until 2:00 a.m. and did result in a broken sink. At this point in their affair, Hughes admits they could have broken up, but he could not stand losing Assia and did not want to be a coward who withdraws. Basically, he wanted to smash his way out of his life in North Tawton. A very short paragraph covers the news of Plath's suicide and the timeline of it from Hughes's perspective. He spent the night with Alliston before returning home in the snow and receiving the call about Plath's death. He recalls sitting with Assia afterward and that moment was fatal—a "fatality," he calls it—for Assia (214). After Shura is born, Hughes recollects Assia pushing the baby carriage and investing great effort in setting up a home for Shura and herself in Clapham after leaving Highbury. Even in Ireland, where she was happiest with Hughes, Assia was desolate when Hughes stayed overnight in Dublin, leaving her and Shura (and Frieda and Nicholas Hughes) in Connemara. Significantly, Hughes directs our attention to the great gaps in his memories and in his writing; he is confounded by them (215). But gaps are a hallmark of trauma in writing and in storytelling. We should expect them in Hughes's reminiscences about Assia and Shura.

Shura is invoked twice on page 219 in the collection of papers. First, she is associated with Assia. In the second mention, Hughes addresses her, remarking that no one will know how lovely she is and what spirit she had. And people may not know how unlucky she was. As for Assia, Hughes likens her to Ophelia and himself to Hamlet, noting that Hamlet's madness kills Ophelia. He faults himself for his folly, stupidity, greed, and conceit, all that he could not own up to or confront with respect to Assia (219). Hughes also lists Plath's ghost and having to live with it in his Assia notes (222). In a draft of a short poem, written in what looks to be an agitated hand and at breakneck pace, Hughes contemplates Assia twenty-four years after she has died; he still thinks about her and assumes she would be a beauty on the cusp of seniority. He wonders about the meaning of her life, what its purpose was, although this line of thinking is couched as a question (223–24). Disturbingly, the collection of archived papers in the "A" box closes with a handwritten and slightly messy poem titled "Ashes," in which Hughes details the ashes that are Assia (he even calls her Ashes) and Shura (referred to as an ashen child) and how he kept Assia's ashes in a casket on a bookshelf in his bedroom. Assia's life, as a refugee from Nazi Germany, was only a reprieve from death, Hughes concludes (230).

In 2022, a notebook containing unpublished poems by Ted Hughes went up for auction in England. Previously the property of Frieda Hughes, the notebook is a medium-blue Challenge Duplicate Book with one hundred pages, of which Hughes wrote on eight of them. Emory University won the item, and I became the first researcher to access it at Emory in

April 2023 after it was processed and made available for reading. Hughes never intended for these pieces to be published; I do not know anyone who knew the notebook existed until it was ready to be auctioned and sold. The poems do not carry titles, and they do not appear to be worked up for any type of dissemination. Rather, they are private poems, offering time and a place for Hughes to process and work through the traumatic deaths of his partner and daughter.

The poem on the first page is written neatly with few cancellations. It initially sets the scene of a world in which the best possibilities exist and nothing is too late; people are smiling, laughing, and hoping. Then death appears and blasts people to ash. In the next stanza, the speaker discusses a game that he and the Assia character would play, and the game would end with smiles and promises. Then she dies, and the speaker realizes she was playing for death, whereas he wanted to play for life. By the third page, the speaker laments that he has failed—utterly—all of them, by which he likely means Assia and Shura.

An important and unique feature of the Emory notebook is the poetry written wholly about Shura. Two poems spotlight her. In the first, Shura wears a lime-green dress and sports a crown; she energetically dances to Bach, flinging her arms, running, and attempting what Hughes dubs broken pirouettes. Soberly, Hughes writes that she will never know who Bach is, and she will never be a good dancer; she will be dead shortly after her fourth birthday. Dancing on the last afternoon she is alive, Shura cannot know that she is destined to die. In a deeply unsettling image, Hughes has death watching Shura out of her mother's eyes, and the poem ends there. The next poem comprises seven lines only, and it addresses Shura directly. She is too young to understand or to know death, Hughes observes, and she is made a victim—dropped into death, as he expresses it—by her hope of safety, by which Hughes underscores Assia's betrayal of Shura; her job as a mother is to keep her daughter safe. The poem ends without punctuation and with the image of Shura lying dead and very pale.

The poetry that follows immediately after the Shura ones concentrates on Assia. Unlike any other poem I have read by Hughes about Assia, the one that immediately follows the second Shura poem reads directly and authentically, without myth mediating the content. Hughes wants to know why Assia did not tell him that, unless he made her happy, she would kill herself. He cannot comprehend why Assia pretended her independence suited her when she symbolically waved him off on his solo voyage, acting as if she did not want desperately to accompany him. This poem, too, ends without punctuation, as does the one that follows it. Perhaps no closure is to be had for Hughes regarding these deaths.

In the last Assia poem in this notebook, Hughes speaks directly to her. He reminds her that he purchased a fern for her when they were both "solidly married," as he terms their relationship status during their affair. Looking back, Hughes avers his marriage to Plath is dead, as if it has been murdered, and Assia is dead, too, as if murdered. All that is left of her as a lovely human being, writes Hughes, are ashes. In a gesture to the great suffering he endured, Hughes confesses that he does not live except as a stone. Like the fern, Hughes lasts. Unlike him, the fern thrives, and Hughes dismisses it as ignorant ([Notebook 31]). Surviving but not thriving, the stone image perfectly captures what the symptoms of posttraumatic stress disorder (PTSD) would feel like.[19] In a different notebook, a diary rather than a creative writing journal, Hughes communicates remorse for the deaths of Assia and Shura. He records that he dreams about Assia every night, and the recurring dream is cruel: she has not yet died, and he believes her suicide is preventable. His analysis of the last telephone conversation he had with Assia, immediately before her death, is that it was all a bitter misunderstanding ([Notebook 11]).

Hughes thought that "he could spend the rest of his life trying to understand and come to terms with what had happened to him," especially in relation to the deaths of Assia and Shura, writes Elaine Feinstein in her biography of Hughes (175). His return to Assia and Shura as subjects of his writing, spanning decades, shores up the difficulty in coming to terms with those traumatic losses. In reading Hughes's manuscripts about Assia in the British Library and Emory University, where the cache of unpublished materials about her lie in drafts in sometimes indecipherable hand, it becomes very evident when Hughes is writing in distress as his handwriting appears chaotic and even less legible than usual. According to Hughes, "Maybe the crucial element in handwriting is that the hand is simultaneously drawing. I know I'm very conscious of hidden imagery in handwriting—a subtext of a rudimentary picture language" ("The Art of Poetry" 65). As for poetry and confession, Hughes reflects, "Maybe all poetry, insofar as it moves us and connects with us, is a revealing of something the writer doesn't actually want to say, but desperately needs to communicate, to be delivered of. Perhaps it's the need to keep it hidden that makes it poetic—makes it poetry." He adds, "Maybe, if you don't have that secret confession, you don't have a poem—don't even have a story. Don't have a writer" (75). In his conversation with the interviewer, Hughes details a kind of confession linked to poetry that keeps it vitalized and rich in its messaging. Furthermore, the way he understands poetry is akin to the function of testifying as it is couched in trauma studies: in Hughes's words, "until the revelation's actually published, the poet feels no release" (76). Indeed, Hughes connects art to healing and therapy later on in the interview after he describes the work of a healer who works in therapy: "the idea occurred to me that art was perhaps this: the psychological component of the autoimmune system. It works on the artist as a healing" (82). Hughes points to poetry as an "intense" art form to work in this capacity, and therefore, more important than other art forms, with the exception of music (82).

Hughes never achieved peace with respect to the memories of Assia and Shura. In May 1969, shortly after they had passed away, Hughes confided the following to Richard Murphy: "If I'd put a ring on her finger she'd still be alive" (Murphy, *The Kick* 279). So much irony is braided into the lives of Assia and Hughes, and another emerges: Hughes did secure a ring from jeweler Patricia Tormey *after* Assia died. Seeing the gold ring Tormey had made, Hughes experiences a jolt: "when I saw it I saw I would have got it for Assia because it is more like her than anything I ever bought her." The irony, of course, is that a ring with a marriage proposal is what Assia desperately desired, and she got the ring, presumably after she died. For, as Hughes writes Tormey in April 1969, just after Assia and Shura's funeral, "When I saw [the ring] I thought I must bury it with her ashes and I think I shall" (292).

Assia always desired Hughes. It is probably impossible to overestimate his charisma in general, and for Assia, his magnetism was powerful. In his memoir, Al Alvarez speculates that Hughes's gifts, as well as his handsomeness and masculinity, attracted Assia, but he also slights her by suspecting she "wanted him to add to her collection, because she saw herself as irresistible" (234). While nothing in Assia's own writing supports Alvarez's interpretation of her motivations or behavior, it remains the case that Assia could not envision her life without Hughes. For his part, as his published and unpublished writings across genres document, he could not imagine a life with her or without her. For the last decade, I have immersed myself in material related to Assia Wevill and, by extension, Ted Hughes, and it is clear to me that there was never a happy fairytale ending in store for them. Hughes says it best in the poem "Folktale" from *Capriccio:* "So they ransacked each other for everything / That could not be found" (lines 27–28).

CONCLUSION

Truly, it is remarkable that we have any writing by Assia at all, that we have anything recorded and extant. As Assia's first biographers chronicle in an e-mail to me, "Indeed, Hughes never wanted Assia's journals to be seen by anyone and certainly not his letters to her, which he asked her to destroy. As far as we know, he and Olwyn emptied her flat after her death and he took it [Assia's writing] with him. . . . Celia only received some personal items in the beautiful wooden crate that her mother brought from Germany" (Negev and Koren, e-mail to the author). Ira Chaikin, Assia Wevill's nephew, understood from his mother that someone who was intimate with Hughes took Assia's letters and journals, knowing that Assia's papers did not belong to or with him. When Yehuda Koren and Eilat Negev interviewed her for their biography of Assia, the woman readily gave the materials to them to safeguard and for safe transport to Canada, where Koren and Negev would interview Assia's sister. Per Ira Chaikin's understanding and that of the Estate of Assia Wevill, what the woman read in Assia's papers enlightened her with respect to her own romantic relationship with Hughes (Ira Chaikin, e-mail to the author). The woman, of course, is Brenda Hedden, whom Assia intensely disliked. But for her part, Hedden felt no animosity toward Assia; instead, she credited Assia with saving her life. What Hedden learned about Hughes from Assia's writing unsettled her. As Negev and Koren report,

> Brenda Hedden, who already had an affair with Hughes at the time of Assia's death, stayed with him at Lumb Bank, where he kept all his papers,

including Assia's. Brenda told us that she owes her life to Assia—that she [Assia] actually saved her life. When Brenda read the materials she saw his modus operandi for women—being the hunter that when they try to break loose, he clamps on them and draws them closer and doesn't let go. . . . After Hughes died in 1998 and she was no longer afraid of him, she wanted Assia's papers to be transferred to the rightful heir. (e-mail to the author).

Assia would never have guessed that Hedden would prove to be the key in helping to safeguard her legacy: the very pieces and fragments of her life that continue to instruct and provide meaningful connections and contexts in Plath studies and Hughes studies specifically and women's, gender, and sexuality studies more broadly.

Hughes's relationship with Assia, even after her death and/or especially because of her death, stayed fraught and complicated. Assia and David Wevill divorced in the early fall of 1968 (David Wevill, e-mail to the author), and it may have easily taken six months—March, the month of her death—for Assia to receive the decree in the mail. What she desired in 1969 was a marriage to Hughes: a husband for her and a recognized father figure for Shura. Assia daydreamed about adding Hughes to her last name—hyphenating it as "Wevill-Hughes"—and she practiced writing it, while living with Hughes in a blended family arrangement with their children in Ireland in 1966 (Koren and Negev 155). Assia sent a photo of Shura to her family in Canada, with "Shura Hughes 1st birthday" inscribed on the back of the photograph (155). However, a secret marriage between Assia and Hughes, though certainly not impossible, likely did not happen; using Hughes as a last name was Assia acting out a fantasy. David Wevill also believes a secret marriage did not happen, though he declines to give interviews about these old and tragic events and understandably so (David Wevill, e-mail to the author). It seems to me a marriage would have given Assia the confidence to continue in a relationship with Hughes: they would be legally committed to each other, if nothing else. Hughes thought his "insane indecisions" were to blame and told Lucas Myers as much (Hughes qtd. in Koren and Negev 215). When Hughes interviewed with Koren and Negev on October 8, 1996, in London, he shared that he thought Assia's death "was avoidable" (Hughes qtd. in Koren and Negev 215). Assia's close friend Mira Hamermesh understood that Assia died "disappointed" because Hughes "would not marry her" (161).

Readers remain fascinated with Assia, just as her own contemporaries were. Harriet Rosenstein suspected that Plath was fascinated—the exact word she used—with Assia because "Assia was in some way her other." Suzette and Helder Macedo confirm Rosenstein's suspicions: Plath admitted it; she saw Assia as a double, believing that she "almost made Assia," in the words of Suzette. Indeed, Suzette believes that Plath willed something to happen between Hughes and Assia, perhaps out of fear or for another reason altogether. Plath harbored an "enormous identification with Assia" in addition to being "fascinated" with her. In the interview with Rosenstein, Suzette herself says that she was "half in love" with Assia, with something of what is described as a schoolgirl's crush on her: Assia "is so enchanting" and "extraordinary," explains Suzette, speaking of her deceased friend in the present tense and signaling that she remains so for her. Together, Suzette and Rosenstein speculate that Plath vicariously had an affair with Assia through Hughes and vice versa, that Assia paradoxically participated in a romantic affair with Plath by virtue of having an affair with Hughes. Rosenstein even suggests that Plath and Assia are antithetical figures, and one could put them together and get one fully rounded person (Suzette Macedo and Helder Macedo, interview recording, parts 3 and 4). Because we want to understand the dynamics in the love triangle involving two of the most famous poets in the twentieth century and the most notorious so-called other woman in the twentieth-century literary and extraliterary imagination, we mine information to learn more and draw conclusions about them. And, because we live in a patriarchal and misogynistic world, we continue to diminish women to the extent that we need two women to represent one whole one.

Many people realized that the sensational aspects of Assia's and Hughes's lives together—and the tragedies that ensued—could be capitalized on for financial gain. Hedden writes to Elizabeth Sigmund about a photograph Hedden possesses of Hughes and Assia ("to*gether*" [sic], she emphasizes) that she is willing to sell for cash (correspondence). Such a photograph would not amount to much if it were not so rare, given Hughes's agenda in minimizing or diminishing Assia's presence in his public life. Assia's coworker Julia Matcham actively participated in that larger project, writing letters to anyone who would listen to her denigrate and deride Assia, including Plath's biographer Linda Wagner-Martin and Sigmund, Plath's friend. In a letter dated January 17, 1987, Matcham focuses on Assia and her affair with Hughes; she informs Sigmund that she "was always amazed that neither then, nor since, has mention been made of their affair, or that it might have contributed to Sylvia's frame of mind." Intent on faultfinding, Macham identifies Assia as a possible architect of Plath's despair, despite admitting that "what happened unfolded like a fascinating novel, many pages of which are frustratingly missing." We may never know what those figurative pages would have told us, but we do have accounts by Assia's contemporaries that have forever frozen their perspectives. For her purposes, Matcham writes Sigmund with a twofold purpose: to relate what she knows about Assia to a receptive audience and to fish for more gossip about her. Just to be clear that Assia was to be viewed on the negative side of a conventional cartesian binary construction, Matcham emphasizes Assia's otherness: "She was about as different from me as any woman could be. I had never met anyone like her." This otherness, also couched as Assia's exoticness, so to speak, runs rampant in documented reminisces.

We need to center stories and narratives, people, identities and subjectivities, positions, issues, values, and the like that are not only important and significant but critical in approaching and understanding our diverse world and its stories, histories, people, and cultures. Feminist recovery efforts and feminist lines of inquiry and activism constitute the very efforts we need to recover, reclaim, surface, and center the underserved, underrepresented, and marginal. The desire to bring about much-deserved attention to women's lives and contributions is a major motivating force for this book. Such consideration of noteworthy women will not eclipse established men, such as Ted Hughes. For instance, Clarissa Roche, a friend of Plath, informs Rosenstein that she does not have many impressions of Hughes, other than he slouched and was a "misfit." According to Roche, Hughes was a "nobody" when Plath taught at Smith College from 1957 to

1958, and, four decades later, in 1997, Hughes writes a letter to Andrew Motion, explaining that he is keenly aware of the "mortifying pressures" of social class consciousness (*Letters of Ted Hughes* 702). Rosenstein interjects in her interview with Roche that Plath worked as the breadwinner in their relationship at that time. In response, Roche develops a dichotomy between the two. As for Hughes, Roche offers, "To go to Cambridge from the tobacco shop, he must have been a big thing in his village," and Plath intended for him to be "the big cheese"; she was going to jump-start his success, as well as her own. And, although he was not born into aristocracy, Hughes overcame seemingly insurmountable odds and orbited around it as the British poet laureate. Moving on, Roche sketches Plath as a "very beautiful" and "attractive young woman." As for Assia, Plath never mentioned her to Roche (interview recording, November 20, 1973, part 2). Hughes partnered two beautiful, vivacious, and intelligent women, who spoke and wrote eloquently, and we would do well to attend to their words in concert with his. One woman need not supplant the other, and centering Assia or Plath need not lead to a cancellation of Hughes in academic study. There is much to learn from studying Assia, Plath, and Hughes in any combination and to varying degrees.

We need diversity to enrich our work, lives, and communities; only with diversity will we be able to imagine a fuller, more panoramic picture that offers and displays possibilities, potentialities, and what already exists and has existed. In tandem with diversity, our work in service of equity will pave the way for feminist futures, futures that promise a better life and world for everyone. We can intentionally embark on the work needed in centering the stories, people, issues, histories, values, and cultures we have neglected in literary studies. By being intentional in examining how we write about women—and by insisting that we write about women, that we make their lives and contributions visible by taking them seriously—we guarantee a bigger and brighter future in Plath studies, Hughes studies, and scholarship in twentieth-century literature. Wonders Assia in her May 19, 1963, journal entry, "What sort of woman am I?" (*Collected Writings* 163). Although writing to Plath's mother about Plath, Hughes believes, "In time everything will be quite clear, whatever has been hidden will lie in the open" (Hughes qtd. in Middlebrook xx). As time progresses, we learn more about Assia, Plath, and Hughes, and the goal of this book is to provide information and additional perspectives and contextualization to enable reinvigorated discussions about all three, with an eye toward contributing in more sustained (because necessary) fashion to Assia's biographical profile and to scholarship about her. As archives open up, what has been hidden and inaccessible will become available. Already that is the case with Hughes's papers about Assia at the British Library in London and Rosenstein's papers about Plath (and Assia and Hughes) at Emory in Atlanta, Georgia.

In the BBC program "*Poems* by Yehuda Amichai by Assia Gutmann," which was prerecorded on June 28, 1968, and aired on BBC Radio 3 on December 12, 1968, Assia read the script she wrote that introduced her English translations of Amichai's poems to British listeners (Wevill, *Collected Writings* 268–80). The only extant recording of her voice, this radio program is archived at the BBC. The BBC transferred the file to the British Library so that I could listen to it on March 29, 2022. It proved to be a stunning experience as her voice sounded nothing like what I anticipated, and Negev anticipated my response as it was hers, too. She had told me to be ready for a surprise (Negev and Koren, e-mail to the author). As I listened to Assia's voice in the Rare Books and Music Room, I struggled to come up with adjectives to describe it and the experience of listening to it. What I had expected from Assia: a voice that was higher pitched, theatrical, soft, and girlish, with more clipped enunciation. I am not a linguist, so the best I can do in describing it is to offer these observations: the quality of her speaking voice is a bit thick, like syrup, with some nasality. Her accent reminds me of English that is being spoken by a speaker whose first language is not English, and, although that is the case, none of her contemporaries, except Hughes in one instance, observed this, and he thought it made her sound even more English than otherwise.[1] From my perspective, the biggest takeaway from listening to the 1968 radio program featuring Assia and Hughes lies in the reminder that these were living, breathing people, whose own lives encompassed more than this moment, more than their successes and tragedies. In the recording, I could hear Assia breathing while Hughes read, especially during "My Parents' Migration" and "As for the World." When she reads, she sounds mature, and she is clearly reading a script, maybe a bit nervously. Despite what I have attempted to describe as the syrupy quality of her voice, she does not speak slowly or theatrically, as Hughes does. (Hughes's performance is star quality, and he, incidentally, sounds like a young man.) The extraliterary aspects of this sound recording—Assia's breathing and Hughes's shuffling of papers—underscore their humanity. The reminder is one we can always use, as is the reminder that there is not one correct interpretation of lives—or voices. Many people have commented upon Assia's voice, remembering it as beautiful, including, by implication, Frieda Hughes.[2] Rather than beautiful, I find her reading voice, as captured in the BBC recording, to be unusual but not remarkably so. My own expectations—that Assia would possess a very feminine voice—were not met, and I realize my own bias means that what I did hear proved startling to me.

Forever captured on that recording, Assia's voice sounds alive and inviting.[3] That voice is present in her writings across genres. In contrast to her accent is Hughes's: while he sounds terrific on the recording, Clarissa Roche notes, "It was most unfashionable to speak with a Northern accent" (interview recording, November 20, 1973, part 2). The program closes with Hughes reading "The United Nations." Though I do not want to begin to close this book with Hughes's voice, which has long defined Assia, I will quote the last stanza of the poem he read aloud on BBC airwaves because those closing words were selected and translated by Assia herself. And it might be fitting to cite this stanza for a myriad of reasons. Assia's life continues to be intertwined with Hughes's in scholarship and popular culture; she inspired and made an impact on him, and he inspired and influenced her.[4] Also, Assia's translations of Amichai's poems constitute her major literary achievements. Finally, this stanza expresses hope, however unwavering or fleeting. Until she could not find any, Assia embodied hope in ventures throughout her life: through travel, love, professional pursuits, and artistic work.

> And hopes come to me like daring sailors
> Like discoverers of continents
> To an island
> And they rest for a day or two,
> And then they sail away. (Wevill, *Collected Writings* 280)

Assia herself did feel bereft of hope, as we know from her journals and letters. And yet, the researchers, writers, teachers, and artists who continue to mine her legacy and rework it surely find hope in their products, agendas, artifacts, art, and the like. Hers is a life, with its contributions, that is worthy of consideration, good and bad. We can learn a lot about biography, midcentury literary culture in London, Sylvia Plath, Ted Hughes, Yehuda Amichai, and twentieth-century literature being written and translated in England in the 1960s through study of her life and contributions. We also learn about the traumatic wound, what it entails and how people may respond. Bessel A. van der Kolk and Alexander C. McFarlane imply that the study of trauma is important because of its universality: "Experiencing trauma is an essential part of being human," they write. Hence the preoccupation with literature that treats "how people cope with the inevitable tragedies of life" (3). "In short," they posit, "the study of trauma confronts one with the best and the worst in human nature, and is bound to provoke a range of intense personal reactions in the people involved" (6). Moreover, we know that surfaces can be deceiving, and the acts of reconstructing and reinterpreting lives reflect our own values and approaches in the twenty-first century. Feminist recovery work often responds to or is initiated by symbolic violence that stems from bias, discrimination, and oppression (often figured as absence or misrepresentations in literary studies); such work aims to counter oppression and violence. "Anti-oppression work *is* anti-violence work," emphasizes Stephanie Cunningham, an activist and preventionist in intimate partner violence.

We can learn more about our world in positioning Assia as a biographical-literary case study. Whatever the case for the interest in Assia as a subject of study, the fact remains that she steadily attracts readers and writers. And, as Paula M. Krebs asserts, "what philosophers and literary critics do is just as essential as what musicians or poets do: they enable us to interpret the world around us and to posit a better one" (1). A little more than a half century ago, Assia suffered erasure and demonization. Since then, her life and its work has undergone restoration, rehabilitation, and reintegration. Now her voice, her life, and her work may be here to stay. The words we use have consequences, and the words we consume shape us. Even if we push back or modify what we are reading and hearing, we still engage with meanings, concepts, arguments, and the material realities of this world. In her research about sexual violence, Linda Martín Alcoff dedicates space to examining the words we use and the impact they make. According to Alcoff, "Concepts never merely describe or refer: they also constitute, engender, and incite. New concepts give people ideas." Concepts need to be unpacked and closely examined not only for "their descriptive adequacy and legal utility but also [for] their normative implications for the formations of subjectivity and power" (150).

In this book, I have wanted to draw our attention to written texts, literary and extraliterary, and audio interviews, to the very words that form the concepts of who Assia Wevill and Ted Hughes are. These concepts constitute, engender, and incite scholarship, pedagogy, and cultural and artistic products. It is a grand irony that it is not difficult to write off or write out a woman like Assia Wevill, whose life lends itself to stories we can learn from, whose work we can enjoy and take in new directions, and who, as unacceptable as she is for taking up any space in a world not designed for her (that is, a woman in a patriarchal society and culture), continues to fascinate us. This book uses the words from numerous people to present, construct, analyze, synthesize, and contextualize the multifaceted portraits of Assia primarily and Hughes secondarily (and Plath when possible) in its pages. Reducing any woman to an archetype or stereotype transforms and flattens her into a secondary character in her own life and diminishes complexity and richness. It is a kind of violence, symbolic violence, in fact, that carries real-world promises of physical ramifications, when we actively annihilate women in writing in attempts to procure or sustain power and the status quo. We need the humanities and the work associated with it "to live a more illuminated life," in the words of Judith Butler. Feminist writing, as well as queer and trans writing, "has always been linked with fundamental questions of how to survive, live, flourish, fight, and pursue the promise of radical transformation," pronounces Butler ("The Future of the Humanities" 3). We know words and stories are powerful and that they shape identities and lives, affect and effect environments, usher in events, and make things happen.

This book would not exist without access to the "new" archival materials at the British Library and Emory University, and it builds upon recent scholarship in Plath, Hughes, and feminist and gender studies. These materials offered the opportunity to expand, correct, and realign the literary record. In continuing to recover and recuperate Assia's biographical story and in fine-tuning or fleshing out part of Hughes's, we gain more diverse, equitable, and inclusive perspectives on lives that continue to engage readers and energize scholars. I took up this project with the hope of more firmly establishing new and reframing old narratives, especially in connection with Assia Wevill, whom I view as a victim in a tragedy with many victims. For it is too simplistic to cast Assia as the foil to Plath and pit them against each other. Assia is more than the cold, destructive, unnatural, and beautiful woman Plath characterized her as, and she is more than the persecuted, dangerous, desirable, destructive, and demonic force Hughes portrayed her as. She is not like Lady Lazarus; she is not a vigilante, though the femme fatale script has been pinned to her. In her actual life, she was driven toward and motivated by love, security, and maybe admiration. Feminist recovery is a critical enterprise that endeavors to recover and recuperate significant women writers and their work, work that has been forgotten or lives that have been erased because of complicated gendered politics and imbalances of power. This is not to say that Assia's life and work are significant only because we are dealing with a woman, although women's lives and contributions have uniquely shaped literature, history, culture, and society that are, to this day, widely unacknowledged and sometimes contested.

I take to heart what David Wevill communicated to me via our e-mail correspondence in March 2022, fifty-three years after Assia's and Shura's deaths. Following the publications of *Reclaiming Assia Wevill* and *The Collected Writings of Assia Wevill*, he wrote that the books were well done and good even, though he holds little to no interest in Plath-Hughes scholarship. Wevill's accounts of Assia and Shura are consistently kind and loving whenever he elects to break his silence on them. Due to the sensational and traumatic nature of the topic, Wevill prefers reticence: fifty years on, Wevill continues to live an entirely different and wonderful life than the one he was living in the 1960s. He remembers Assia sent him a postcard in the spring of 1969, wishing him a happy life. In March 1969, she and Shura died, and Wevill could not help but mourn those deaths because he loved them. His advice to me: to not become emmeshed in the Plath-Hughes-Assia maelstrom. "The beauty of poetry, and of lives, goes on," writes Wevill, "The world offers much." Those might be exactly the right words for the conclusion of a book about poetry, lives, and a world that keeps changing while remaining the same in many respects.

Documents related to Assia (and Hughes and Plath) will surface in the future, but others have been lost to time. While it may be disheartening to readers (as it is to me) that we do not have access to more materials, what we do have is valuable: we can learn from biographies of Assia Wevill, Ted Hughes, and Sylvia Plath, told and retold. These stories show us ourselves and the world in which we live, then and now. This conclusion will end with words from the poem "If with a Bitter Mouth," a poem by Amichai that Assia translated for publication. We will close with it because Assia's translations remain an important part of her legacy.

> And it is written in the book that we shall not fear.
> And it is also written, that we also shall change,
> Like the words,
> In future and in past,
> In the plural or in isolation.

And soon in the coming nights
We shall appear, like strolling players,
Each in the other's dream.

And into these dreams
There shall also come strangers
We did not know together. (*Collected Writings* 231)

NOTES

1. SETTING THE SCENE

1. Recent books about Assia Gutmann-Steele-Lipsey-Wevill refer to her by her first name because of the ephemeral nature of her last names, due, in part, to her three marriages, and this book follows that practice. For example, Assia used her maiden name, Gutmann, when translating Amichai's poetry in the late 1960s, although her legal name was Wevill from 1960 to 1969.

2. In an interview with Malcolm, Anne Stevenson describes her research experiences and revelations in the archives at Indiana University, work that informed her biography of Plath. Stevenson reflects, "I came to feel in Indiana that I had finally met Sylvia Plath; that I was fonder of her because I knew her. I went back to her journal and reread it with renewed understanding" (77). What Stevenson felt working with archival materials at IU is similar to what I felt working with archival materials, especially those related to Assia and Hughes, at Emory University. The recorded interviews with their contemporaries provided various and sometimes new perspectives on people who all have biographies dedicated to them. I would, however, add the caveat that it also seems to me that it is impossible to perfectly pin down or portray Assia, Hughes, or Plath. New facts, details, and stories will emerge, new interpretations will surface, and any record will likely be forced to leave something unknown.

3. From my perspective, the four photographs, taking up a full page, of Assia in the photo insert between pages 768 and 769, continue to inspire awe. Two of the photos are published for the first time in this book and could only be published under these conditions: Clark needed to select them from the restricted-from-photography folder at Emory, where they are buried among Ted Hughes's papers, and Carol Hughes needed to grant permission for the publication of them. I have handled these photographs in person more than once because they are, by far, among the most revealing and special photographs of Assia, as I discuss in *Reclaiming Assia Wevill*. Now these photographs can be viewed, enjoyed, and studied by any reader, along with a disarming photograph that Clark had printed from 1959 and a remarkable one in color that features Hughes, Assia, and Shura from the mid-1960s.

4. For example, Edward Lucie-Smith, a friend of Assia, dismisses Plath's poetry as limited in range (interview recording, July 28–29, [?]). In a different interview, he faults Plath

for Assia's suicide (interview recording, July 28, [?]), which explains his animosity toward Plath, and by extension, her work. By the same token, Plath disparages Assia as not a real writer at the time that she is angry with her about the affair with Hughes, as we see in this November 7, 1962, letter to her mother: Assia "has only her high-paid ad agency job, her vanity & no chance of children & *everybody* wants to be a writer, like me" (*Letters* 899).

5. Elizabeth Compton Sigmund tells Rosenstein that she knows of a story concerning Brenda Hedden, whom Sigmund describes as a social worker with bleached blonde hair. Hedden, Sigmund sets forth, was one of Hughes's girlfriends, and she tried to burn down Hughes's home after he hit her (Sigmund, interview recording, part 6).

6. Assia writes to her sister Celia Chaikin in a letter dated March 11, 1967, that Hedden is "my real enemy. . . . I beat her hollow in intelligence and experience but she feels that I have usurped her place as the rightful soul of Court Green. . . . She hates me, has clearly hated me right away, but is either, or was, rather, too stupid or too cocksure to bother concealing it as Vati [Assia and Celia's father] will testify. . . . She *is* a bore, Earth Mother, mean, acutely mean" (*Collected Writings* 188).

7. Harriet Rosenstein asks the interviewee about Assia's sex life (Orr [and Beben?], interview recording, July 30, [?]). She also asks if Assia found she could not have children with her third husband and whether she wanted children (Fainlight, interview recording, undated, side B).

8. With respect to his own breaking of silence in his review of *Lover of Unreason*, a biography about Assia, Porter writes, "For me to have waited till the main actors are dead to lay at the door of Ted Hughes and the literary establishment the cruelty of excising Assia's true part in the Hughes/Plath heritage, assigning her only the role of marginal temptress, may seem a cowardly act."

9. Conversely, Porter, who claims Assia as a close friend, reminisces, "She [Assia] had wit, charm and generosity, and while she could be wilful [sic] and self-dramatising, she was also natural and straightforward—never in my eyes the 'femme fatale.'" He continues, "I found Assia's beauty no strain—she was gestural and extravagant but more usually quiet and serious-minded."

10. Much as Plath and Assia are compared and contrasted, Plath and Hughes are even more so. David Compton provides the following in his dual description of Plath and Hughes, which becomes a binary. Plath, judges Compton, was "the most American person I ever met." She displayed an un-English enthusiasm, ingenuousness, and vividness. Being very warm and very open, Plath was "very unlike Ted," says Compton. From his vantage point, Compton viewed Hughes as a "weak-willed man" who did not know what to do with himself and needed Plath's discipline and direction to make something of him. He was a "weak, muddled, intuitive man," pronounces Compton (Compton, interview recording, December 7, 1973). Astutely, Rosenstein tells Compton, "Everyone has his or her own Sylvia" (Compton, interview recording, December 7, 1973).

11. Carolyn G. Heilbrun agrees in *Writing a Woman's Life:* "We can only retell and live by the stories we have read or heard. We live our lives through texts." She adds, "Whatever

their form or medium, these stories have formed us all; they are what we must use to make new fictions, new narratives" (37).

12. As Mary Talbot reasons, "Discourses are historically constituted bodies of knowledge and practice that shape people, giving positions of power to some but not to others. But they can only exist in social interaction in specific situations. So discourse is both action and convention" (119). Thus, this book cites and is otherwise informed by various texts, spanning academic books to archival materials to interviews.

2. ASSIA AND HUGHES AS SUBJECTS IN INTERVIEWS AND THE LIVES OF OTHER PEOPLE

1. Please compare Alvarez's take on Assia with what Mary Talbot explains in *Language and Gender*. Talbot lays out the inherent sexism in language, like what we see in Alvarez's writing about Assia: "[W]omen are often defined in terms of physical attributes, such as hair colour (a blonde, a redhead), attractiveness to men, or otherwise (stunner, dog). [Feminists] have also taken issue with the extent to which women are defined in terms of the home and family and, in particular, in terms of their relationships with men" (31–32).

2. In parallel fashion, Edward Lucie-Smith retells a story that Assia related, about Plath throwing herself at Alvarez, who "cruelly rejected" her. Lucie-Smith chalks up this tale as a tall tale, dismissing Assia as a liar (interview recording, July 28, [?]), though there is speculation that Alvarez rejected romantic overtures from Plath at the end of her life. See chapter 16 in Rollyson's *The Last Days of Sylvia Plath*. Rollyson interviewed Alvarez, who "blurted out: '[Plath] was in love with me'" (150). See also Heather Clark's *Red Comet*, esp. 831–33, 835, 840, and 874. See, too, Jonathan Bate's *Ted Hughes: The Unauthorised Life*, in which he writes about Plath offering herself to Alvarez (202) and Alvarez's rejection of Plath (314–15).

3. Tarn is the pen name of Michael Mendelson, who was trained as an anthropologist and who is a writer. In 1968, he edited a special issue of *Afrasian*, featuring Latin American, African, and Middle Eastern poetry, to which Assia contributed translations of Yehuda Amichai's "It's a Long Time Since Anybody's Asked," "You Also Were So Tired," "Farewell," and "The Place Where I've Not Been," under the name Anastassia Gutmann. He also served as the general editor at Cape Goliard Press, which published the first lauded English translations of Amichai's poems, *Selected Poems*, translated by Assia, under the name Assia Gutmann. These poems were also part of a BBC radio program in which Assia wrote and read introductions to the Amichai poems she had translated, and Hughes read Assia's translations in the broadcast. See *The Collected Writings of Assia Wevill*, 268–80, for the script of the radio broadcast. It aired on BBC Radio 3 on December 12, 1968.

4. See his diary, archived at Stanford University (Nathaniel Tarn Papers).

5. Commenting also that David Wevill was famous in England in the 1960s, Tarn implied that David Wevill may have greater name recognition than Assia Wevill at a national literature conference, albeit in the United States. However, he may have wished to underscore the fact that Assia was married when the "appalling nightmare" started.

6. In his diary entry for October 1, 1962, Tarn describes himself as a spectator in the affair between Hughes and Assia, which he dubs a Greek play, with David Wevill and Plath as characters in the drama (Nathaniel Tarn Papers).

7. Assia died before the book was completed, and Baker shelved it for decades. Upon revisiting the manuscript, Baker determined to finish it to honor the memories of Assia and Shura. (Hughes did not contribute any writing.) The book was published in 2021, and my article about it, Baker, Assia, and Hughes, "'You Horrible Lovely Genius': Assia Wevill, Storytelling, and Feminist Recovery," was published in 2022.

8. Baker compiled the recordings of Assia he possesses and uploaded them to *YouTube*: https://youtu.be/LI_lqV8hYhU ("Unfinished 1968"). Viewers will see the unfinished film Assia embarked on with Martin and others, as well as the aforementioned candid recordings and photographs of Assia and Shura.

9. Julia Matcham, a contemporary of Assia and someone who worked closely with her in advertising, wanted Assia to assume responsibility for Plath's suicide. When Assia explained that Plath's death was a result of Plath being prescribed harmful medication that exacerbated her depression and suicidal tendencies rather than helping her, Matcham outright dismissed such an explanation, even though Assia was repeating what Hughes had told her. For Matcham, Assia deceives herself by jettisoning responsibility. However, even Matcham eventually notices Assia's dampened spirits, referring to her as melancholy during the time that she and Shura lived alone; this observation, Matcham notes, was made shortly before Assia and Shura died (correspondence).

10. Assia's health suffered, according to Elaine Feinstein, and she consumed vitamin B tablets to calm her rattled nerves (*Ted Hughes* 156).

11. Myers also believed that Hughes would have reconciled with Plath, had she not died, within seven days (Feinstein, *Ted Hughes* 143).

12. Emory purchased the research materials from the rare book and manuscript dealer Peter Grogan, who, in turn, had acquired them from Ken Lopez Bookseller, which had received the bundle from Rosenstein in 2017 (Harriet Rosenstein Research Files).

13. In her book *Loving Sylvia Plath: A Reclamation*, Emily Van Duyne investigates Rosenstein's place and legacy in Plath studies. She notes that Rosenstein dedicated time to researching a proposed Plath biography from 1969 to 1978 (1). The archival papers and interviews became available to researchers in January 2020 (159). For a sustained discussion about the fraught history of Rosenstein's archive and her unsuccessful biographical pursuit, see *Loving Sylvia Plath*, especially the beginning of the "Gaslight" chapter and the entire "Harriet the Spy" chapter.

14. In reading the manuscript of this book on October 4, 2023, Peter K. Steinberg remarked that Plath did not have a headstone until Assia and Shura had died; Plath's grave acquired a headstone likely around 1970.

15. In his interview with Rosenstein on July 28, [ca. early 1970s], Lucie-Smith conjectures that running Court Green "must have been a great strain," as one of Assia's responsibilities was cooking three meals for six or more people every day. Cooking was one of many

responsibilities Assia held, and Court Green proved to be a hostile environment for her emotionally and psychologically.

16. For a discussion of the statistics regarding Assia's situation, see Goodspeed-Chadwick, *Reclaiming Assia Wevill*, 108–9.

17. Mira Hamermesh, a contemporary of Assia and a personal friend, sets forth the following in her memoir:

> The carefree time included an encounter with a girl about my age, who unbeknown to her had made an impact on me once before, while she was boarding a bus in Tel Aviv. Even then, during the short bus ride, I was mesmerised by her looks. She was the most beautiful and graceful young person I had seen outside the glamour of a cinema screen. There was an aura of crispness about her striking good looks. I could not keep my eyes off her and took in every detail about her appearance: the silver choker round her long neck, the crisp, off-the-shoulder white cotton blouse edged with black velvet, the Roman sandals and the leather, bucket-shaped shoulder bag. Soon after setting eyes on the stranger, I strove to imitate her and began to wear chokers and asked my brother to get me a bag like hers.
>
> I spotted her promenading on the upper deck, looking fresh and well-groomed when most of the other passengers looked windblown or seasick. Her poise and melodious voice won adoring looks from other passengers as well, particularly from men.

Hamermesh adds this caveat, "Her attractiveness had less to do with her striking good looks than with her personality" (158–59). And yet, Hamermesh admits, "Next to her sophistication, my provincialism made me feel wanting and for the second time in my life I wished to be like her. I even began to comb my hair in imitation of her hairstyle, letting it fall over my left eye" (160).

18. Per Assia's biographers, Assia informed David Wevill, Nathaniel Tarn, and Celia Taylor, the wife of the supervisor at the advertising agency where David Wevill worked, that Hughes had raped her (see Koren and Negev, *Lover of Unreason*, 98–99).

19. In a striking parallel, Rosenstein informs Lucie-Smith that Plath was scared "shitless" of Olwyn Hughes; it is no wonder, Lucie-Smith replies, because Olwyn is a female version of Ted (Lucie-Smith, interview recording, July 28, [ca. early 1970s]).

20. An unnamed man in Lucie-Smith's interview pipes up and announces that, while Assia was the most feminine woman he had ever met, she also struck him as "hard as nails" (Lucie-Smith, interview recording, July 28, [ca. early 1970s]).

21. See chapter 9, "Work Inside and Outside the Home," in Susan M. Shaw and Janet Lee's *Gendered Voices, Feminist Visions* for a thorough explanation of this type of situation, one common to women even today. On average, women complete two-thirds of domestic work, and they tend to assume responsibility for "reproductive labor," meaning the kind of work involved in kin keeping, such as taking care of children and other family members (458). According to Shaw and Lee, "Sociologists suggest that once married, women do about twice the amount of work in the home as their spouses, increasing their stress and anxiety.

When women marry, unfortunately most gain an average of 14 hours a week of domestic labor, compared with men, who gain an average of 90 minutes. Husbands tend to create more work for wives than they perform" (461).

22. Assia may have been referring to "The Munich Mannequins," which Plath finished on January 28, 1963.

23. Writes Assia, "I should never have looked into Pandora's box, but now that I have I am forced to wear [Plath's] love-widow's sacking" (*Collected Writings* 163).

24. Tarn explains what Assia told him about the novel: the Wevills are "the Goof-Hoppers," and the manuscript "shocked Assia by its portrait of David who is presented as detestable & contemptible. A[ssia] is of course the icy barren woman. In the novel, apart from SP who is full of poems, kicks & kids, there are only saints and miserable sinners. She hopes TH will destroy this" (Nathaniel Tarn Papers).

25. In a May 3, 1970, letter to Chaikin, held at Emory University, Hughes asks that she return the manuscripts to him after Chaikin notified him that she had them (and she does mail them back). In that letter, Hughes discloses that he knew Assia had some things of Plath's in her possession and that he does not know why she took ownership of such items because they depressed her.

26. The lack of empathy may be traced to Sigmund's determination to equate Assia as the instigator and perpetrator: according to Sigmund, Assia "destroyed everything" (Sigmund, interview recording, undated, part 1).

27. For a catalogue and description of the contents of archived and unpublished letters in which Hughes makes promises to Assia that remained unfulfilled, see Goodspeed-Chadwick, *Reclaiming Assia Wevill*, 188–89n14.

28. Plath expressed her idea of a good life as part and parcel of these synecdoches: "Books & Babies & Beef stews" (*Unabridged Journals* 269).

29. See *The Bell Jar*, 77, for this famous gendered parable.

30. Plath, too, valued beauty as gendered currency. In a letter to his brother, Gerald, Hughes writes in December 1962, "[I]t was cruelly unfortunate that the one woman Sylvia envied for her appearance should happen to get tangled up in my departure. That hurt her more than any other thing" (*Letters of Ted Hughes* 210). Wolf writes about how women learn to fear other women's beauty because that is where value is located; the fear is that a woman's vaunted beauty is a "weapon to be used against" other women and that it impinges on other bodies (284).

31. As Bruce D. Perry, an M.D. and Ph.D. who specializes in trauma, underscores, "Isolated and disconnected, we are vulnerable. In community, we can protect one another. . . . Relational glue keeps our species alive, and love is relational superglue" (77). Per Perry, a "major finding is that your history of relational health—your connectedness to family, community, and culture—is more predictive of your mental health than your history of adversity. . . . This is similar to the findings of other researchers looking at the power of positive relationships on health. Connectedness has the power to counterbalance adversity" (108). Unfortunately, belonging to an "out-group" can result in long-term traumatic effects (103).

32. See his "Draft Constitution," archived at Emory, and see discussions of it in Goodspeed-Chadwick, *Reclaiming Assia Wevill*, 110, 137, 161, 189n14, 191n7, and 192n9.

33. It is noteworthy that Plath cannot escape the gendered bind of the beauty expectations either. Rosenstein informs the Smith College faculty in an interview in 1971 that, after Plath arrived in England, she had "awful hair, awful dress" and was "dowdy." Rosenstein spends a significant amount of time discussing with some of Plath's former professors and colleagues whether she was considered physically attractive (Gibian and Smith College English Faculty).

34. With respect to Plath, Rosenstein hammers questions at Kay Burton, asking whether Plath dyed her hair and whether Plath came across as vain. Burton responds that Plath was not vain but "made the best of herself" (interview recording).

35. In an interview, Anthony Thwaite, a BBC producer and judge of poetry contests, provided a different interpretation of Plath as a person. Plath was "quick on the uptake, warm, friendly," and professional. Thwaite remembers her as a "bright American woman graduate who knew her own mind." Klein perceived Plath as the smartest girl, who was "loving, generous, warm" and not crazy (interview recording, undated, part 1).

36. For example, see Plath's September 22, 1962, letter to Ruth Tiffany Barnhouse Beuscher in *The Letters of Sylvia Plath*, vol. 2: *1956–1963* (827–32): "Ted beat me up physically a couple of days before my miscarriage: the baby I lost was due to be born on his birthday" (830). A bit later, Plath confides that she hopes to move to Ireland with her children: "The children would love this, I would be safe from Ted, & get the first months of separation underway in a fresh setting" (831).

37. A "key practice in enactments of masculinity is violence" (Talbot 159). Acknowledging that masculinity and violence are associated does not excuse violent acts.

38. Janos Csokits recounts how Hughes invited him to have tea when the following happened: "Then we walked to the train station with little Shura. All of a sudden, Ted said a quick goodbye, and walked straight to the train, without looking back. Shura understood only too well what was happening, and flew into a tantrum, crying, shouting, Daddy! Daddy! She was stamping her feet, and Assia wept" (Csokits qtd. in Koren and Negev 194). Shura suffered from the toxic and unstable relationship, too. Fay Weldon informed Assia's biographers she witnessed Hughes giving Shura, a toddler at the time (she was probably two or three years old), wine. "It was very sadistic on his part," says Weldon, "and I'm sure he would not have dared to do the same to Frieda" (qtd. in Koren and Negev 213).

39. Negev and Koren, e-mail to the author, Jan. 22, 2023.

3. ASSIA

1. The world in which they lived was also misogynistic, and some women internalized this hate for other women. Rosenstein likens Plath's destruction of Hughes's poems to "murder" and exclaims, "I'd hit her!" These remarks were made after a discussion of the domestic violence incident that Plath alleged caused her miscarriage (Richard Murphy, interview recording, April 19, 1974, part 2).

2. Assia identifies herself on her résumé thus: "I'm half Russian, half German, and half Jewish" (*Collected Writings* 151).

3. The contrast between the reactions she was accustomed to getting in the mid- to late 1950s versus a decade later must have been demoralizing. A friend of Assia, Pam Gems, remembers, "To be with Assia was like being admitted into the presence of Aphrodite. We were stopped in the streets—one man clutched at her sleeve, and stared and stared before apologizing" (Gems qtd. in Koren and Negev 53). Assia was showstopping—almost literally—in the 1950s, as we see in this recollection, but her value was located in her physical appearance and unusual beauty, something subjective and ephemeral. Philip Hobsbaum designated Assia as "one of the most beautiful, if not the most beautiful woman" during this same time period (Hobsbaum qtd. in Koren and Negev 66). In such a damaging environment, where women's worth is tied to their bodies, Assia found it very difficult to retain a healthy outlook on future prospects for herself and her daughter. The world could be cruel and was not designed to lift her up, she discovered. Her friend and coworker Edward Lucie-Smith recounts, "Her figure was rather dumpy, heavy legs and thick ankles, and being a perfectionist, she was very conscious of these defects. Curiously she was unaware of the beauty which made one overlook these flaws. If you paid her a compliment on her beauty, she was rather put out. I remember Marisa and I reduced her to tears by telling her the whole morning how beautiful she was" (Lucie-Smith qtd. in Koren and Negev 77). Martin Baker corroborates: "She was very critical of her looks, edgy when people looked at her, and uptight when complimented on her beauty" (Baker qtd. in Koren and Negev 180).

4. For close readings of Assia's translated Amichai poems and for discussions of the content of those poems within the context of her life, see Goodspeed-Chadwick, *Reclaiming Assia Wevill*, 124–35.

5. Bateson continues in provocative and convincing fashion: "You can't 'have it all'—nature doesn't work that way, and finally there are only so many hours in the day. It is, however, almost always possible to have more; having less often means producing less" (185).

6. In short, according to Judith Herman, traumatic reactions are responses "to a situation of helplessness and terror and shame" ("The Politics of Trauma" 141).

7. Hughes wonders why Assia did not take herself to a hospital to get help in "The Error" and gestures to her desperation in a crisis in "Flame."

8. Trying to secure a safe place where she belonged was a lifelong pursuit for Assia. Hamermesh characterizes Assia's desire to relocate to England as "the surge towards a new beginning" and "an escape from a wounding past" (160).

9. Eda Megged spent time with Assia in March 1969 and was stunned at how "heavy and awkward" Assia was and how depressed. Megged believes that Assia was putting everything into finding a house and making a home with Hughes (Megged qtd. in Feinstein 170).

10. The National Suicide Prevention Lifeline in the United States operates twenty-four hours a day and can be reached at 800–273–8255.

11. Anne Sexton may be considered one such victim; she "identified Plath's suicide as an enviable career move" (Middlebrook 216), believing that "the world would now pay

more serious attention to Plath's poetry than was otherwise conceivable" (217). Even though Sexton did not want to appear to be a copycat, she perished by suicide, a little over a decade after Plath died.

12. As Assia's biographers document, "The Gutmann family had not been spared [during World War II]; the Nazis murdered Vanya [Assia's paternal uncle] . . . together with his wife and small daughter" (Koren and Negev 55). Understandably, the intergenerational and transhistorical trauma of the Holocaust affected Assia; she battles what seem to be symptoms of trauma after revisiting Germany in 1954, twenty years after her immediate family fled to other countries for safety (55). Periodically, Assia's mental health suffered; she "had made a few attempts on her life in the past, but they seemed to be demonstrative, a plea for sympathy" (Koren and Negev 163). When she was twenty, Assia had her stomach pumped after swallowing aspirins; she had been "shocked and outraged" that her husband at the time, John Steele, had decided to move to Canada from England without consulting her, and she responded in extreme fashion (Koren and Negev 41). During her second marriage, to Richard (Dick) Lipsey, Assia swallowed pills in despair in front of her husband on two different occasions because she "felt cheated, thinking she was entitled to a better life" (Koren and Negev 57). Lipsey understood Assia's suicide attempts as "a clear cry for help, and not a deliberate attempt to end her life" (Lipsey qtd. in Koren and Negev 57). Toward the end of her life, when her life was at its most unstable and insecure, Assia's friends recount that she talked of suicide more than once (Koren and Negev 195–97). Assia confided in Chris Wilkins, her former coworker, "that she was worried about her insecurity, and wanted to marry again and settle, but things were not going right with Ted" (Koren and Negev 197). Assia revealed "that she couldn't stand the state of things as they were, and if it didn't change, she would kill herself" (Wilkins qtd. in Koren and Negev 197).

13. Writes Hughes to Chaikin on April 14, 1969, "I know if only I had moved—if I had only given her hope in slightly more emphatic words in that last phone conversation, she would have been O.K." (*Letters of Ted Hughes* 290).

14. Koren and Negev ponder the dynamics at play: "In her will, Assia clearly indicated that she wished to be buried. Did Hughes choose cremation in order to obliterate any trace of his daughter and of Assia? Was he apprehensive of the revealing epitaph [Assia specified], 'Lover of Unreason'? The fact remains that Assia, who was an unwilling wanderer on earth, and throughout her life yearned to strike roots, found no repose even in death" (220).

15. For instance, in what became a well-known interview, Hughes relates, "Several of my favorite pieces in my book *Crow* I wrote traveling up and down Germany with a woman and a small child—I just went on writing wherever we were" (Hughes, "The Art of Poetry" 63). Despite Assia being his partner and Shura his child and *Crow* dedicated to them both, Hughes opts to refer to them generically, withholding their special relationships to him, in the retelling of his life and craft. That interview took place in 1995, long after they had died. For context, we can turn to Murphy's account of their life together in 1966; Hughes and Assia were living as a family unit with Frieda Hughes, Nicholas Hughes, and Shura Wevill in Ireland, and Murphy saw them regularly during the first six months of 1966. They were

getting along so well that Murphy remembers: "They were thinking of settling in Ireland, and Ted even offered to sell me Court Green" (*The Kick* 251). While he was in Ireland, Murphy notes, Hughes began writing the *Crow* poems (251).

16. Though it is not a well-known fact, Assia worked as a teacher when she was twenty-six and delighted in the role. In a May 22, 1953, letter to her sister, Assia writes, "This is the best thing that has happened to me since October 1952—I love it, and apparently the children like me. The last school I was at, presented me with large bunch of flowers on my last day. I nearly cried. . . . I teach in the toughest districts in London. . . . But they are good, [sic] children, responding quickly to fair-play and kindness" (*Collected Writings* 54–55).

17. Jonathan Bate also makes this observation ("It was as if they were losing a second mother, and a sister") and details how Frieda and Nicholas Hughes were distraught when Assia and Shura moved out of Court Green: "The children did not want her [Assia] to go, Frieda saying so vociferously, Nick concurring more silently" (*Ted Hughes* 255).

18. See chapter 5 in *Reclaiming Assia Wevill: Sylvia Plath, Ted Hughes, and the Literary Imagination*, where I examine in detail these subjects and Frieda Hughes's poetic responses to Assia in her book *Alternative Values* (2015).

19. Manne elaborates: if a man has "enough material and social resources—or alternatively, a heart-rending 'down on his luck' story—then we will often fight with all our might to defend his honor, maintain his innocence" (215). Whereas victims are held to be lying generally, we might also disparage and dismiss them as "stupid, crazy, or hysterical" or call their victimhood into question on moral grounds (217–18).

20. The imperfectness of victims can induce us to keep silent on their behalf. As Manne states, "we ourselves may elect to hold our tongues, given the likely social penalties for defending imperfect victims of misogynistic vitriol—moral disgust, counter-shaming, and ostracism" (290).

21. For Plath's poetic treatment of Assia, see chapter 2 in Goodspeed-Chadwick, *Reclaiming Assia Wevill*.

22. Some have maintained that Assia killed herself out of rage, Rosenstein being one of them at one point (Murphy, interview recording, April 19, 1974, part 3).

23. For example, Rosenstein relates that she heard seven versions of the story about Assia's name on a scrap of paper floating down to Plath from Plath cleaning the grate or, alternately, setting up a magical ritual and burning Hughes's "invisible particles." One source, says Rosenstein, claimed a different name (Dido Merwin). Declares Rosenstein, "Assia told this story" and "loved to tell the story" (Murphy, interview recording, April 19, 1974, part 2).

24. A selection of poems from *A Full House* can be found in Ted Hughes, *Collected Poems* 731–36.

25. Despite having little time to dedicate to such a task, Assia persisted in producing the translations, which resulted in a modest volume in 1968 and an expanded volume in 1969. Her tireless dedication to the project, even when her life was crumbling around her, shores up Audre Lorde's argument that poetry is not a luxury, especially not for women and people harboring marginalized identities. Lorde maintains: "The quality of light by which we scrutinize our lives has direct bearing upon the product which we live, and upon the changes

which we hope to bring about through those lives. It is within this light that we form those ideas by which we pursue our magic and make it realized. This is poetry as illumination, for it is through poetry that we give name to those ideas which are—until the poem—nameless and formless, about to be birthed but already felt" ("Poetry Is Not a Luxury" 37).

4. TED HUGHES

1. See Goodspeed-Chadwick, *Reclaiming Assia Wevill*, chap. 5.
2. See *The Collected Writings of Assia Wevill*, 151.
3. Per Mary Talbot, "We need to consider in what institutions, in what situations and in what genres men can and do dominate women, and how those institutions, situations and genres help them to do so" (99).
4. In his memoir, Huws comments that he could feel quite relaxed around Assia, though that was never the case with Plath (47). There are always multiple competing views about who a person is, and this study engages those whenever possible, while presenting never-before-cited material whenever possible.
5. Kai Erikson insists, "Traumatized people . . . look out at the world through a different lens. And in that sense they can be said to have experienced not only a *changed sense of self* and a *changed way of relating to others* but a changed *worldview*." He elaborates that traumatized people feel they "have lost an important measure of control over the circumstances of their own lives and are thus very vulnerable" and "that they have lost a natural immunity to misfortune and that something awful is almost *bound* to happen." According to Erikson, "One of the crucial tasks of culture, let's say, is to help people camouflage the actual risks of the world around them—to help them edit reality in such a way that it seems manageable, to help them edit it in such a way that the dangers pressing in on them from all sides are screened" (194).
6. Bessel A. van der Kolk and Alexander C. McFarlane cite research that shows writing personal accounts of trauma "plays a critical role in maintaining personal and psychological health" (18). They add the caveat: "Merely uncovering memories is not enough; they need to be modified and transformed (i.e., placed in their proper context and reconstructed in a personally meaningful way)" (19).
7. Hughes states in a letter to Leonard Baskin, dated July 16, 1969, "I have two nice children [Frieda and Nicholas Hughes] who make life a great pleasure. They come to the States every summer. I had a third [Shura Wevill], a little marvel, but she died with her mother" (*Letters of Ted Hughes* 293). Jonathan Bate documents that Hughes gave a statement to police after Assia died, in which he stated that he and Assia, in the words of the police report, "became intimate, and there was a girl born of this union" (*Ted Hughes* 275).
8. It also runs unfettered in *Capriccio*, where, Jo Gill argues, "Hughes orientalizes Assia, by which I mean that he projects onto her his own forbidden, disavowed fears and desires" (61). Another way to interpret the letter is to read Hughes as being ironic about colonialist ideology, as one reader of this book's manuscript has suggested: it is the middle- to fringe aristocratic classes that show such cruelty, violence, and attitudes, not the working class.

9. Blackness signifies in various ways in various poems in *Crow*. As an outside reader noted, there are additional referents that may exist: "the blackness of actual crows, the black faces of Yorkshire miners among whom [Ted Hughes] was raised, his own sense of a heritage that has elements of 'Black Irish'/Spanish/Romany."

10. In *Unclaimed Experience: Trauma, Narrative, History*, Cathy Caruth explains that repetition is a hallmark of trauma, stating, "catastrophic events seem to repeat themselves for those who have passed through them" (1), and "repetition [is] at the heart of catastrophe" (2). It is "the unwitting reenactment of an event that one cannot simply leave behind" (2).

11. In a September 29, 1984, letter, fifteen years after Assia's and Shura's deaths, Hughes writes the following to Lucas Myers: "I wonder sometimes if things might have gone differently without the events of 63 [Plath's suicide] & 69 [Assia's suicide and Shura's death]. I have an idea that those two episodes as giant steel doors shutting down over great parts of myself, leaving me that much less, just what was left, to live on. No doubt a more resolute artist would have penetrated the steel doors—but I believe big physical changes happen at those times, big self-anaesthesias. Maybe life isn't long enough to wake up from them" (*Letters of Ted Hughes* 489).

12. In "Ted Hughes and the Challenge of Gender," Nathalie Anderson articulates "the accepted wisdom: Hughes kills. Hughes is inimical—no, downright dangerous to women." Attempting to soften "the accepted wisdom," Anderson argues that "Hughes's disquieting presentation of women is part of a larger indictment—ultimately of a society which represses not only what Hughes perceives as a female principle within the psyche, but actual women as well. If we cannot define Hughes as a feminist—and I certainly do not propose to do so—we can nevertheless acknowledge that feminists too endorse this position." Much of *Crow* is a "dramatisation of violent men and devouring women," writes Anderson, and the violence against women equates to "a feminist's nightmare." Anderson concludes that readers keep returning to *Crow* because of its "continuing power to fascinate, to influence, and—emphatically—to disturb."

13. See "Snow" and "The Coat."

14. Elaine Feinstein began the work of restoring Assia in *Ted Hughes: The Life of a Poet* in 2001, after Hughes had died. The first full-length biography, *Lover of Unreason* by Koren and Negev, appeared in 2006.

15. In the much-publicized acceptance speech that she gave for the 1999 Whitbread Book of the Year prize on behalf of her father, who had passed away in the previous year, Frieda Hughes read the following from a letter by her father: "How strange that we have to make these public declarations of our secrets, but we do. If only I had done the equivalent 30 years ago I might have had a more fruitful career—certainly a freer psychological life" ("Posthumous Whitbread Prize for Ted Hughes").

16. See chapter 3 of that book.

17. See chapter 27 in its entirety in Bate's *Ted Hughes: The Unauthorised Life*. Among the unforgettable memories are these: "Assia at the Beacon, 'sitting in that chair by the phone while Hilda screamed at her, and she helpless to defend herself.' To hear again Assia at Lumb Bank, her horror at its darkness and damp. To remember Assia in her ponyskin coat

waiting for a train at Clapham Junction in the last month of her life. To capture the image of her in a pub, wearing a skirt of brown Thai silk and holding an Embassy cigarette. To recapture the energy and freedom of the beginning of their affair in London: the newness of everything, the shine of her black handbag, the thick scent of her Dior perfume, the smell of Mayfair in 1962" (453).

18. Baskin collaborated with Hughes, producing cover art for *Crow, Capriccio,* and *Howls & Whispers.*

19. According to the American Psychiatric Association's *Diagnostic and Statistical Manual of Mental Disorders (DSM 5)*, PTSD can occur after a person learns about the violent or accidental death of a close family member or friend. For a PTSD diagnosis, intrusive symptoms related to the trauma persist longer than a month, with the *DSM* specifying how many of the following must be met under each criterion: recurring distressing memories; recurring distressing dreams in which the content or affect pertain to the traumatic event; flashbacks; intense or prolonged psychological or physiological distress and reactions with traumatic triggers; avoidance of or attempt to avoid upsetting memories, thoughts, feelings, and external reminders related to the trauma; negative changes in cognitions and mood, such as dissociative amnesia, persistent and exaggerated negativity in connection with beliefs about oneself and the world, blaming oneself or others, persistent negative emotionality (e.g., horror, anger, guilt, and shame), diminished interest in activities, detachment, and inability to experience positive emotions; irritable behavior and outbursts; reckless and/or self-destructive behavior; hypervigilance; heightened startle response; concentration problems; and sleep disturbances (*DSM* 5 pp. 271–72).

CONCLUSION

1. See Hughes's letter to Jutta and Wolfgang Kaussen, dated November 19, 1997, in *Letters of Ted Hughes* 696.

2. Frieda Hughes remembers Assia's beauty and voice through an implied metaphor in the poem "Assia Gutmann," collected in *Out of the Ashes:*

> Her beauty frightened me
> Carved as she was of piano keys,
> Her hair the black flats,
> Her voice on the pedals. (185)

3. An unidentified friend of Assia appears on an interview recording with Rosenstein, and this female friend cites the BBC program featuring Assia and Hughes as one she enjoyed, so much so that she invited Assia and Hughes to visit her in London (Orr [and Beben?]).

4. See my article "'He's Busy Espalliering Sylvia': Ted Hughes, Sylvia Plath, and Assia Wevill" for a detailed discussion of how Hughes, Plath, and Assia influenced, inspired, and made an impact on one another.

WORKS CITED

Afrasian, no. 1, 1968.
Alcoff, Linda Martín. *Rape and Resistance*. Polity, 2018.
Alexander, Paul. *Rough Magic: A Biography of Sylvia Plath*. Viking, 1991.
Alvarez, Al. *Where Did It All Go Right?* Bloomsbury, 1999.
American Psychiatric Association. "Trauma- and Stressor-Related Disorders." *Diagnostic and Statistical Manual of Mental Disorders: DSM-5*, 5th ed., American Psychiatric Publishing, 2013, pp. 265–90.
Amichai, Yehuda. *Poems*. Translated by Assia Gutmann [Wevill], Harper & Row, 1969.
———. *Selected Poems*. Translated by Assia Gutmann [Wevill], Cape Goliard, 1968.
Anderson, Nathalie. "Ted Hughes and the Challenge of Gender." *Poetry Criticism*, edited by Michelle Lee, vol. 89, Gale, 2008. *Gale Literature Resource Center*. Rpt. of Nathalie Anderson, "Ted Hughes and the Challenge of Gender." *The Challenge of Ted Hughes*, edited by Keith Sagar, St. Martin's Press, 1994, pp. 91–115.
"Apocalypse Terminable and Interminable: An Interview with Arthur S. Blank Jr." *Listening to Trauma: Conversations with Leaders in the Theory and Treatment of Catastrophic Experience*, interviews and photography by Cathy Caruth, Johns Hopkins UP, 2014, pp. 270–95.
Avery, John. Interview recording. Undated. Side A. Harriet Rosenstein Research Files on Sylvia Plath, Stuart A. Rose Manuscript, Archives, and Rare Book Library, Emory University, Atlanta, GA.
Baker, Martin. "Assia Gutmann, 1927–69." Unpublished memoir, 2022, pp. 94–114.
———. *Wellington the Tin Soldier*. Berti, 2021.
Baskin, Leonard. Interview recording. December 16, 1971. Side A. Harriet Rosenstein Research Files on Sylvia Plath, Stuart A. Rose Manuscript, Archives, and Rare Book Library, Emory University, Atlanta, GA.

Bate, Jonathan. *Bright Star, Green Light: The Beautiful Works and Damned Lives of John Keats and F. Scott Fitzgerald.* Yale UP, 2021.

———. *Ted Hughes: The Unauthorised Life.* Harper, 2015.

Bateson, Mary Catherine. *Composing a Life.* Grove Press, 1989.

Burton, Kay. Interview recording. December 11, [undated]. Part 2, side B. Harriet Rosenstein Research Files on Sylvia Plath, Stuart A. Rose Manuscript, Archives, and Rare Book Library, Emory University, Atlanta, GA.

Butler, Judith. *The Force of Nonviolence: An Ethico-Political Bind.* Verso, 2020.

———. "The Future of the Humanities Can Be Found in Its Public Forms." *MLA Newsletter,* vol. 52, no. 4, winter 2020, pp. 2–3.

Caruth, Cathy. *Unclaimed Experience: Trauma, Narrative, and History.* Johns Hopkins UP, 1996.

Chaikin, Ira. E-mail to the author. Feb. 19, 2022.

Clark, Heather. *The Grief of Influence: Sylvia Plath and Ted Hughes.* Oxford UP, 2011.

———. *Red Comet: The Short Life and Blazing Art of Sylvia Plath.* Knopf, 2020.

Collins, Patricia Hill. *Intersectionality as Critical Social Theory.* Duke UP, 2019.

Compton, David. Interview recording. December 7, 1973. Side A. Harriet Rosenstein Research Files on Sylvia Plath, Stuart A. Rose Manuscript, Archives, and Rare Book Library, Emory University, Atlanta, GA.

———. Interview recording. Undated. Side A. Harriet Rosenstein Research Files on Sylvia Plath, Stuart A. Rose Manuscript, Archives, and Rare Book Library, Emory University, Atlanta, GA.

Cottom, Tressie McMillan. *Thick and Other Essays.* New Press, 2019.

Crowther, Gail. *Three-Martini Afternoons at the Ritz: The Rebellion of Sylvia Plath and Anne Sexton.* Simon and Schuster, 2021.

Cunningham, Stephanie. "Intimate Partner Violence." Introduction to Women's Studies, Dec. 6, 2022, Indiana University Columbus. Featured course speaker.

Davies, Winifred. Interview recording. 1970. Part 2, side A. Harriet Rosenstein Research Files on Sylvia Plath, Stuart A. Rose Manuscript, Archives, and Rare Book Library, Emory University, Atlanta, GA.

———. Interview recording. Undated. Part 1, side B. Harriet Rosenstein Research Files on Sylvia Plath, Stuart A. Rose Manuscript, Archives, and Rare Book Library, Emory University, Atlanta, GA.

Ely, Steve. "The Key of the Sycamore." *Ted Hughes Society Journal,* vol. 8, no. 2, 2020, pp. 42–64.

Enniss, Stephen C., and Karen V. Kukil. *"No Other Appetite": Sylvia Plath, Ted Hughes, and the Blood Jet of Poetry.* Grolier Club, 2005.

Erikson, Kai. "Notes on Trauma and Community." *Trauma Explorations in Memory,* edited by Cathy Caruth, Johns Hopkins UP, 1995, pp. 183–99.

Fainlight, [Ruth]. Interview recording. Undated. Side A. Harriet Rosenstein Research Files on Sylvia Plath, Stuart A. Rose Manuscript, Archives, and Rare Book Library, Emory University, Atlanta, GA.

———. Interview recording. Undated. Side B. Harriet Rosenstein Research Files on Sylvia Plath, Stuart A. Rose Manuscript, Archives, and Rare Book Library, Emory University, Atlanta, GA.

Farrar, Hilda. "Letters to Olwyn Hughes from Friends and Family, Undated." MS 88948/2. Folder 1. Western Manuscripts, British Library, London.

———. "Letters to Olwyn Hughes from Friends and Family, Wednesday." MS 88948/2. Folder 1. Western Manuscripts, British Library, London.

Feinstein, Elaine. *Ted Hughes: The Life of a Poet.* Norton, 2003.

Felski, Rita. *Hooked: Art and Attachment.* U of Chicago P, 2020.

"A Ghost in the House of Justice: A Conversation with Shoshana Felman." *Listening to Trauma: Conversations with Leaders in the Theory and Treatment of Catastrophic Experience,* interviews and photography by Cathy Caruth, Johns Hopkins UP, 2014, pp. 320–53.

Gibian, George, and Smith College English Faculty. Interview recording. 1971. Side B. Harriet Rosenstein Research Files on Sylvia Plath, Stuart A. Rose Manuscript, Archives, and Rare Book Library, Emory University, Atlanta, GA.

Gill, Jo. "Ted Hughes and Sylvia Plath." *The Cambridge Companion to Ted Hughes,* edited by Terry Gifford, Cambridge UP, 2011, pp. 53–66.

Goodspeed-Chadwick, Julie. "'He's Busy Espalliering Sylvia': Ted Hughes, Sylvia Plath, and Assia Wevill." *Influence and Inspiration,* special issue of *Journal of the Midwest Modern Language Association,* edited by Deborah M. Mix, vol. 55, no. 1, spring 2022, pp. 11–30.

———. *Reclaiming Assia Wevill: Sylvia Plath, Ted Hughes, and the Literary Imagination.* LSU P, 2019.

———. "'You Horrible Lovely Genius': Assia Wevill, Storytelling, and Feminist Recovery." *ANQ: A Quarterly Journal of Short Articles, Notes, and Reviews,* July 2022, https://www.tandfonline.com/doi/full/10.1080/0895769X.2022.2104200. Rpt. in *ANQ: A Quarterly Journal of Short Articles, Notes and Reviews,* vol. 37, no. 2, spring 2024, pp. 288–92.

Gordon-Reed, Annette. "Writing the Lives of the Well Known and the Unknown." Annual Leon Levy Biography Lecture: Annette Gordon-Reed, May 4, 2022, City University of New York, Zoom.

Hamermesh, Mira. *The River of Angry Dogs: A Memoir.* Pluto, 2019.

Harriet Rosenstein Research Files on Sylvia Plath. Stuart A. Rose Manuscript, Archives, and Rare Book Library, Emory University, Atlanta, GA. https://findingaids.library.emory.edu/documents/rosenstein1489/. Accessed 18 January 2022.

"The Haunted Self: An Interview with Onno van der Hart." *Listening to Trauma: Conversations with Leaders in the Theory and Treatment of Catastrophic Experience,* interviews and photography by Cathy Caruth, Johns Hopkins UP, 2014, pp. 178–211.

Hedden, Brenda. Correspondence: Brenda Hedden to Elizabeth Sigmund. Box 1, folder 21, item 41. Elizabeth Sigmund Collection of Photographs and Correspondence Related to Sylvia Plath, Mortimer Rare Book Collection, MRBC-MS-00441, Smith College Special Collections, Northampton, MA.

Heilbrun, Carolyn G. *Writing a Woman's Life.* Norton, 2008.

Herman, Judith. *Trauma and Recovery: The Aftermath of Violence—from Domestic Abuse to Political Terror.* Basic, 1997.

Horder, John. Interview recording. Harriet Rosenstein Research Files on Sylvia Plath, Stuart A. Rose Manuscript, Archives, and Rare Book Library, Emory University, Atlanta, GA.

Hughes, Frieda. *Out of the Ashes.* Bloodaxe, 2018.

Hughes, Olwyn. Copy of Correspondence by Olwyn Hughes to Clarissa Roche, in which Hughes refers to Trevor Thomas and the "party." 1987-09-25. Box 1, folder 17, item 34. Elizabeth Sigmund Collection of Photographs and Correspondence Related to Sylvia Plath, Mortimer Rare Book Collection, MRBC-MS-00441, Smith College Special Collections, Northampton, MA.

———. Correspondence: Olwyn Hughes to Clarissa Roche, 1986-03-24. Box 1, folder 12, item 22. Elizabeth Sigmund Collection of Photographs and Correspondence Related to Sylvia Plath, Mortimer Rare Book Collection, MRBC-MS-00441, Smith College Special Collections, Northampton, MA.

Hughes, Ted. "The Art of Poetry." Interview by Drue Heinz. *Paris Review,* vol. 71, spring 1995, pp. 54–94.

———. *Birthday Letters.* Farrar, Straus, and Giroux, 1998.

———. Capriccio, ca. 1967–Nov. 8, 1993. MS 88918I//17. Western Manuscripts, British Library, London.

———. *Collected Poems.* Farrar, Strauss and Giroux, 2003.

———. *Crow: From the Life and Songs of the Crow.* Faber, 1970.

———. Foreword. *The Journals of Sylvia Plath,* edited by Frances McCullough, with Hughes as consulting editor, Anchor, 1998, pp. xi–xiii.

———. Hughes, Ted, to Celia Chaikin. May 3 1970. MSS 1058. Box 1, folder 4. Ted Hughes, Letters to Assia Wevill, Stuart A. Rose Manuscript, Archives, and Rare Book Library, Emory University, Atlanta, GA.

———. Letters from Ted Hughes: Letters from Ted Hughes and Others to Elizabeth Compton, Afterwards Sigmund; 1963–1976. Undated. MS 88612. Western Manuscripts, British Library, London.

———. *Letters of Ted Hughes*. Selected and edited by Christopher Reid, Farrar, Straus and Giroux, 2007.

———. Letters to Olwyn Hughes from Friends and Family. Undated. MS 88948/2. Folder 1. Western Manuscripts, British Library, London.

———. "Lovesong." *Northwest Review*, vol. 9, no. 2, fall-winter 1967–68, pp. 56–57.

———. [Notebook 11]. Spiral Bound Shorthand Notebook. Undated [ca. 1968–69]. MSS 644. Box 57, folder 10. Ted Hughes Papers, 1940–1999, Stuart A. Rose Manuscript, Archives, and Rare Book Library, Emory University, Atlanta, GA.

———. [Notebook 31]. Poems Written Following the Deaths of Assia and Shura Wevill. Undated [ca. 1970]. MSS 644. Box 190. Ted Hughes Papers, 1940–1999, Stuart A. Rose Manuscript, Archives, and Rare Book Library, Emory University, Atlanta, GA.

———, previous owner. *Selected Poems*. By Yehuda Amichai, translated by Assia Gutmann [Wevill], Cape Goliard, 1968, Stuart A. Rose Manuscript, Archives, and Rare Book Library, Emory University, Atlanta, GA.

Huws, Daniel. *Memories of Ted Hughes: 1952–1963*. Nottingham, England: Richard Hollis, 2010.

Jenkins, Alan, and Nan Jenkins. Interview recording. December 4, 1973. Side A. Harriet Rosenstein Research Files on Sylvia Plath, Stuart A. Rose Manuscript, Archives, and Rare Book Library, Emory University, Atlanta, GA.

Kane, Marvin. Interview recording. Nov. 27, 1973. Side B. Harriet Rosenstein Research Files on Sylvia Plath, Stuart A. Rose Manuscript, Archives, and Rare Book Library, Emory University, Atlanta, GA.

Kavanagh, P. J. "An Awkward Shyness." *The Guardian*, July 12, 1968, p. 6.

"Kimberlé Crenshaw Discusses 'Intersectional Feminism.'" Oct. 15, 2015. *YouTube*, https://www.youtube.com/watch?v=ROwquxC_Gxc.

Kirkus Reviews, June 18, 1969.

Klein, Elinor. Interview recording. Undated. Part 1, side A. Harriet Rosenstein Research Files on Sylvia Plath, Stuart A. Rose Manuscript, Archives, and Rare Book Library, Emory University, Atlanta, GA.

———. Interview recording. Undated. Part 2, side B, Harriet Rosenstein Research Files on Sylvia Plath, Stuart A. Rose Manuscript, Archives, and Rare Book Library, Emory University, Atlanta, GA.

Kolodny, Annette. "Dancing through the Minefield: Some Observations on the Theory, Practice, and Politics of a Feminist Literary Criticism." *Falling into Theory: Conflicting Views of Reading Literature*, edited by David H. Richter, 2nd ed., Bedford, 2000, pp. 302–9.

Koren, Yehuda, and Eilat Negev. *Lover of Unreason: Assia Wevill, Sylvia Plath's Rival and Ted Hughes's Doomed Love*. Da Capo, 2007.

Krebs, Paula M. "Acknowledging Humanities Expertise." *MLA Newsletter*, vol. 54, no. 4, winter 2022, p. 1.

Kukil, Karen V. "Sylvia Plath in the Round." *The Bloomsbury Handbook to Sylvia Plath*, edited by Anita Helle, Amanda Golden, and Maeve O'Brien, Bloomsbury, 2022, pp. 300–305.

Lee, Hermione. *Biography: A Very Short Introduction*. Oxford UP, 2009.

Levy, Lisa. Interview recording. Undated. Side B. Harriet Rosenstein Research Files on Sylvia Plath, Stuart A. Rose Manuscript, Archives, and Rare Book Library, Emory University, Atlanta, GA.

Lorde, Audre. "Learning from the 60s." *Sister Outsider: Essays and Speeches*, by Lorde, Crossing Press, 2007, pp. 134–44.

———. "Poetry Is Not a Luxury." *Sister Outsider: Essays and Speeches*, by Lorde, Crossing Press, 2007, pp. 36–39.

———. "The Master's Tools Will Never Dismantle the Master's House." *Sister Outsider: Essays and Speeches*, by Lorde, Crossing Press, 2007, pp. 110–13.

Lucie-Smith, Edward. Interview recording. July 28, [ca. early 1970s]. Harriet Rosenstein Research Files on Sylvia Plath, Stuart A. Rose Manuscript, Archives, and Rare Book Library, Emory University, Atlanta, GA.

———. Interview recording. July 28–29, [ca. early 1970s]. Side A. Harriet Rosenstein Research Files on Sylvia Plath, Stuart A. Rose Manuscript, Archives, and Rare Book Library, Emory University, Atlanta, GA.

Macedo, Alda [Helder]. Interview recording. December 1, 1973. Side A. Harriet Rosenstein Research Files on Sylvia Plath, Stuart A. Rose Manuscript, Archives, and Rare Book Library, Emory University, Atlanta, GA.

———. Interview recording. December 1, 1973. Side B. Harriet Rosenstein Research Files on Sylvia Plath, Stuart A. Rose Manuscript, Archives, and Rare Book Library, Emory University, Atlanta, GA.

Macedo, Suzette. Interview recording. November 27, [1973?]. Harriet Rosenstein Research Files on Sylvia Plath, Stuart A. Rose Manuscript, Archives, and Rare Book Library, Emory University, Atlanta, GA.

———. Interview recording. Undated. Roll 1. Harriet Rosenstein Research Files on Sylvia Plath, Stuart A. Rose Manuscript, Archives, and Rare Book Library, Emory University, Atlanta, GA.

Macedo, Suzette, and Helder Macedo. Interview recording. December 1, 1973. Parts 3 and 4, side A. Harriet Rosenstein Research Files on Sylvia Plath, Stuart A. Rose Manuscript, Archives, and Rare Book Library, Emory University, Atlanta, GA.

———. Interview recording. December 1, 1973. Parts 3 and 4, side B. Harriet Rosenstein Research Files on Sylvia Plath, Stuart A. Rose Manuscript, Archives, and Rare Book Library, Emory University, Atlanta, GA.

Malcolm, Janet. *The Silent Woman: Sylvia Plath and Ted Hughes.* Vintage, 1994.
Manne, Kate. *Down Girl: The Logic of Misogyny.* Oxford UP, 2019.
Marcus, Laura. *Auto/Biographical Discourses: Theory, Criticism, Practice.* Manchester UP, 1994.
———. *Autobiography: A Very Short Introduction.* Oxford UP, 2018.
Mardorossian, Carine M. *Framing the Rape Victim: Gender and Agency Reconsidered.* Rutgers UP, 2014.
Matcham, Julia. 1990–91. Wagner-Martin MSS. Lilly Library Manuscript Collections, Indiana University, Bloomington.
———. Correspondence: Julia Matcham to Elizabeth Sigmund. Refers to Assia Wevill, 1987-01-17. Box 1, folder 21, item 42. Elizabeth Sigmund Collection of Photographs and Correspondence Related to Sylvia Plath, Mortimer Rare Book Collection, MRBC-MS-00441, Smith College Special Collections, Northampton, MA.
McCullough, Frances. Editor's Note. *The Journals of Sylvia Plath,* edited by McCullough, with Ted Hughes as consulting editor, Anchor, 1998, pp. ix–x.
Merwin, W. S. Interview recording. Undated. Side A. Harriet Rosenstein Research Files on Sylvia Plath, Stuart A. Rose Manuscript, Archives, and Rare Book Library, Emory University, Atlanta, GA.
Micir, Melanie. *The Passion Projects: Modernist Women, Intimate Archives, Unfinished Lives.* Princeton UP, 2019.
Middlebrook, Diane. *Her Husband: Hughes and Plath—A Marriage.* Viking, 2003.
Minton, Nathaniel. *A Memoir of Ted Hughes.* Westmoreland Press, 2015.
Murphy, Richard. Copy of correspondence by Richard Murphy to an unknown correspondent. Box 1, folder 19, item 38. Elizabeth Sigmund Collection of Photographs and Correspondence Related to Sylvia Plath, Mortimer Rare Book Collection, MRBC-MS-00441, Smith College Special Collections, Northampton, MA.
———. Interview recording. April 19, 1974. Part 1. Harriet Rosenstein Research Files on Sylvia Plath, Stuart A. Rose Manuscript, Archives, and Rare Book Library, Emory University, Atlanta, GA.
———. Interview recording. April 19, 1974. Part 2, side B. Harriet Rosenstein Research Files on Sylvia Plath, Stuart A. Rose Manuscript, Archives, and Rare Book Library, Emory University, Atlanta, GA.
———. Interview recording. April 19, 1974. Part 3, side B. Harriet Rosenstein Research Files on Sylvia Plath, Stuart A. Rose Manuscript, Archives, and Rare Book Library, Emory University, Atlanta, GA.
———. *The Kick.* Granta, 2002.
Myers, Lucas. *Crow Steered, Bergs Appeared: A Memoir of Ted Hughes and Sylvia Plath.* Proctor's Hall, 2001.

Negev, Eilat, and Yehuda Koren. E-mail to the author. e-mail to the author, Jan. 22, 2023.

———. E-mail to the author. Feb. 24, 2022.

Nelson, Maggie. *The Argonauts*. Graywolf Press, 2015.

Oluo, Ijeoma. *So You Want to Talk about Race*. Seal, 2019.

Orr, Peter, [and Pennah Beben?]. Interview recording. July 30, [undated]. Harriet Rosenstein Research Files on Sylvia Plath, Stuart A. Rose Manuscript, Archives, and Rare Book Library, Emory University, Atlanta, GA.

Perry, Bruce D., and Oprah Winfrey. *What Happened to You? Conversations on Trauma, Resilience, and Healing*. Flatiron Books, 2021.

Plath, Sylvia. *The Bell Jar*. 1963. Harper Perennial, 2005.

———. *The Letters of Sylvia Plath*. Vol. 2: *1956–1963*, edited by Peter K. Steinberg and Karen V. Kukil, HarperCollins, 2018.

———. *The Unabridged Journals of Sylvia Plath*. Edited by Karen V. Kukil, Anchor, 2000.

"*Poems* by Yehuda Amichai." By Assia Gutmann [Wevill], with poems read by Ted Hughes. BBC Radio 3, Dec. 12, 1968.

"The Politics of Trauma: A Conversation with Judith Herman." *Listening to Trauma: Conversations with Leaders in the Theory and Treatment of Catastrophic Experience*, interviews and photography by Cathy Caruth, Johns Hopkins UP, 2014, pp. 130–51.

Porter, Peter. Review of *Lover of Unreason*, by Yehuda Koren and Eilat Negev, *The Guardian*, Oct. 28, 2006, https://www.theguardian.com/books/2006/oct/28/featuresreviews.guardianreview8.

"Posthumous Whitbread Prize for Ted Hughes." *BBC News*, Jan. 27, 1999, http://news.bbc.co.uk/2/hi/entertainment/263541.stm.

Rape Crisis Scotland. *Briefing: False Allegations*, 2021.

Robinson, Lillian S. "Treason Our Text: Feminist Challenges to the Literary Canon." *Falling into Theory: Conflicting Views of Reading Literature*. Edited by David H. Richter, 2nd ed., Bedford: 2000, pp. 152–66.

Roche, Clarissa. Interview recording. November 30, 1973. Part 1, side B. Harriet Rosenstein Research Files on Sylvia Plath, Stuart A. Rose Manuscript, Archives, and Rare Book Library, Emory University, Atlanta, GA.

———. Interview recording. November 20, 1973. Part 2, side A. Harriet Rosenstein Research Files on Sylvia Plath, Stuart A. Rose Manuscript, Archives, and Rare Book Library, Emory University, Atlanta, GA.

———. Interview recording. November 20, 1973. Part 3, side B. Harriet Rosenstein Research Files on Sylvia Plath, Stuart A. Rose Manuscript, Archives, and Rare Book Library, Emory University, Atlanta, GA.

———. Interview recording. November 1973. Part 4, side A. Harriet Rosenstein Research Files on Sylvia Plath, Stuart A. Rose Manuscript, Archives, and Rare Book Library, Emory University, Atlanta, GA.

———. Interview recording. Undated. Part 5, side B. Harriet Rosenstein Research Files on Sylvia Plath, Stuart A. Rose Manuscript, Archives, and Rare Book Library, Emory University, Atlanta, GA.

Roche, Paul. Interview recording, November 21, [undated]. Side A. Harriet Rosenstein Research Files on Sylvia Plath, Stuart A. Rose Manuscript, Archives, and Rare Book Library, Emory University, Atlanta, GA.

———. Interview recording, November 21, [undated]. Side B. Harriet Rosenstein Research Files on Sylvia Plath, Stuart A. Rose Manuscript, Archives, and Rare Book Library, Emory University, Atlanta, GA.

Rollyson, Carl. *The Last Days of Sylvia Plath*. UP of Mississippi, 2020.

Rosenthal, Jon. Interview recording. 1971. Harriet Rosenstein Research Files on Sylvia Plath, Stuart A. Rose Manuscript, Archives, and Rare Book Library, Emory University, Atlanta, GA.

Sanger-Katz, Margot. "The Science Behind Suicide Contagion." *New York Times*, Aug. 13, 2014, https://www.nytimes.com/2014/08/14/upshot/the-science-behind-suicide-contagion.html.

Shaw, Susan M., and Janet Lee. *Gendered Voices, Feminist Visions: Classic and Contemporary Readings*. 7th ed., Oxford UP, 2020.

Sigmund, Elizabeth Compton. Interview recording. Undated. Part 1, side A. Harriet Rosenstein Research Files on Sylvia Plath, Stuart A. Rose Manuscript, Archives, and Rare Book Library, Emory University, Atlanta, GA.

———. Interview recording. Undated. Part 2, side B. Harriet Rosenstein Research Files on Sylvia Plath, Stuart A. Rose Manuscript, Archives, and Rare Book Library, Emory University, Atlanta, GA.

———. Interview recording. Undated. Part 3, side A. Harriet Rosenstein Research Files on Sylvia Plath, Stuart A. Rose Manuscript, Archives, and Rare Book Library, Emory University, Atlanta, GA.

———. Interview recording. Undated. Part 4, side B. Harriet Rosenstein Research Files on Sylvia Plath, Stuart A. Rose Manuscript, Archives, and Rare Book Library, Emory University, Atlanta, GA.

———. Interview recording. Undated. Part 5, side A. Harriet Rosenstein Research Files on Sylvia Plath, Stuart A. Rose Manuscript, Archives, and Rare Book Library, Emory University, Atlanta, GA.

———. Interview recording. Undated. Part 6, side B. Harriet Rosenstein Research Files on Sylvia Plath, Stuart A. Rose Manuscript, Archives, and Rare Book Library, Emory University, Atlanta, GA.

Steinberg, Peter K. "'They Will Come Asking for Our Letters': Editing *The Letters of Sylvia Plath*." *The Bloomsbury Handbook to Sylvia Plath*, edited by Anita Helle, Amanda Golden, and Maeve O'Brien, Bloomsbury, 2022, pp. 307–15.

Steiner, Nancy Hunter. Interview recording. Undated. Part 1, side B. Harriet Rosenstein Research Files on Sylvia Plath, Stuart A. Rose Manuscript, Archives, and Rare Book Library, Emory University, Atlanta, GA.

———. Interview recording. Undated. Part 2, side A. Harriet Rosenstein Research Files on Sylvia Plath, Stuart A. Rose Manuscript, Archives, and Rare Book Library, Emory University, Atlanta, GA.

Stern, Marcia. Interview recording. Undated. Side A. Harriet Rosenstein Research Files on Sylvia Plath, Stuart A. Rose Manuscript, Archives, and Rare Book Library, Emory University, Atlanta, GA.

———. Interview recording. Undated. Part 2, side B. Harriet Rosenstein Research Files on Sylvia Plath, Stuart A. Rose Manuscript, Archives, and Rare Book Library, Emory University, Atlanta, GA.

Stimpson, Catharine. "Beginning Again and Again." Keynote, Feminist Pedagogies / Understanding the Past, Inventing the Future: An International Seminar, Sept. 10, 2020, Ca'Foscari University, Venice, Italy.

Talbot, Mary. *Language and Gender*. 3rd ed., Polity, 2020.

Tarn, Nathaniel. "Nathaniel Tarn's Auto-Anthropology: A Reading and Responses." The Louisville Conference on Literature and Culture, Feb. 22, 2020, University of Louisville.

———. Nathaniel Tarn Papers. M1132. Dept. of Special Collections, Stanford University Libraries, Stanford, CA.

Tennant, Emma. *Burnt Diaries*. Edinburgh, Scotland: Canongate, 1999.

Thwaite, Anthony. Interview recording. Undated. Part 1, side A. Harriet Rosenstein Research Files on Sylvia Plath, Stuart A. Rose Manuscript, Archives, and Rare Book Library, Emory University, Atlanta, GA.

Trevor, William. *Excursions in the Real World: Memoirs*. Penguin, 1995.

"Unfinished 1968: Fragments of a Film by Assia Wevill and Martin Baker." *YouTube*, uploaded by Martin Baker, April 9, 2020, https://www.youtube.com/watch?v=LI_lqV8hYhU.

van der Kolk, Bessel. *The Body Keeps the Score: Brain, Mind, and Body in the Healing of Trauma*. Penguin, 2014.

van der Kolk, and Alexander C. McFarlane. "The Black Hole of Trauma." *Traumatic Stress: The Effects of Overwhelming Experience on Mind, Body, and Society*, edited by van der Kolk, McFarlane, and Lars Weisaeth, Guilford Press, 2007, pp. 3–23.

Van Duyne, Emily. *Loving Sylvia Plath: A Reclamation*. Norton, 2024.

Wagner-Martin, Linda. Correspondence: Linda Wagner-Martin to Elizabeth Sigmund. Box 1, folder 18, items 36–37. Elizabeth Sigmund Collection of Photographs and Correspondence Related to Sylvia Plath, Mortimer Rare Book Collection, MRBC-MS-00441, Smith College Special Collections, Northampton, MA.

Walsh, Chad. "The New Poetry—Ragas, Koans—and Sonnets, Too." *Chicago Tribune*, Feb. 15, 1970.

Weldon, Fay. Interview recording. November 19, [undated]. Harriet Rosenstein Research Files on Sylvia Plath, Stuart A. Rose Manuscript, Archives, and Rare Book Library, Emory University, Atlanta, GA.

Wevill, Assia. *The Collected Writings of Assia Wevill*. Edited by Julie Goodspeed-Chadwick and Peter K. Steinberg, LSU Press, 2021.

———, previous owner. *Anna Karenin*. By Leo Tolstoy, Penguin, 1954, Stuart A. Rose Manuscript, Archives, and Rare Book Library, Emory University, Atlanta, GA.

———, previous owner. *The Art of Loving*. By Erich Fromm, George Allen and Unwin, 1960, Stuart A. Rose Manuscript, Archives, and Rare Book Library, Emory University, Atlanta, GA.

———, previous owner. *The Film Sense*. By Serge Eisenstein, Faber, 1968, Stuart A. Rose Manuscript, Archives, and Rare Book Library, Emory University, Atlanta, GA.

———, previous owner. *Oedipus*. Adapted by Ted Hughes and translated by David Anthony Turner, London: National Theatre, 1967, Stuart A. Rose Manuscript, Archives, and Rare Book Library, Emory University, Atlanta, GA.

———, previous owner. *Tess of the d'Urbervilles*. By Thomas Hardy, Macmillan/St. Martin's, 1966, Stuart A. Rose Manuscript, Archives, and Rare Book Library, Emory University, Atlanta, GA.

———, previous owner. *Wodwo*. By Ted Hughes, Harper, 1967, Stuart A. Rose Manuscript, Archives, and Rare Book Library, Emory University, Atlanta, GA.

Wevill, David. E-mail to the author. March 2, 2022.

Wolf, Naomi. *The Beauty Myth: How Images of Beauty Are Used Against Women*. Harper Perennial, 2002.

INDEX

Alcoff, Linda Martín, 145
allegiances, 20–21, 41
Alliston, Susan, 131
Alvarez, Al, 24–26, 65, 75–76, 136, 151n1, 151n2
Amichai, Yehuda, 28–29, 68–69, 78, 90–91, 97–98, 121, 142–44, 147–48, 151n3
Anderson, Nathalie, 160n12
"An Intruder into the Family Myth" (Hughes), 130
"As for the World" (Amichai), 143
"Ashes" (Hughes), 132
"Assia Gutmann" (Hughes), 78–79, 161n2
attachment, 20–21
autobiographical writing, 76, 120–23
Avery, John, 51–52, 54

Baker, Martin, 28–30, 59, 99, 152n7, 156n3
Baskin, Leonard, 15, 122–24, 159n7, 161n18
Baskin, Lisa, 122–23
Bate, Jonathan, 7–8, 25, 32, 59, 72, 105, 151n2, 158n17, 159n7
Bateson, Mary Catherine, 19, 69, 96–97, 156n5
Beacon in Heptonstall, 100, 104, 160n17
Becker, Jillian, 30–31

"A Bedtime Story" (Hughes), 117–18
"Beginning Again and Again" (Stimpson), 83
The Bell Jar (Plath), 47
binary oppositions, 15–17, 140, 150n10
biographies and biographical studies, 5–18, 22, 33–34
Birthday Letters (Hughes), 13, 38, 79, 103–4, 112, 117–18, 120–21
blackness, 110–14, 120, 126, 160n9
Blank, Arthur, 124
Burton, Kay, 155n34
Butler, Judith, 33, 146

canon, 22–23
Capriccio (Hughes): "Chlorophyl," 129; "Descent," 107; drafts from, 124–28; "The Error," 70; "Fanaticism," 79, 111; "Flame," 70, 118, 128, 156n7; "Folktale," 107, 136; and healing, 121–23; literary foils, Plath and Assia as, 103–4; "Lovesong" from *Crow*, 118–19; misogyny, 82–83; "The Other," 29; "The Pit and the Stones," 67; poems from to be translated, 107; "Rules of the Game," 38; "Shibboleth," 86, 107–9, 125; "Systole Diastole," 118; and trauma, 13
"Capriccios" (Hughes), 103
Caruth, Cathy, 105–6, 118, 160n10

Chaikin, Celia, 35, 43, 71, 74, 87, 103, 137, 150n6
Chaikin, Ira, 137
Chicago Tribune, 68
"Chlorophyl" (Hughes), 129
Clapham Common, South London, 131–32, 161n17
Clark, Heather, 7–8, 26, 30–31, 37–38, 59, 111, 149n3
Cleggan, Ireland, 88
"The Coat" (Hughes), 128
collaboration, 28, 96–97, 124, 161n18
Collected Poems (Hughes), 38, 158n24
The Collected Writings of Assia Wevill, 39, 61, 68, 147
Collins, Patricia Hill, 66
colonialist ideology, 107–11, 159n8
Composing a Life (Bateson), 69
Compton, David, 15, 104, 150n10
Connemara, Ireland, 132
Cottom, Tressie McMillan, 48–49, 110
Court Green, Devon, England, 27, 32, 51–54, 87, 89, 94, 104, 106–7, 129, 152–53n15, 158n17
Crenshaw, Kimberlé, 66–67
Crow (Hughes), 111–20, 124, 157n15, 160n9
"Crowcolour" (Hughes), 113–15
"Crow's Fall" (Hughes), 113–14
"Crow's First Lesson" (Hughes), 115
"Crow's Undersong" (Hughes), 115–16
Crowther, Gail, 7
Csokits, Janos, 155n38
Cunningham, Stephanie, 82, 144

Davies, Winifred, 15, 47, 65, 77
"Descent" (Hughes), 107, 109
Difficulties of a Bridegroom (Hughes), 38
"Do Not Pick Up the Telephone" (Hughes), 118
Double Exposure (Plath), 43

Down Girl (Manne), 82
"Dreamers" (Hughes), 38, 79, 103
"Dream of A" (Hughes), 130

"Edge" (Plath), 117
Eliot, T. S., 26
Elm Hotel, 99
Ely, Steve, 35
Enniss, Stephen C., 105
erasure, 34, 69, 116, 145
Erikson, Kai, 159n5
"The Error" (Hughes), 70, 127, 156n7
"Examination at the Womb-Door" (Hughes), 115
exercise books, 130–31

Fainlight, Ruth, 31, 35, 48, 59, 94
"Fanaticism" (Hughes), 79, 111
Farrar, Hilda, 94–95
Feinstein, Elaine, 7, 12–13, 37, 48–49, 72, 134, 152n10, 160n14
Felman, Shoshana, 124
Felski, Rita, 20–21
feminist recovery work, 8–9, 19, 140–42, 144, 146
"Flame" (Hughes), 70, 118, 128, 156n7
"Folktale" (Hughes), 107, 136
The Force of Nonviolence (Butler), 33
A Full House (Hughes), 97

Gems, Keith, 68
Gems, Pam, 156n3
gendered expectations, 40, 45, 52–53, 69, 73, 115–17, 154n30, 155n33
gendered violence. *See* intimate partner violence
Gill, Jo, 122–23, 159n8
Gordon-Reed, Annette, 10
"Grand Canyon" (Hughes), 117
"The Grey Cairn" (Hughes), 127
The Grief of Influence (Clark), 111

The Guardian, 68–69
Gutmann, Lonya, 30, 71

Hamermesh, Mira, 26, 139, 153n17, 156n8
Hardy, Thomas, 18–19, 98
Hart, Onno van der, 50
Haworth, Yorkshire, 99
Heaney, Seamus, 120–21
Hedden, Brenda, 10, 74–75, 84, 87–88, 137–40, 150n5
Hedden, Trevor, 87
Heilbrun, Carolyn G., 45, 150–51n11
Heinz, Drue, 3, 18
Heptonstall, West Yorkshire, England, 93, 104
Herman, Judith, 105, 156n6
Highbury, North London, 132
himpathy, 85
Hooked (Felski), 20–21
Horder, John, 50
Hughes, Edith, 32
Hughes, Frieda, 72, 77–80, 99, 132, 143, 157n15, 158n17, 159n7, 160n15, 161n2
Hughes, Nicholas, 72, 77, 80, 99, 120–21, 132, 157n15, 158n17, 159n7
Hughes, Olwyn, 13–14, 32, 35–36, 39, 46, 72, 93–95, 137, 153n19
Hughes, Ted, 3–5, 102–36; art and healing, 120–24, 135; Assia's beauty, 79; Assia's letters, 85–90; Assia's stepparenting role, 80; biographical studies, 6–18; collaboration, 96–97; colonialist ideology, 107–11; and Davies, 47; deaths of Assia and Shura, 72–75; diminishing Assia's presence, 137–40; diverse narratives, 140–42; extended family, 93–95; and Hedden, 137–38; intimate partner violence, 37–38, 55–57, 81–85; journal writing, 75–77, 99–101; and Lucie-Smith, 40–41; masculine literary establishment, 65–66; and Minton, 57–61; and Myers, 31–32; narratives about Assia, 102–9; "*Poems by Yehuda Amichai by Assia Gutmann*" (radio program), 142–44; privileged and entitled men, 82–83; Rosenstein interviews, 30–57; secret marriage, 138–39; Tennant's story, 21; textual erasure, 34–35; and trauma, 102–6; unpublished materials, 123–36
Hughes, Ted, works by: "An Intruder into the Family Myth," 130; "Ashes," 132; "A Bedtime Story," 117–18; *Birthday Letters*, 13, 38, 79, 103–4, 112, 117–18, 120–21; "Capriccios," 103; "Chlorophyl," 129; "The Coat," 128; *Collected Poems*, 38, 158n24; *Crow*, 111–20, 124; "Crowcolour," 113–15; "Crow's Fall," 113–14; "Crow's First Lesson," 115; "Crow's Undersong," 115–16; "Descent," 107, 109; *Difficulties of a Bridegroom*, 38; "Do Not Pick Up the Telephone," 118; "Dreamers," 38, 79, 103; "Dream of A," 130; "The Error," 70, 127, 156n7; "Examination at the Womb-Door," 115; "Fanaticism," 79, 111; "Flame," 70, 118, 128, 156n7; "Folktale," 107, 136; *A Full House*, 97; "Grand Canyon," 117; "The Grey Cairn," 127; "The Locket," 79, 82; "Lovesong," 117–20; "The Mythographers," 82; "Notes for a Little Play," 115; "Opus 131," 125; "The Other," 29, 38, 103; "The Pit and the Stones," 67; "Possession," 82; "Revenge Fable," 115–17; "Rules of the Game," 38; "Shibboleth," 86, 107–9, 125; "Smell of Burning," 82; "Snow," 125; "Systole Diastole," 82, 118; "Truth Kills Everybody," 117–18; "Two Legends," 113; *Wodwo*, 112
Huws, Daniel, 103, 159n4

identification, 20–21, 41
identity politics, 31, 111
"If with a Bitter Mouth" (Amichai), 147–48
intersectionality, 66–68, 113
intimate partner violence, 37–38, 55–57, 81–85
Ireland, 87, 132, 138

Jenkins, Alan, 52–54
Jenkins, Nan, 54
journal writing, 75–77, 85–87, 93, 99–101, 137

Kane, Marvin, 71
Kaussen, Jutta and Wolfgang, 107–10
Kavanagh, P. J., 68–69
Kirkus Reviews, 68
Klein, Elinor, 12, 15, 52–54, 155n35
Kolodny, Annette, 22–23
Koren, Yehuda, 3, 72, 74, 79, 84, 97, 137–39, 157n14
Krebs, Paula M., 145
Kukil, Karen V., 8–9, 105

Landels, Angela, 79
Language and Gender (Talbot), 151n2
Larschan, Richard, 84
"Learning from the 60s" (Lorde), 67–68
Lee, Hermione, 5–6
Lee, Janet, 153–54n21
"Lesbos" (Plath), 46
The Letters of Sylvia Plath, 8–9
Levy, Lisa, 71
literary shocks, 18–20
"The Locket" (Hughes), 79, 82
London, England, 26–27, 52–54
Lorde, Audre, 19–20, 66–68, 158–59n25
Louisville Conference on Literature and Culture, 26–27
Lover of Unreason (Koren and Negev), 3, 150n8, 160n14

"Lovesong" (Hughes), 117–20
Lucie-Smith, Edward, 35, 39–42, 120, 149–50n4, 151n2, 152–53n15, 153n19, 153n20, 156n3
Lumb Bank, Heptonstall, England, 35, 74, 104–5, 129, 160n17

Macedo, Helder, 16, 92–93, 139
Macedo, Suzette, 14, 16–17, 35–40, 66, 92–93, 139
Malcolm, Janet, 5–6, 106, 149n2
Manne, Kate, 82–83, 85, 158n19, 158n20
Marcus, Laura, 76, 122
Mardorossian, Carine M., 70
"The Master's Tools Will Never Dismantle the Master's House" (Lorde), 18–19
Matcham, Julia, 10–11, 13, 73–75, 103–4, 140, 152n9
McCullough, Frances, 75
McFarlane, Alexander C., 144, 159n6
medium-blue Challenge Duplicate Book, 132–34
Megged, Eda, 156n9
Mendelson, Patricia, 27, 30, 36, 88–89, 94, 95
mental illness, 72–73
Merwin, Dido, 16, 44
Merwin, W. S., 65–66
Micir, Melanie, 9
Middlebrook, Diane, 4, 23, 73, 76–77, 110
Minton, Nathaniel, 57–61
misogyny, 22, 34, 82–83, 85, 109, 155n1
Motion, Andrew, 141
Murphy, Richard, 13–14, 35, 36, 45–46, 65, 95–96, 135, 157–58n15
Myers, Lucas, 31–33, 76–77, 95, 138, 152n11, 160n11
"My Parents' Migration" (Amichai), 143
"The Mythographers" (Hughes), 82

Negev, Eilat, 3, 72, 74, 79, 84, 97, 137–39, 142, 157n14

Nelson, Maggie, 22, 79–80
New Yorker, 65
North Tawton, England, 49, 51, 54, 104, 131
Northwest Review, 118–19
"Notes for a Little Play" (Hughes), 115

Ogilvy and Mather, 28
Okeover Manor, 29
Oluo, Ijeoma, 110–11
"Once There Was a Large, Flat Stone" (Wevill), 100–101
oppression, 49, 66, 82, 110, 144
"Opus 131" (Hughes), 125
"The Other" (Hughes), 29, 38, 103
Out of the Ashes (Hughes), 78, 161n2

The Passion Projects (Micir), 9
patchwork paradigm, 69
patriarchal societies, 46–47, 54–55
Perry, Bruce D., 31, 154n31
"The Pit and the Stones" (Hughes), 67
Plath, Aurelia, 39, 44, 84, 91
Plath, Sylvia, 4–5, 21–22; and Alvarez, 25–26; and Avery, 51–52; *The Bell Jar*, 47; biographical studies, 6–18; compared and contrasted with Assia, 92–93, 139; competing interpretations of, 53–55; and Davies, 47; diverse narratives, 140–42; *Double Exposure*, 43; "Edge," 117; femininity, 36–37, 40–42; gendered expectations, 53, 154n30, 155n33; Hughes's autobiographical writing, 120–23; insecurities, 92–93; intimate partner violence, 37–38, 55–57, 81–82, 84; journal writing, 75–76, 93; "Lesbos," 46; as literary foil, 103–4; and Lucie-Smith, 39–41; and Macedo, 35–39; masculine literary establishment, 65–66; and Matcham, 140, 152n9; and Murphy, 45–46; poem that Assia wrote about, 38–39; posthumous presence, 30–32, 80–81; racialization of, 111–13; Rosenstein interviews, 30–57; and Sigmund, 43–45; suicide, 30–31, 70–74, 96, 104–6, 121, 131–32, 156n11; Tarn's diary, 27; theft of manuscripts, 43; as victim, 50, 70
Plath, Warren, 39
Poems (Amichai), 68, 83
"*Poems* by Yehuda Amichai by Assia Gutmann" (radio program), 142–44, 151n3
Porter, Peter, 13, 112, 150n8, 150n9
"Possession" (Hughes), 82
post-traumatic stress disorder (PTSD), 124, 134, 161n19

race and racism, 107–15
rape, 37, 84–85, 153n18
Reclaiming Assia Wevill (Goodspeed-Chadwick), 3, 33, 34, 48, 83, 102, 106, 122–23, 147, 149n3
Red Comet (Clark), 7–8
repetition, 77, 112, 160n10
"Revenge Fable" (Hughes), 115–17
Robinson, Lillian S., 23
Roche, Clarissa, 4, 16–17, 35–38, 55–56, 93, 140–41, 143
Roche, Paul, 54–55, 66
Rollyson, Carl, 25, 75–76, 151n2
Roose, Chris, 28
Rosenstein, Harriet, 4, 12, 14–15, 16–17, 30–57, 65, 81, 92–93, 102, 139, 140–41, 150n7, 152n13
Rosenthal, Jon, 54
"Rules of the Game" (Hughes), 38

Sagar, Keith, 104, 112, 117, 121
Selected Poems (Amichai), 78, 83, 151n3
sexism, 25, 34, 83, 110, 151n1
Sexton, Anne, 156–57n11
Shaw, Susan M., 153n21
"Shibboleth" (Hughes), 86, 107–9, 125

INDEX 179

Sigmund, Elizabeth Compton, 10–13, 25, 35, 43–45, 49, 57, 73–74, 104, 106–7, 139–40, 150n5, 154n26
"Smell of Burning" (Hughes), 82
"Snow" (Hughes), 125
social class, 106–7, 109, 141
Sokolov-Amichai, Hana, 88, 91, 121
Steinberg, Peter K., 8–9, 39, 152n14
stepmothers, 79–80
Stern, Marcia, 54, 56, 81
Stevenson, Anne, 106, 149n2
Stimpson, Catharine, 83
"Systole Diastole" (Hughes), 82, 118

Talbot, Mary, 111, 151n1, 151n12, 159n3
Tarn, Nathaniel, 25–27, 38, 84, 94, 151n3, 151n5, 152n6, 153n18, 154n24
Taylor, Celia, 84, 153n18
Ted Hughes (Bate), 7
Ted Hughes (Feinstein), 7, 160n4
Tennant, Emma, 21, 48, 56, 60
Tess of the d'Urbervilles (Hardy), 18–19, 98
"'They Will Come Asking for Our Letters'" (Steinberg), 8
Three-Martini Afternoons at the Ritz (Crowther), 7
Thwaite, Anthony, 155n35
Tormey, Patricia, 135
trauma, 10, 13–14, 30–32, 50, 70, 102–6, 112–18, 120–29, 132–35, 144, 154n31, 159n5, 159n6. *See also* intimate partner violence; victims
Trevor, William, 37, 59
"Truth Kills Everybody" (Hughes), 117–18
"Two Legends" (Hughes), 113

The Unabridged Journals of Sylvia Plath, 8–9
Unclaimed Experience (Caruth), 160n10
"The United Nations" (Amichai), 143
unpublished materials, 123–36

van der Kolk, Bessel A., 70, 103, 123, 144, 159n6
Van Duyne, Emily, 152n13
victims, 50, 69–70, 81–85, 158n20

Wagner-Martin, Linda, 10–11, 13, 25, 74, 140
Walsh, Chad, 68
Weldon, Fay, 35, 42, 71–72, 155n38
Wellington the Tin Solider (Baker), 28, 99
Wevill, Assia, 3–5, 21–22, 65–101; acceptance and belonging, 67–68, 71, 104–7, 156n8; achievements, 68–69; and Alvarez, 24–26; and Baker, 28–30, 156n3; beauty, 15–17, 36–37, 41–42, 46, 48–52, 79, 92, 111, 129–30, 161n2; biographical studies, 6–18; blackness, 110–14, 120, 126, 160n9; body, 47–49, 111; and children, 77–80; compared and contrasted with Plath, 92–93; competing interpretations of, 53–55; David Wevill's accounts of, 147; declining mental health, 86–90; empathy for, 30–31, 44–45, 107–8, 154n26; femininity, 36–37, 40–42, 44; gender as a subject in Hughes's *Crow*, 115–20; gendered expectations, 52–53, 116; and Hedden, 137–38; Hughes's autobiographical writing, 121–23; Hughes's narratives, 102–9; intersectionality, 67–68; intimate partner violence, 37–38, 55–57, 81–85; journal writing, 75–77, 99–101; letters, 85–90; as literary foil, 103–4; literary London, 26–27; and Lucie-Smith, 39–42, 156n3; and Macedo, 35–39; masculine literary establishment, 65–66; and Matcham, 140, 152n9; and Minton, 57–61; motherhood, 95–96; and Murphy, 45–46; "Once There Was a Large, Flat Stone," 100–101; personal

library, 97–99; Plath's death, 30–32; Plath's presence, 80–81; "*Poems by Yehuda Amichai by Assia Gutmann*" (radio program), 142–44; poem written about Plath, 38–39; Rosenstein interviews, 30–57; secret marriage, 138–39; and Sigmund, 43–45; social class, 106–7; suicide, 99, 104–6, 121, 124, 128, 157n12; Tarn's diary, 27; textual erasure, 34–35; translations, 28–29, 68–69, 78, 90–91, 97–98, 142–44, 147–48, 158n25; unpublished writing about, 123–36; voice, 142–43, 161n2; and Weldon, 42; work situation, 91–92

Wevill, David, 14, 26–27, 43, 47, 84, 87, 138, 147, 151n5, 152n6, 153n18, 154n24

Wevill, Shura: Assia's mental health, 87–88; Assia's motherhood, 95–96; and Baker, 28–30; *Crow* poems, 111, 115, 120; David Wevill's accounts of, 147; death of, 71–74; Hughes family, 93; Hughes's trauma, 104–7; and Murphy, 45–46; neglect of, 43–44; Tennant's story, 21; textual erasure, 35; unpublished writing about, 127, 129–35

White, Eric Walter, 68

Wilkins, Chris, 28, 88, 157n12

Wodwo (Hughes), 103, 112

Wolf, Naomi, 48–49, 52, 69, 154n30

women: binary oppositions, 16; biographical enterprise, 9–15; body positivity, 48–49; domestic work, 40, 52–53; gendered expectations, 45, 69, 99–100; intersectionality, 66–68; intimate partner violence, 55–57, 81–85; literary shocks, 18–20; masculine literary establishment, 65–66; physicality, 111; privileged and entitled men, 82–83; stereotypes about, 80; value of lives and contributions, 21–22. *See also* feminist recovery work

Woolf, Virginia, 5

Writing a Woman's Life (Heilbrun), 45, 150–51n11

www.ingramcontent.com/pod-product-compliance
Lightning Source LLC
Chambersburg PA
CBHW050217240925
33081CB00001B/1